D0775131

# A LIFE OF PRAYER

# A LIFE OF PRAYER

*Faith and Passion for God Alone*

ST. THERESA OF AVILA

Edited by
JAMES M. HOUSTON

Introduction by
CLAYTON L. BERG

REGENT COLLEGE PUBLISHING
VANCOUVER, BRITISH COLUMBIA

**A LIFE OF PRAYER**
Copyright © 1983, 1998 by James M. Houston

Originally published by Multnomah Press in 1983.

This edition published 2003 by Regent College Publishing
5800 University Boulevard, Vancouver, B.C. V6T 2E4 Canada
www.regentpublishing.com

The views expressed in works published by Regent College Publishing are those of
the author and do not necessarily represent the official position of Regent College.

Scripture quotations are from the King James Version of the Bible or are a para-
phrase by St. Theresa of Avila.

Pen and ink drawing of St. Teresa of Avila by Sarah Chamberlain

National Library of Canada Cataloguing in Publication Data

Teresa, of Avila, Saint, 1515-1582
    A life of prayer: faith and passion for God alone / St. Teresa of
Avila; edited by James M. Houston; introduction by Clayton L. Berg.

(Classics of faith and devotion)
Includes bibliographical references and index.
ISBN 1-55361-088-1 (Canada)
ISBN 1-57383-247-2 (United States)

    1. Prayer—Christianity—Early works to 1800. 2. Spiritual
life—Catholic authors—Early works to 1800. I. Houston, J. M. (James
Macintosh), 1922- II. Title. III. Series.

BV209.T47 2003        248.3'2                    C2003-910501-6

# CONTENTS

# PREFACE TO THE CLASSICS OF
# FAITH AND DEVOTION

With the profusion of books now being published, most Christian readers require some guidance for a basic collection of spiritual works that will remain life-long companions. This new series of Christian classics of devotion is being edited to provide just such a basic library for the home. Those selected may not all be commonly known today, but each has a central concern of relevance for the contemporary Christian.

Another goal for this collection of books is a reawakening. It is a reawakening to the spiritual thoughts and meditations of the forgotten centuries. Many Christians today have no sense of the past. If the Reformation is important to them, they jump from the apostolic Church to the sixteenth century, forgetting some fourteen centuries of the work of the Holy Spirit among many devoted to Christ. These classics will remove that gap, and enrich their readers by the faith and devotion of God's saints through all history.

And so we turn to the books, and to their purpose. Some books have changed the lives of their readers. Notice how Athanasius's *Life of Antony* affected Augustine or William Law's *A Serious Call to a Devout and Holy Life* influenced John Wesley. Others, such as Augustine's *Confessions* or Thomas à Kempis's *Imitation of Christ*, have remained perennial sources of inspiration throughout the ages. We sincerely hope those selected in this series will have a like effect on our readers.

Each one of the classics chosen for this series is deeply significant to a contemporary Christian leader. In some cases, the thoughts and reflections of the classic writer are mirrored in the leader's genuine ambitions and desires today, an unusual pairing of hearts and minds across the centuries. And thus these individuals have been asked to write the introduction on the book that has been so meaningful to his or her own life.

## EDITING THE CLASSICS

Such classics of spiritual life have had their obstacles. Their original language, the archaic style of later editions, their length, the digressions, the allusions to by-gone cultures—all make the use of them discouraging to the modern reader. To reprint them (as was done on a massive scale in the last century and still so today) does not overcome these handicaps of style, length, and language. To seek the kernel and remove the husk, this series involves therefore the abridging, rewriting, and editing of each book. At the same time we sought to keep to the essential message given in the work, and to pursue as much as possible the original style of the author.

The principles of editing are as follows. Keep sentences short. Paragraphs are also shortened. Material is abridged where there are digressions or allusions made that are time-binding. Archaic words are altered. Spelling is that of Webster's Dictionary. Logical linkage may have to be added to abridged material. The identity of theme or argument is kept sharply in mind. Allusions to other authors are given brief explanation. And marginal readings are added to provide concise summaries of each major section.

For the Christian, the Bible is the basic text for spiritual reading. All other devotional reading is secondary and should never be a substitute for it. Therefore, the allusions to Scripture in these classics of devotion are searched out and referenced in the text. This is where other editions of these books may ignore the scriptural quality of these works, which are inspired and guided by the Bible. The biblical focus is always the hallmark of truly Christian spirituality.

## PURPOSE FOR THE CLASSICS: SPIRITUAL READING

Since our sensate and impatient culture makes spiritual reading strange and difficult for us, the reader should be cautioned to read these books slowly, meditatively, and reflectively. One cannot rush through them like a detective story. In place of novelty, they focus on remembrance, reminding us of values that remain of eternal consequence. We may enjoy many new things, but values are as old as God's creation.

The goal for the reader of these books is not to seek information. Instead, these volumes teach one about living wisely. That takes obedience, submission of will, change of heart, and a tender, docile spirit. When John the Baptist saw Jesus, he reacted, "He must increase, and I must decrease." Likewise, spiritual reading decreases our natural instincts, to allow His love to increase within us.

Nor are these books "how-to" kits or texts. They take us as we are—that is, as persons, and not as functionaries. They guide us to "be" authentic, and not necessarily help us to promote more professional activities. Such books require us to make time for their slow digestion, space to let their thoughts enter into our hearts, and discipline to let new insights "stick" and become part of our Christian character.

James M. Houston

*Dr. James M. Houston was born to missionary parents who served in Spain. Dr. Houston served as University Lecturer at Oxford University, England, from 1949-1971. He was a Fellow of Hertford College during the period between 1964-1971, and held the office of Principal of Regent College from 1969-1978. From 1978 to the present he has served as Chancellor of Regent College.*

*Dr. Houston has been active in the establishment and encouragement of lay training centers across the continents. These include the C. S. Lewis Institute in Washington, D.C., and The London Institute for the Study of Contemporary Christianity. In addition to his work with the Classics series, he has published a book entitled, I Believe in the Creator (Eerdmans, 1978.)*

St. Teresa of Avila
1515-1582

# EDITOR'S NOTE
## ABOUT TERESA OF AVILA AND
## THE RELEVANCE OF THIS CLASSIC

The lack of prayer as a way of life among Christians makes this anthology of Teresa's writings a timely one. But I hope the intensity of Teresa's life of prayer, with its mystical experiences of locutions and visions, and her single-mindedness in her desire for God, will not seem too much for the ordinary Christian.

My mother, a Protestant missionary to Spain, was stoned out of a village near Avila, the place where Teresa lived. With that experience as a child, I never thought that I would come to admire the devotion of this Catholic woman. Yet the more I have tried to understand the spirit of Teresa, the more I feel the depth of devotion in her fervor to God, in her desire to be like Christ, and in her practical realism as the founder of seventeen convents.

Across the distance of four centuries and the prejudices of religious differences, Teresa reaches out to us all. She fills us with the breath of prayer, and she challenges us to enrich our interior lives more fully with the presence of Christ. Dr. Alexander Whyte wrote an anthology on a few of Teresa's works in 1897.

> . . . the greatest and best talent that God gives to any man or woman in this world is the talent of prayer—it was this that first drew me to Teresa. It was her singular originality in prayer and her complete captivity to prayer. It was the time she spent in prayer, and the refuge, and the peace, and the sanctification, and the power for carrying on hard and unrequited work that she, all her life, found in prayer. It was her fidelity and

her utter surrender of herself to this first and last of all
her religious duties, until it became more a delight,
and, indeed more an indulgence, than a duty. With
Teresa it was prayer first, and prayer last, and prayer always. With Teresa literally all things were sanctified,
and sweetened, and made fruitful by prayer.[1]

## TERESA'S WRITINGS

If prayer is much neglected today, prayer was also much under
suspicion in Teresa's day. In 1525, the Inquisition condemned
some forty-eight propositions of the *alumbrados* (those who sought
mystical experiences by interior inspiration). The fear of demon-
possession was another concern of the times.

And so the society of Spain in that day was not a propitious one
for women like Teresa, or anyone who had mystical experiences of
prayer. She took the sensible action under these circumstances to
seek out spiritual advisors and to be open in describing the whole
state of her soul. She did this in a number of documents that were
subsequently published.

First, she composed a number of *Spiritual Relations* for the infor-
mation of her confessors. Then she embarked on a full-length ac-
count of her *Life* in 1562 at the request of Father Garcia de Toledo.
Properly speaking, it is not an autobiography, any more than
Augustine's *Confessions* or Bunyan's *Grace Abounding* are biog-
raphies. Rather, it is an apologia for the growth of her spiritual life.
She herself disclaimed it to be her life story, preferring to call it
*The Mercies of God.*

When another of her counselors, Domingo Bañez, refused to let
her nuns read *The Life,* they begged her to write them some simple
directions on vocal prayer. *The Way of Perfection* (1566) was her
response to write "some things about prayer." Three years later,
she revised this work. In it she emphasizes that unceasing prayer is
the true life of the Christian because Christ is present with the
Christian all the time.

Teresa had also written her *Meditations on the Song of Songs* possibly in 1566; she revised it in 1572-75. This was a daring thing to
do in view of Fray Luis de León's imprisonment in 1572-77 for
translating the Song of Solomon into the vernacular. Indeed,

Teresa had no knowledge of Latin, so her access to the Scriptures was only by understanding the biblical references in the breviary —a book containing prayers, hymns, etc. that Catholic clerics committed to memory—and other books.

A further request was made by Father Gratian in 1577 for Teresa to write another book on the spiritual life since the Inquisition had taken possession of her *Life*. She was sixty-two years old, and having had five years to contemplate the life of union with God, Teresa wrote *The Interior Castle* in a few months. It is possibly her spiritual masterpiece on the life of prayer. As some of her letters show, it was a difficult year for her, filled with persecution and slander. Yet it was also a year of spiritual richness.

Teresa wrote *Maxims* or "Admonitions to her nuns" in 1582; these were published with *The Way of Perfection*. After she died, Fray Luis de León edited her *Meditations* or "Soliloquies of the Soul to God" in 1588. They reveal some of the most intimate religious feelings of Teresa. *The Book of the Foundations* was started as a journal of the beginnings of each of her houses. It was begun in 1576 and completed in 1582. It was published in 1610.

Her other minor works which are not included in this present anthology are: *Constitutions Given to Her Nuns*, 1568; *Judgment*; and *Method of Visitation of Convents to Discalced Carmelite Nuns*. She wrote a number of poems and hymns, some interspersed in her correspondence and other manuscripts. Allison Peers has collected thirty-one of them. Some 441 letters by her have also been collected and edited together with twenty-seven other fragments, material that is dated between 1546-1582.[2]

## THE IMAGERY OF TERESA'S WORKS

Teresa has made an incredible impact on many Christians since her time. The fervor and the submissiveness of her love for God are profound. Thus the poet Crashaw begins his poem with the words:

Let me so read thy life, that I
Unto all life of mine may die.
("Hymn to the name of the admirable Saint Teresa")

But her images are also vivid and living. Fray Luis de León, in his edition of Teresa's writings in 1588, says: "I never knew, or saw, Mother Teresa while she lived on earth . . . but now that she lives in Heaven I do know her, and I see her almost continuously in two living images of herself which she left us in her daughters and her books."

Except perhaps for Cervantes, no other writer is better known in the Spanish-speaking world than she is. Scholar and simple reader alike are enchanted by her, not because she is learned—she is not. Nor are readers impressed simply because of her devotion—though she does inspire all with her deep experience of life as the experience of prayer. People are impressed because she is just herself, in unconscious self-forgetfulness. And practical, too; oh so practical! Terse, vigorous, alive, she speaks to us in vivid metaphors that illuminate the way of the spirit, delicately and unaffectedly.

Literary images can deeply affect us. They are the language of the soul. The first of Teresa's images is the journey or pilgrimage of the soul. It has infinite possibilities, because it is the journey to God coupled with the experience of being near God. It is a journey composed of a series of transformations, for it is God's purpose for man that by creation, man should bear the image of God; and by redemption, man should be transformed into the image of His Son. Teresa's images explore these purposes of Scripture and so are essentially biblical allusions. They are also intrinsically human images.

The dominant image which she portrays is that of the Castle. It is an image of the wholeness of the soul. It is the place for experiences of the whole person with God and in His indwelling presence, God being the King of Kings whom Teresa fondly calls "His Majesty." She tells us that this image came in an instant, as "a most beautiful crystal globe." This indicated the preciousness of each unique person before God whom God would indwell. In place of the narrowness of the lonely soul without God, Teresa sees the infinite vastness of experiencing alone the presence of God within the interior life. For it is God's presence within the soul of man that gives it such spaciousness and delight. How contrastive is Kafka's *Castle* with its fearful absence of the landlord, depicting not only the absence of the earthly father of the novelist, but also Kafka's alienation from God.

This is, perhaps, the heart of the biblical revelation about man.

For he is created to be a worshiper of God. Worship, then, is but the spirit of allegiance that the subject man has with God as "His Majesty."

Likewise, the purpose of all pilgrimage is to come home where we are intended to live; namely, with God. This Teresa sees as ultimately no less than union with God. Each stage of the journey has its own stipulations which, without fulfilling, make it impossible to make further progress.

Teresa sees first in mansions one to three that the soul is the domicile of His Majesty. This requires us to adopt the manners and protocol of the court; namely, a godly life. So the unclean animals, snakes, and other crawling creatures of sin and passion must be eradicated where possible. In the last four mansions, the closeness of His Majesty becomes ever more intimate. One moves from His near presence, to His friendship, to His betrothal, and ultimately to union with Him.

Water is another image that Teresa dwells upon. Its scarcity in the arid steppes of Castile and the irrigation practices Spain inherited from the Moors were familiar to her. Water, too, is a primordial image of life frequently used in Scripture. She thinks of it as an image of the entire life, saying, "I do not find anything more appropriate to explain such spiritual experiences than water" (*Interior Castle*, IV, 2, 2).

In particular, water for Teresa was the differing types of prayer—the true sources of spiritual vitality—which are experienced in the life of the Christian. First, she links water drawn from the well with buckets to the exercise of active meditation. This is also the experience of God in the first three mansions.

The second experience of prayer she associates with the metaphor of an aqueduct, or channel, that takes water from a spring or fountain. She associates this with prayer that focuses entirely upon the presence of God. It produces great personal joy and peace which are not the result of any human effort. This is what she experiences in the fourth to sixth mansions.

Then she speaks of the refreshment of rains that saturate the earth as the ultimate union the soul has with God. This is experienced in the seventh mansion.

Thus Teresa merges the three sets of images—the Journey, the Interior Castle, and Water in the Garden. However, unlike secular psychology that seeks to know by self-knowledge, Teresa admits: "In my opinion, we shall never completely know ourselves if we do not strive to know God" (*Interior Castle,* I, 2, 8).

Another delightful image she gives us is that of the butterfly. It represents the fresh yet fragile life which so beautifully appears when the soul comes out from the darkness of its self-centered cocoon into the light of the love and union with God. Freeing oneself for a relationship with God requires transformation; it is God's presence that can give this liberation and subsequent transformation. Prayer is the secret of it all. The cocoon is the alienated self, separation from God by sin. The struggle of the soul to be freed is the whole story of the seven Mansions. Teresa recounts her struggles so vividly, struggles in her sufferings which are compounded by both sinfulness and yet the desire for God. "What exterior and interior trials the soul suffers before one reaches the seventh dwelling place!" (*Interior Castle,* VI, 1, 1,).

Such images are intended by Teresa to be an encouragement and a guide in living a life that is centered on prayer. She reminds us that there is a fourth dimension to our existence beyond the spheres of the empirical and scientific, beyond the aesthetic, and even beyond the personal. This fourth dimension is the sphere of prayer and union with God. It is the realm of worship before His Majesty.

In the compilation of this anthology, I have consulted a number of other anthologies, notably those of Alexander Whyte[3] and Pierre Serouet.[4] I used several commentaries as well, such as those of Ruth Burrows[5] and Trueman Dicken,[6] and the biographies of Stephen Clissold,[7] Mary Terese Donze,[8] and Allison Peers.[9]

Perhaps too much stress has been made traditionally on the categories and stages of prayer that Teresa describes. She believed herself that not everyone would experience what she did, and so I believe her emphasis lies rather in the individual's relationship with God in Christ, not whether every Christian should take her directions to repeat all that she had experienced. I have therefore arranged the materials as they reflect the varied aspects of prayer in this remarkable woman. The condensation of the *Interior Castle*—the most closely developed synthesis of all her works—has also been the hardest to abridge. Readers are encouraged to read the full text of this classic in other publications.

The text is based on a revision of the following basic sources:

Lewis, David. *The Life of St. Teresa of Avila* (including the *Relations or Manifestations of Her Spiritual State*). London: Thomas Baker, 1854.

Dalton, John. *The Way of Perfection* (including *Conceptions of Divine Love, Letters, Maxims*). London: C. Dolman, 1852.

Dalton. *The Interior Castle* (and *Letters*). London: Catholic Publishing and Bookselling House, 1859.

I am also grateful to have been able to consult modern translations such as those of Allison Peers[10] and Kieran Kavanaugh and Otilio Rodriguez.[11]

*The marginal numbers appearing infrequently throughout the text are the notations that were used in the nineteenth century translated editions. The lack of consistency in the numbering is due to the abridgement work which was done for this volume.*

We are grateful to Dr. Clayton Berg for his introductory essay on Teresa of Avila. This missionary statesman of one of the largest Protestant missions in Latin America expresses his profound respect for Teresa's life of prayer with an ecumenicity of devotion that true prayer engenders. I am also indebted to Miss Cheryl Bjorklund for typing the manuscript, and to Mr. Craig Gay for his research assistance.

James M. Houston

[1]Alexander Whyte, *Saint Teresa, an Appreciation.* (London: Oliphant, Anderson, & Ferrier, 1897), pp. 18-19.

[2]Efren de la Madre de Dios & Otger Steggink, *Santa Teresa de Jesus, Obras Completas* (Madrid: Biblioteca Autores Cristianos, 1974), pp. 667-1126.

[3]Whyte, *Saint Teresa, an Appreciation.*

[4]Pierre Serouet, *Sainte Terese d'Avila* (Amour et Priere: Paris, Editions du cerf, 1965).

[5]Ruth Burrows, *Fire Upon the Earth [The Interior Castle Explored]* (Denville, N.J.: Dimension Books, 1981).

[6]Trueman Dicken, *The Crucible of Love* (New York: Sheed & Ward, 1963).

[7]Stephen Clissold, *Saint Teresa of Avila* (London: Sheldon Press, 1979).

[8]Mary Terese Donze, *Teresa of Avila* (New York: Paulist Press, 1982).

[9]E. Allison Peers, *Mother of Carmel* (Wilson Ct.: Morehouse-Barlow, Co., 1944).

[10]Peers, *The Complete Works of Saint Teresa of Jesus*, 3 vols. (London: Sheed & Ward, 1946).

[11]Kieran Kavanaugh & Otilio Rodriguez, *St. Teresa of Avila*, 2 vols. (Washington, D.C.: Institute of Carmelite Studies, 1976, 1980).

# INTRODUCTION

It was the late 1950s. I was a young missionary fresh out of Spanish language studies and serving as a pastor in a rural, still fanatically Roman Catholic area in the beautiful Costa Rican mountains. I had also just begun my teaching in the *Seminario Bíblico Latinoamericano* in the capital city of San Jose.

As a missionary, there were of course the usual language struggles. And there was the urgent need to understand as completely as possible and identify with the people whom I would be serving for the next thirteen years. In the midst of these cross-cultural struggles we also discovered the more general problems of establishing self-identity and nurturing spiritual growth. Spiritual growth was especially desired in reference to prayer.

It was around this time that missionary colleague John Stam introduced me to the writings of the "Spanish mystics" from the 16th century. (Besides Santa Teresa, a partial list of Spanish mystics included St. Ignatius of Loyola, Luis de Granada, Francisco de Osuna, San Juan de la Cruz, Luis de León, and Juan de los Angeles.) General readings assisted me in understanding the "Spanish mind" and its distinctive religious culture. The works of Saint John of the Cross (San Juan de la Cruz) were particularly helpful along this line.

But it was the writings of Santa Teresa de Avila that pricked my understanding of what true spirituality and prayer *in practice* are all about. Seeds of new insights were planted. While I would like to say that these insights were transformed immediately into fresh patterns in my experience, in all honesty I must confess that only the surface was scratched. However, subsequent travels in Spain and my recent studies of her writings, as well as works about her life and ministry, have brought me to an even greater appreciation of *Teresa de Avila*. This study has also resulted in a deeper commitment to my Lord.

But who was this Teresa of Spain? From whence did she come?

October 4, 1982, marked the four hundredth anniversary of the death of Teresa Sánchez de Cepeda y Ahumada—the woman commonly known as *Santa Teresa de Avila*. Forty years after her death (1622) she was canonized by Pope Gregory XV.

In 1972 Pope Paul VI named Teresa of Avila and Catherine of Siena "doctors of the church." They were the first women to join that select group. Finally, on November 1, 1982, in Avila, Spain, Pope John Paul II paid homage to Santa Teresa before two hundred thousand enthusiastic Spaniards. He stated that the sixteenth century mystic's life of poverty and meditation was an example for Christian women around the world.

## LIFE AND CONTEXT OF SANTA TERESA

Santa Teresa de Jesús (as she is also known) was born in 1515 to a prominent and prestigious Spanish family. She had six brothers—all of them soldiers. Her mother died when she was quite young.

Teresa turned as a child to the motherhood represented symbolically in the Virgin Mary, "Our Lady." She read incessantly first of the lives of saints and then books of chivalry. She was apparently a charming and attractive girl. Marriage and a comfortable life could have been her lot, but she was led otherwise.

After Teresa's mother died and her elder half-sister was married, her father sent her away to boarding school at the age of sixteen for about eighteen months. Allison Peers summarizes as follows: "As a child Teresa had been moved by hopes of Heaven; as an adolescent she was swayed by thoughts and fears of Hell. Yet, in her mature life [many years later], she was to be surpassed by none for her complete selflessness" (*Mother of Carmel*, p. 6).

Teresa's place of birth and the place of her early years of service was Avila, which stands alone on the Castilian plateau. Its grim medieval walls reflect its title: "Avila of the Knights." For several centuries until the Reconquest in 1492, Avila was the pivotal post in the great struggle of the Christians against the Moors.

Recognition of this military backdrop is important in understanding at least in part the almost masculine characteristic in her ministry. Even her verses about the church of God were often reflections of martial themes, such as the following:

> All ye who with our Master fight,
> And 'neath His banner take your stand,
> Oh, sleep not, sleep not, 'tis not night:
> There is no peace in all the land.
>
> Poems, XXIX (III, 309)

During her latter teen years, Teresa suffered from ill health. But it was also in this crucial period of her life that she discovered her religious vocation. In 1536 she left home to become a novice at the Convent of the Incarnation and a few months later she made her profession as a Carmelite nun.

The Order of Carmel claimed descent from Elijah and the "sons of the prophets" as well as from early Christian hermits who lived austere lives on sacred mountains. Friars and Carmelite sisters were added to the Order in the fifteenth century. At the time of Teresa the Order lived under "Mitigated Rule" or hard severities, even though inconsistencies along this line led her to significant reforms.

These early years were marked by Teresa's serious illness including paralysis. In 1542, however, she recovered and attributed her cure to the intercession of St. Joseph.

Shortly afterwards, Teresa began to grow lukewarm and she gave up the practice of "mental prayer." These several years of spiritual deadness are pinpointed by Teresa's confession:

> Very often, over a period of several years, I was more occupied in wishing my hour of prayer were over, and in listening whenever the clock struck, than in thinking of things which were good. Again and again I would rather have done any severe penance that might have been given than practice recollection as a preliminary to prayer. . . . Whenever I entered the oratory . . . I had to summon up all my courage to make myself pray (Life, VIII [I, 51]).

In 1555, the Jesuits came to Avila, and Teresa confessed to Father Juan de Padranos. Just before that, she had a life-changing vision of the wounded Christ which she describes in her *Life* (Chapter IX, 1). This was the beginning of Teresa's mystical life. It also represented the beginning of opposition from her confessors and other friends who pronounced her to be possessed.

After experiencing several locutions and seeking God's direction to lead her either by "another way" or "show the truth of this," she experienced a vision known as the "Mystical Betrothal" (*Life*, Chapters XXVII, XXVIII).

This, her "second conversion," led Teresa to seek solitude to become vividly aware of the lax state of the Convent of the Incarnation where she had spent the first twenty years of her religious life. Worldliness was rampant. She found herself totally dissatisfied with the state of affairs.

God inspired her to found the Convent of St. Joseph's in 1562 and the other foundations or convents. Most of the rest of her ministry was engaged in this great endeavor. The other sixteen foundations with their years of founding include: Medina del Campo (1567), Malagón (1568), Valladolid (1568), Toledo (1569), Pastrana (1569), Salamanca (1570), Alba de Tormes (1571), Segovia (1574), Beas (1574), Sevilla (1575), Caravaca (1576), Villanueva (1580), Palencia (1580), Soria (1581), Granada (1582), and Burgos (1582). In 1571, Teresa reluctantly accepted nomination as Prioress at her former convent, the Incarnation, where she served for three years.

Mention must be made in this brief account of two major points of opposition and conflict which confronted Teresa in her ministry. The first has to do with the Inquisition.

In early 1567, the General of the Carmelite Order visited Avila and approved the reform initiated and maintained by Teresa. However, certain nuns left the convent at Pastrana in 1574 on account of difficulties raised by the troublesome Princess of Eboli. The Princess then denounced Teresa's *Life* to the Inquisition. More difficulty followed later when an aggrieved novice brought charges to the Inquisition against her. The General then disapproved the Reform and ordered Teresa back from the South to Castile. Later, she was restored to good standing by the forces of the Inquisition.

The other controversy had to do with the dispute between the

Calced and Discalced (or "Barefoot") which reached its height in 1578 within the Carmelite Order. Teresa led the Discalced faction to practice their Order's strict Rule in all its ancient rigors, zeal, and poverty. Even though she and Father Garcián Fracián were held in disfavor, she was permitted to resume her travels a bit later.

As a woman of her epoch, Teresa de Avila followed a road very different in many ways from that which we follow today. However, the vitality of her faith in Jesus Christ and the incredible significance of her life and work are eternal; they speak very clearly in a language which we can, and should, understand.

## THE WORKS OF SANTA TERESA AND THEIR SIGNIFICANCE

Teresa was born in exciting Spanish times. The sixteenth century in Spain was the golden age of its history. It flaunted the likes of Miguel de Cervantes, El Greco, Lope de Vega, and Ignatius Loyola.

Twenty-three years before Teresa's birth, Christopher Columbus discovered America and claimed it for King Philip II of Spain and the Roman Catholic Church. The beginnings of the Reformation came a few years later. Both the riches of the new World and Teresa's reaction to the alleged heresies of the *Luteranos* shaped some of her later writings. Teresa lived in the background of the Counter-Reformation and, in fact, was a part of it.

Despite a lack of profound formal education, Teresa has left us with vigorous, passionate, and terse literature. She has a natural style of exceptional merit which is very human. Some have said that no other literature by a Spanish author is as widely known in Spain with the exception of Cervantes' *Don Quixote*.

A list of her works in chronological order includes: *The Book of Her Life* (her autobiography); *Constitution*; *The Way of Perfection*; *Conceptions of the Love of God*; *Exclamations*; *Book of the Foundations* (of the Reforms); *Interior Castle*; *Relations*; *Conceptions*; some minor works: poems, hymns and other verses, and numerous letters.

## PRAYER AND SANTA TERESA

Most of us would agree with these words of Jacques Ellul even when applied to ourselves:

> The man of our time does not know how to pray; but much more than that, he has neither the desire nor the need to do so. He does not find the deep source of prayer within himself. I am acquainted with this man. I know him well. It is I myself (*Prayer and Modern Man*, p. vi).

We live in an age that opposes meditation, contemplation, and prayer. The cultural values of our society have unduly permeated the worship, life, and service of the church. To a great extent, all of us are faced with a mind-set characterized by the success syndrome, pragmatic functionalism (if it works, it's good), the myth of self-fulfillment, materialism, a fragmentation and impersonality of life, a frenetic pursuit of pleasure, and the tyranny of timepieces, schedules, computers, jet flights, and telephones.

Coupled with this spirit of the times is a marked confusion among many Christians concerning the great framework of God's grace in our spirituality and prayer life. A major problem we have is our failure to recognize that our God and heavenly Father is waiting, ready, and able to help us in our prayers to Him. All too often we fail to trust God and fail to realize the enabling power of His Spirit in and among us.

The life and writing of Teresa of Avila can help us greatly in this vital dimension of *prayer in life*. Her thoughts and example are significant indeed for the church of Jesus Christ these four centuries later.

## 1. Prayer in Life Is Faith.

Prayer in life for Teresa began always and foremost with God. Very clearly the greatest reality for her in all of her experience was that her life was hidden with Christ in God.

Therefore, her constant and consistent emphasis was not so much what one does. Instead, her emphasis was "only to look to Him." And so, as in her *Way of Perfection*, the reader is given the impression that, in every inch of the way, he is guided by one who never strayed from belief in the grace of God and in the dependence of the traveler on that Father of grace.

There is the ever-present need of the commitment called trust and the ability to believe our complete acceptance in Christ. We come with empty hands, and, therefore, are free to give all of our selves to God.

Prayer for Teresa is much more than just "saying our prayers." It is God giving Himself and we receiving Him. Thus, when we are really in earnest, steadily pursuing God's will, in an attitude of faith and an act of trust and commitment, it will not be long before we are blessed by His life-giving touch. This is the vital reality which permeates her life and writing.

Ruth Burrows states it this way: "The coming of the Kingdom into the individual heart, the great earthquake, the overturning of this world order in the Easter event, is what Teresa's teaching is all about" (*Fire Upon the Earth*, p. 4).

A series of beautiful affirmations preserve Teresa's simple but heroic creed in delicate song.

> Let nothing perturb you, nothing frighten you.
> All things pass;
> God does not change.
> Patience achieves everything.
> Whoever has God lacks nothing.
> God alone suffices.

Teresa calls us with great urgency to have communion with God. "Souls without prayer are like people whose bodies or limbs are paralyzed: they possess feet and hands but they cannot control them." She urges us to make a first step of beginning or of renewal. There is no other means of growth, no other way of entering the castle (her "Interior Castle") than by prayer and meditation.

So, prayer is a state of being with our Lord as well as a stage of growth as a person. In her *Life*, she refers to "those who are beginning to be servants of love."

It is the life of faith which this world in the latter decades of the twentieth century needs so greatly. This is what the church of Jesus Christ needs. It is the all-surpassing need which you and I have.

## 2. Prayer in Life Is Humility.

Teresa's humility characterized her life and writings. It springs directly from her faith in God. She believed with all of her being that God dwelt in the very center of her soul. Her belief in God was always intensely *personal.*

The wonder of it all is that the "King of Glory" dwelt in Teresa in all of His beauty and grace and glory. Her consistent response gives us an illuminating idea of what God will do in a heart wholly committed to Him.

I was struck by her abnegation in the very first lines I read. In her introduction to *Interior Castle,* as a woman over sixty years old, she writes:

> Few tasks which I have been commanded to undertake by obedience have been so difficult as this present one of writing about matters relating to prayer: for one reason, because I do not feel that the Lord has given me either the spirituality or the desire for it. . . . Their only excuse for crediting me with it [the ability to solve difficulties concerning prayer among the nuns of the Carmel convents] could be their having as little understanding as I have ability in these matters, should the Lord of His mercy not grant it to me.

The personality of Teresa is clearly seen in her voluminous correspondence. It throws light on her relations with dominating personages such as Pedro Gracián and St. John of the Cross. And it reveals her as a living, human woman, not some kind of an unearthly idol. She manifested imperfections and a certain crudeness. But she also had a wonderful grace of manner, amazing efficiency and energy, a great sense of humor, and a self-abasement.

Teresa liked taking her turn in the kitchen. Apparently she was an excellent cook and could work wonders with meager provisions. "The Lord walks amongst the pots and pans," she was fond of telling her colleagues.

It has been observed that she seemed to be both Martha and Mary. Allison Peers described it in this way.

> Such in broad outline is Teresa the woman, combining the practical efficiency of a Martha and the calm, rapt devotion of a Mary, sharing the joys and the troubles

peculiar to each and offering them as a gift to her Master *(Studies of the Spanish Mystics,* I, 151).

Teresa constantly urged the nuns to criticize her own faults as they would those of others. She would also submit to humiliating mortifications with all the meekness that she would expect of her daughters. This would be repugnant if we did not recognize the all-important value she attached to the practice of humility. Humility was the chief of all virtues in her eyes.

This was all the more remarkable when we consider a prevailing cultural Spanish characteristic which Clissold discusses.

> In a Spain dominated by the cult of "honor"—pride of lineage, disdain for plebian occupation and manual work, and a touchiness which led to ferocious revenge for every imagined injury—the practice of self-abasement stood in dramatic contrast. Even her pious father and brothers had not been immune from the poisonous obsession with "honor" and Teresa feared the contagion might spread to the Discalced *(St. Teresa of Avila,* p. 109).

Certainly the surest antidote to this terrible obsession was the practice of humility. Closely related to humility is obedience, which Teresa identified as the touchstone of the spiritual life. Our modern mind may find it difficult to accept—much less approve—Teresa's personal practice of unquestioned obedience to her Order's Rule, to her superiors and confessors, and even to her revelations.

A side to Teresa's character which may be related to humility is her incredible sense of humor. She professed to dislike "moody people" and asked to be delivered from "frowning saints." As a matter of fact, at the heart of her life of poverty and penance throbbed a tremendous joy and spontaneity. Furthermore, this profound inner joy seemed to be developed even further by privation.

There is her famous dialogue with the Lord when, fighting with a river crossing in her advanced age, she complained to the Lord that she had a sore throat and high temperature. She added, therefore, that this prevented her from enjoying the incidents of the journey as she might. The Lord was alleged to have said, "But that is how I treat My friends," to which she readily replied: "Yes, my Lord, and that is why Thou hast so few of them."

Finally, Teresa's great concern about the danger of seeking favors in prayer underscores her humility in trusting in God. Once again she emphasized that God chooses to give Himself only to the humble—only to those who have earned nothing.

It would be expected that on her deathbed her last words, repeated over and over again, were the lines from a Psalm of David: "A sacrifice to God is an afflicted spirit: a contrite and humbled heart, O God, Thou wilt not despise" (Psalm 51:17).

## 3. Prayer in Life Is a Singleness of Purpose.

Teresa's life and writings ring with authenticity. Here is a person who *knows* where she is going. She singles it out as the effect of mystical grace.

One does not find in Teresa fear of illusion or any frenetic search for assurance. She shows us that God does not lead His children ambiguously, but along straight paths. Her complete certainty overwhelms the reader.

What is marvelous in her life is the way everything served God's purpose. It was due in large part to her singleness of heart. She really did want the Lord to receive all of the honor and glory.

As Ruth Burrows comments, this undergirding, basic mind-set of authenticity and singleness of purpose is ". . . that which Jesus was proclaiming, that which Paul, John, and others have tried to express of man's ultimate destiny of being with Christ in God, one spirit with Him who is Spirit, had become even in this life, a living reality in her" (*Fire Upon the Earth*, p. 1).

I suppose further that Burrows is correct when she observes that Teresa had a special, living, vital knowledge and that she was called to communicate this knowledge to others. It is a unique dimension of human existence which can never be known theoretically but only by moving into it and living there.

Teresa's singlemindedness is seen in her denouncing of any studied approach to prayer. This would tend to contrive, create painful efforts to produce a state, or emphasize special techniques. In this connection, she decried the tyranny of "careful schedules" in which we run the risk of using "sacred time" for self-culture.

The essence of prayer for Teresa was found in the inner attitude of the person; for it brings the sins of the spirit or the "creatures from the moat" to life. Therefore, a self-knowledge is called for. But this is not attained by "endless poking into ourselves, trying to turn over this stone and see what reptiles live beneath, but by looking constantly at Jesus Christ our Lord" (Burrows, p. 19). We also need the help of others in this regard. She warns that under the cover of spirituality we can be terribly self-willed.

So, for Teresa, holiness had to do with very ordinary things: truthfulness, courtesy, kindness, gentleness, consideration of others, contentment with our lot, honesty, courage, and reliability. But from sheer experience she unequivocally affirmed, "Without Him, you can do nothing." Over and over again Teresa emphasized the need for self-knowledge "until the end of our life." She practiced it until her dying day.

Another area of her ministry which reflected this singleness of purpose was her continuing care for the foundations.

> Teresa's care for her convents did not cease with their foundation. She followed their fortunes with close affectionate attention, watching over the material and spiritual progress of each with shrewd, motherly solicitude, and keeping up a tireless correspondence with her prioresses, with the protectors and protagonists of the Reform, and with her own family (Clissold, *St. Teresa of Avila*, p. 196).

The hard core of Santa Teresa's "spiritual virility" is found in her words from her *Life*, (XIII [I, 80]): ". . . come what may the great thing to do is for us to embrace the cross." What great common sense she possessed! Allison Peers in his *Mother of Carmel* has commented on her unflinching realism. "When we make minor allowances for the age and the country in which she lived—both very different from our own—we find her amazingly modern" (p. 52).

## 4. Prayer in Life Is the Cultivation of the "Inner Being."

Santa Teresa de Avila is classified in the *Encyclopaedia of Religion and Ethics* as follows: "Mysticism, Christian, Roman Catholic . . . the most complete and vivid description ever penned of the successive phenomena of the inner experience of a saint" (Peers,

*Studies of Spanish Mystics*, I, 163).

It is difficult for many of us in this modern, electronic age to comprehend that prayer is a miracle. It is not a technical procedure. Furthermore, the prayer beyond all prayer, as practiced by Teresa, is quite foreign to historic Protestantism—my particular background.

Prayer in mysticism confuses and even frightens us. It is overpowering. "Whether suddenly or gradually, the person ceases to be conscious of self; he is no longer capable of speaking" (Ellul, *Prayer and Modern Man*, p. 9). It can even pass beyond speaking with tongues (glossolalia). The senses and knowledge become blurred, but there is an inexpressible awareness of God's presence. Ellul makes a comparison of the mystical experience with what the youth of today seek in drugs. Mystics find it in prayer.

A problem for us is that the term "mysticism" is used in describing a great variety of religious experience. It can be an experience firmly based in the Scriptures along the lines of Galatians 2:20, or John 14:17, 20, 23, or Paul "caught up into paradise . . ."—these are some of the most rapturous and hysterical of trances.

It is also well to keep in mind when reading the Spanish mystics—and Teresa in particular—that mysticism was an actual, vital reality in sixteenth century Spain. It was not merely a theory or a doctrine experienced only by a few individuals on numerous occasions. For the special mystics, it meant a contemplative yearning toward and the achievement of a unique and ineffable union with God Himself.

Teresa kept her visions and locutions secret as long as she could. Only when others began to take note of her ecstatic seizures did she divulge them; this with great reluctance. These experiences of ecstasy served as a form of prayer in which she herself played almost no part, but she testified that everything stemmed from the mighty power of God.

She also emphasized that spiritual blessings were the ultimate test of ecstatic experiences. Furthermore, she declared that it is possible to have most lofty spiritual experiences and yet, "be a mere embryo when it comes to capacity with God." Again we see the practical common sense of this remarkable saint of the Lord.

It is well to bear in mind that "Just as *visions* . . . were something perceived by the mind's eye, so the *locutions* communicated themselves as silently uttered 'inner voices,' directing her in things great and small, instructing her to do this or refrain from doing that, warning, encouraging, occasionally rebuking" (Clissold, St. Teresa de Avila, p. 44).

Teresa categorized both visions and locutions in three ways, in ascending order of perfection: (1) *corporeal,* manifested to the bodily eye; (2) *imaginary,* or representation by the action of the imagination alone, without the involvement of the eye; (3) *intellectual,* or perception by the understanding without the manifestation of any sensible image, neither with the "eyes of the body nor with those of the soul" *(Life,* XXVII).

What can one say by way of evaluation of Teresa's mystical experiences?

She believed wholeheartedly that many of her supernatural experiences were sent directly from God. We ourselves can hardly believe they were not. Alexander Whyte, the staunchest of Protestants, and yet one of the most fervent of her admirers, has said that the disbeliever in such happenings may be suspected of disbelief also in Christ's own words that both He and the Father will manifest themselves to those who love Him and keep His word.

> I am driven in sheer desperation to believe such testimonies and attainments as those of Teresa, if only to support my failing faith in the words of my Master. I had rather believe every syllable of Teresa's so staggering locutions and visions than be left to this, that ever since Paul and John went home to heaven our Lord's greatest promises have been so many idle words. It is open to any man to scoff but I cannot any longer sit with them in the seat of the scorner (Whyte, *Santa Teresa, an Appreciation,* pp. 25-26).

All I can say is that I have been made more aware by Teresa of Avila of this wholeness and integration with the Lord, within myself, and with others through prayer that is more than words. This matches in many instances what I have observed in Latin America's burgeoning and dynamic church. Reflection, meditation, ecstasy, special communion—call it what you may, it involves by God's Spirit the cultivation of the "inner being" in Christ Jesus.

## 5. Prayer in Life Is a Practical Manifestation.

Marriage with Jesus for Teresa meant a total immersion into His love and becoming a vehicle of love. Some of her last words to the readers are the need to do away with romantic notions and any kind of artificial manifestation of spirituality. "From foolish devotions may God deliver us!" (*Life*, XIII [I, 80]). We are to buckle down to the work God has given us to do, with our eyes fixed on the Crucified One, totally dedicated to others, regardless of self.

Throughout her writing and teaching we find the presentation of the ideal of the good life, and practice of the principles of the Sermon on the Mount. She vividly emphasizes its cardinal virtues and the double duty of man, to God and to his neighbor.

Teresa also makes the point that spiritual growth in the Lord produces growth in generosity. Using her terminology, mystical grace shows itself in increasing generosity by the gift of self. This reflects a growing resolution to put self aside and devote oneself utterly to others.

She further underscores that such fruitage (profound faith, humility, generosity) does not normally spring forth from a single mystical encounter. As a matter of fact, her warning is one of the peril of falling back after such experiences. Our temptations become more subtle and powerful and our responsibility becomes all the greater.

Clissold's description of the background and implications of the "Discalced" phenomenon is an expression of Teresa's lifestyle.

> A return to the primitive simplicities and virtues was no new aspiration in Spain. Various efforts had indeed been made in that direction for more than half a century. Most of the Orders possessed, or would come to possess, their reformed—Barefoot or "Discalced"—brethren who sought to practice their Rule in all its ancient rigor, zeal, and poverty. Hitherto reform movements had been restricted almost entirely to the friars" (*St. Teresa of Avila*, p. 70).

An illustration from Teresa's early ministry in rich Toledo demonstrates how this "Discalced concept" worked out in experience. "I do not know why it was unless God wished us to prove the blessings of poverty. I did not ask her [the wealthy Doña Luisa de la

Cerda] for anything, as I dislike worrying people, and she may perhaps not have thought of it" (*Foundations*, XV, [III, 74]).

When gifts began coming to them in abundance, three of her nuns who had been genuinely rejoicing in holy poverty hardly knew what they were about. Seeing her companions sad, she asked what was the matter. "What do you think, Mother, is the matter?" they replied. "We do not seem to be poor any longer" (*Foundations*, XV [III, 75]).

Clissold offers the added thought about life and luxury in Toledo:

> Teresa nevertheless found life in the grand lady's [Doña Luisa] entourage a heavy cross. "The luxury of the place was a great torment to me," she wrote, "and the fuss they made over me filled me with fear." Pitfalls and temptations surrounded so that she dared not relax her guard for a moment. Whenever she could, Teresa escaped to the solace of the discipline and her prayers (*St. Teresa of Avila*, p. 85).

O that we of the twentieth century in affluent ambiences were as sensitive to the traps and snares of materialism and the need to affirm constantly the presence of the Lord in our personal devotion to Him!

Ellul has put it well and provides an able summary of this section: "Action really receives its character from prayer" (Ellul, *Prayer and Modern Man*, p. 172). He goes on to say: "Thus, the act of private prayer is the act through which history is structured in Christ, and it is at this point that the transition from 'I' to 'We' is inevitable" (Ibid., p. 177).

Prayer has its full measure as we are placed in the midst of the always present combat against "nothingness in action." Prayer then gives consistency to life, action, human relations, and to the facts of human existence, both small and great. "Prayer holds together the shattered fragments of the creation. It makes history possible" (Ibid.).

## CONCLUSION

The points which strike the greatest sparks in my encounter with Teresa de Avila are, first, that she was faced with most of the basic problems that face me in my work—unending correspondence and reports; urgently needed fundraising; supervision and oversight of professional religious workers; incessant travel; basic administration; communication with the constituency (my board is her order); and spiritual and pastoral direction. And in it all, she came to know and reveal the fullness of God's presence and the power of His spirit.

Second, I am convinced that the major obstacle to that wholeness and completeness in my life is that to which she so eloquently confesses on several occasions—the hard work that is required to detach ourselves from ourselves through the practice of virtues and fidelity to prayer.

God's promise is true and a source of hope for His children.

> Likewise the Spirit helps us in our weakness; for we do not know how to pray as we ought, but the Spirit himself intercedes for us with sighs too deep for words. And he who searches the hearts of man knows what is the mind of the Spirit because the Spirit intercedes for the saints according to the will of God.
>
> Romans 8:26-27

Dr. Clayton L. Berg, Jr.
President, Latin America Mission

*Dr. Clayton Berg has served for many years as Professor of Christian Education and Academic Dean of the Latin America Biblical Seminary. He has published in both Spanish and English and he has been President of Latin America Mission for the last ten years.*

## Bibliography

The works I have found most helpful in understanding Teresa de Avila include:

**Primary Sources:**

Santa Teresa de Jesús. *Obras Completas.* Madrid: Biblioteca de Autores Cristianos, 1975. 1184 páginas.

Santa Teresa of Avila. *Interior Castle.* E. Allison Peers, translator and editor. Garden City, N.Y.: Image Books, 1961. 235 pages.

St. Teresa of Avila. *The Life of St. Teresa of Jesus.* David Lewis, translator. London: Thomas Baker, 1925. 516 pages. (Also includes *The Relations or Manifestations of Her Spiritual State which St. Teresa Submitted to Her Confessors.*)

St. Teresa of Avila. *The Way of Perfection.* E. Allison Peers, translator and editor. Garden City, N.Y.: Image Books, 1964. 280 pages.

**Secondary Sources** (works about Santa Teresa and her writings):

Burrows, Ruth. *Fire Upon the Earth* (Interior Castle Explored). Denville, N.J.: Dimenson Books, 1981. 122 pages.

Clissold, Stephen. *St. Teresa of Avila.* London: Sheldon Press, 1979. 272 pages.

Lauzeral, P.; M. Kieffer; G. Demonchy. *Teresa de Jesús (1515-1582).* Album del 4 Centenario: 1582-1982. Madrid: Ediciones Paulinas, 1981. 96 páginas.

Peers, E. Allison. *Handbook of the Life and Times of St. Teresa and St. John of the Cross.* Westminster, Md.: Newman Press, 1954. 277 pages.

_____. *Mother of Carmel.* Wilton, Ct.: Morehouse-Barlow Co., 1944. 220 pages.

_____. *Studies of the Spanish Mystics.* 2 vols. London: Sheldon Press, 1927. (Also, New York: Macmillan Company.)

## Supplementary Sources about Prayer:

Del Bene, Ron. *The Breath of Life* (A Simple Way to Pray). Minneapolis: Winston Press, 1981.

Ellul, Jacques. *Prayer and Modern Man.* New York: Seabury Press, 1979. 178 pages.

# I

# TERESA'S EARLY YEARS OF FAILURE AND LATER YEARS OF DIFFICULTIES IN PRAYER

## I. INTRODUCTION

It is not without reason that I will dwell so long on that which has been the most difficult portion of my life. I did not lean on my strong pillar of prayer, and so I passed nearly twenty years of my life on a stormy sea, constantly tossed with the tempest and never coming to the harbor. It was the most painful life that can be imagined, because I had no sweetness in God, and certainly no sweetness in sin.

I was often very angry with myself on account of the many tears that I shed for my faults. I could not help seeing how little improvement all my tears made in me. My tears did not keep me from sinning until I came to look on my tears as little short of a delusion; yet in reality they were not.

It was the goodness of the Lord to give me such a prick of conscience, even when it was not as yet accompanied with complete reform. I have discovered that the whole root of my evil lay in not thoroughly avoiding all occasions of sin. My spiritual directors helped me very little at that time, I might add. If they had only told me what a dangerous road it was that I was traveling on, and that I needed to break off all occasions of sin. I believe, without any doubt, that the matter would have been remedied more quickly.

1

**2**  Nevertheless, I can trace distinctly the mercy of God to me. During all that time, I had still the courage to pray. I say courage, because I know nothing in the whole world that requires greater courage than plotting treason against the King, knowing that He knows it, and yet continuing to frequent His presence in prayer.

**4**  I spent more than eighteen years in that miserable condition, attempting to reconcile God and my life of sin.

**5**  The reason that I tell and repeat this often is so that all who read my writings may understand how great is that grace of God which works in the wayward soul. He gives the wandering soul the desire to pray on, even when it has not yet left off all sin.

*Only prayer helps to amend our lives.*

If the soul perseveres, in spite of sin and temptation and many relapses, our Lord will bring that soul at last to the harbor of salvation, to which He is surely bringing myself.

**6**  I say this from experience: Let him never cease from prayer, who has once begun to pray, ever though his life is ever so bad. For prayer is the only way to amend one's life, and without prayer it will never be mended. Let him not be tempted of the devil, as I was, to give up prayer on account of one's unworthiness. Let such a one rather believe that if he will only repent and pray, our Lord will still hear and answer.

**10**  Very often I was more occupied with the wish to see the end of my hour for prayer. I used to actually watch the sandglass. And the sadness that I sometimes felt on entering my prayer-chapel was so great that it required all my courage to force myself inside. In the end, our Lord came to my help. And when I had persisted in this way, I found far greater peace and joy than when I prayed with excitement and emotional rapture.

If our Lord bore so long with me in all my wickedness, why should anyone else despair, however wicked he or she may be? Let him have been ever so wicked up until now, but he will not remain in his wickedness so many years as I did after receiving so many graces from our Lord. And this more I will say: prayer was the true door by which our Lord gave of all His grace so liberally to me.

**11**
With Teresa's example, why despair for yourself?

Prayer and trust. I used indeed to pray for help. But I now see that I committed the fatal mistake of not putting my whole trust in His Majesty. I should have utterly and thoroughly distrusted, and detested, and suspected, myself. I sought help. I sometimes took great pains to get it. But I did not understand of how little use all that is until we root all confidence out of ourselves and place it once and forever, and absolutely, in God. Those were eighteen miserable years (*Life*, VIII).

**18**
Prayer is utter trust in God.

## II. A Godly Family Life

I had a father and mother who were devout and who feared God. Our Lord also helped me with His grace. All this would have been enough to make me good if I had not been so wicked.

**1**

My father was very much given to the reading of good books; he had them in Spanish so that his children might be able to read them. These books, with my mother's careful upbringing to make us say our prayers and to bring us up with a devout attitude toward God, began to make me think seriously when I was six or seven years old.

It helped me, too, that I never saw my father and mother respect anything but goodness. They were very good themselves.

Her parents' good example

My father was a man of charity toward the poor, compassion for the sick, and consideration for the servants. He never could be persuaded to keep slaves for he pitied them so much. A slave belonging to one of his brothers was once in my father's house; my father treated her with as much tenderness as he did his own children. He used to say that he could not endure the pain of seeing that she was not free.

My father was a man of great truthfulness. No one ever heard him swear or speak ill of anyone. His life was most pure.

**Her sick mother** ^2
My mother was also a woman of great goodness, but her life was spent in great infirmities. She was singularly pure in all her ways. Although she possessed great beauty, yet it was never known that she gave any account whatever to it. She was only thirty-three years old when she died, and yet her appearance was already that of an old woman. She was very calm and had a great dignity. The sufferings that she went through during her life were grievous, but her death was so Christian.

**Her sisters and brothers** ^3
I had two sisters and nine brothers. All, by the mercy of God, resembled their parents in goodness except myself. This was so although I was the most cherished of my father. I think God had some reason for this, because I am filled with sorrow whenever I think of the good desires with which our Lord inspired me and the pitifully wretched use I made of them *(Life, I)*.

### III. ROMANTIC IDEALS OF ADOLESCENCE

^4
One of my brothers was only four years older than I. It was he whom I most loved. He was very fond of the rest of the family, and, by God's love, they were fond of me.

My favorite brother and I used to read the lives of saints together. When I read of the martyrdom that was undergone by the saints for the love of God, it struck me that the vision of God was very cheaply purchased. And so I had a great desire to die a martyr's death. It was not out of any love of God of which I was conscious. But I desired that I might most quickly attain to the fruition of those great joys which I had read were reserved for the suffering saints in heaven. So I used to discuss with my brother how we could become martyrs.

We decided to go together to the country of the Moors, begging God that we might there be beheaded. Our Lord, I believe, had given us courage even at so tender an age. If we *had* found the means possible to proceed, we would have done so. But our greatest difficulty seemed to come from our father and mother.

**Her childhood escapades with her brother**

It greatly astonished us to find it said in what we were reading that bliss and pain were eternal. We often talked about this together. We had great pleasure in repeating frequently, "Forever, ever, and ever." Through the constant uttering of these words, the Lord was pleased that I should receive an abiding impression of the way of truth when I was still such a child.

**5**

As soon as I saw that it was impossible to go to any place where people would put me to death for the sake of God, my brother and I set about becoming hermits. In the orchard belonging to the house we attempted to build hermitages by piling up small stones one upon the other. They of course fell down immediately.

**6**

So it came to pass that we found no way of accomplishing our wish. Even now, I have a feeling of devotion whenever I consider how God gave me in my early childhood what I lost later by my own fault. I gave alms as I could, and I could give but little.

I used to try to be alone for the sake of saying my prayers. They were indeed many, especially the rosary. My mother had great devotion to it and had made us appreciate this as she did herself. I used to greatly delight with other children in building monasteries and pretending that we were nuns. I thought that I wished to be a nun, not so much however as I might like to be a martyr or even a hermit (*Life*, I).

I often think now how wrong it is of parents not to be careful what their children see to be good. For although my mother was as I have just said—so very good herself—

nevertheless when I was old enough to think, I did not derive so much good from her as I ought to have done. Indeed, I derived almost nothing at all from her.

Her mother's
love of tales of
chivalry boldly
influenced
Teresa.

Instead, the evil I had learned from my mother did me
much harm. She was very fond of reading books of
chivalry. This pastime did not hurt her because she never
wasted her time in this literature. But it hurt me much
more. As her children, we were free to read them all.
Perhaps she did this to distract her thoughts from her own
great sufferings and to entertain the children so that they
might not go astray in other ways. But it annoyed my
father very much; we had to be very careful that he never
saw us read.

Thus I concentrated the habit of reading these books
voraciously. Looking back, this little fault which I observed in my mother was the beginning of lukewarmness
in my own good desires, and the occasion of my falling
away in other respects. I thought there was no harm in it
when I wasted many hours night and day in such a stupid
occupation, even when I kept it a secret from my father.
So completely did I become mastered by this passion that I
thought I could never be happy without always having a
new book.

2
To the day of her
death, Teresa
fussed about
clean clothes.

I also began to make a fuss about my dress. I wanted to
please others by my appearance. I took pains with my
hands and my hair, used perfumes, and indeed, exercised
all the vanities that were within my reach. They were
many, for I was much given to them. I had no evil intent,
because I never dreamt that anyone like me should offend
God. But this fussiness about excessive neatness lasted
some years. Indeed, so did other practices which I thought
were not at all harmful. But now I see how wrong all this
must have been (*Life*, II).

## IV. COMPANIONS, BAD AND GOOD

I had a sister who was much older than myself. Her modesty and goodness were great, but I learned nothing from them. Unfortunately I learned every evil from our cousin who was often in the house. She was so light and frivolous that my mother took great pains to keep her out of the house. My mother anticipated the evil that I might learn from my cousin.

**4**
**Maria, her**
**half-sister**

But my mother could not succeed in preventing my cousin's coming; there were so many reasons for her visits. I was very fond of her company; I gossiped and talked with her. She helped me in all the amusements that I liked to take up; and what is more, she found some for me and communicated to me her own vanities. I did not know her—I mean she was not friendly with me and did not communicate with me—until I was about fourteen years old.

**She meets a**
**cousin two years**
**after her mother's**
**death.**

At that time I never wanted to turn away from God in willful sin, or lose the fear of Him. For this reason I never wholly forfeited my good name (of virginity). As for that, there was nothing in the world for which I would have bartered it away, and nobody in the world that I liked well enough who could have persuaded me to indulge in this sin. Thus I might have had the strength never to do anything against the honor of God if I had seen His honor as being equivalent with my honor.

I never observed, however, that I was failing in any other way. In vainly seeking after my honor, I was extremely careful. But in the use of the means necessary for preserving my honor I was utterly careless. I was anxious only not to be lost altogether.

This friendship with my cousin distressed my father and sister exceedingly. They often blamed me for it. But as they could not hinder that person from coming into the house, all their efforts were in vain. And I was very clever in doing anything that was wrong.

**5**

Now and then I was amazed at the evil that one bad

companion can bring into another's life. The conversation of this person so changed me that not one trace was left of my soul's natural disposition to virtue. I became a reflection of her and of another that was given to the same kinds of amusements.

**6**
**The advantage of**
**good friends**
I know from this the great advantage that there is of having good companions. I am certain that if at that tender age I had been thrown among good people, I should have persevered in virtue. For if at that time I had found anyone to teach me the fear of the Lord, my soul would have grown strong enough not to fall away.

Afterwards, the fear of God had utterly departed from me and the fear of dishonor alone remained. That was a torment to me in all that I did. When I thought that nobody would ever know, I ventured upon many things that were neither honorable nor pleasing to God.

**7**
In the beginning, these conversations did no harm. The fault was not hers, but mine. For afterwards my own wickedness was enough to lead me astray along with the servants about me, whom I found ready enough for all evil. If any one of these had given me good advice, I might have perhaps profited by it. But they were blinded by self-interest, as I was by passion.

Still, I was never inclined to much evil, for I hated naturally anything dishonorable. I was simply fond of the amusement of a pleasant conversation. The occasion of sin, however, was a danger at hand, and I exposed it to my father and brothers. God delivered me out of it all so that I should not be lost in a manner that was visibly against my will. On the other hand, it was not so secret as to allow me to escape without the loss of my good name or to avoid the suspicions of my father.

**8**
**There were forty**
**nuns in the**
**convent to which**
**Teresa was sent.**
I had not, I think, spent three months in these vanities when they took me to a monastery in the city (Augustinian Monastery of Our Lady of Grace) where I lived.

**10**
For the first eight days, I suffered intensely. But it was

more from the suspicion that my vanity was known to the nuns than from fearing the monastery itself. I was already weary of myself, and although I offended God, I never ceased to have a great fear of Him. I determined to go to confession as quickly as I could. For I was very uncomfortable.

But after eight days, or maybe sooner, I was much more contented than I had been in my own home. All the nuns were pleased with me. For our Lord had given me the gracious spirit to please everyone wherever I might be. So I made quite a fuss in the monastery. Though at this time I hated to be a nun, yet I was delighted at the sight of nuns that were so good. They were very good in that house; very prudent, observant of the Rule, and serene.

I shared conversation with one of them, possibly confiding in her about my own desires for marriage (*Life*, II). **12**

I began gradually to like the good and holy conversation of this nun. How well she used to speak of God! She was a person of great discretion and sanctity. I used to listen to her with delight. There was never a time when I was not glad to listen to her.

**1**
**The good influence of a godly nun**

She began by telling me how she came to be a nun through the mere reading of the words of the Gospel: "many are called, and few are chosen" (Matthew 20:16). She would speak of the reward which our Lord gives to those who forsake all things for His sake.

This good companionship began to root out the habits which bad companionship had formed, and brought my thought back to the desire of eternal things. It also banished in some measure the great dislike I had had to be a nun. This had been very great. And if I saw anyone weep in prayer, or express devotion in some other way, I envied that person so much. For my heart was now so hard that I could not shed a tear even if I read through a Psalm. This was a great grief to me.

I remained in the monastery a year and a half, and I was very much the better for the experience. I began to say **2** many prayers and ask all the nuns to pray for me so that if God should put me into their position, I would be willing to serve Him. But for all this, I secretly did not wish to be a nun. I deceived myself that God did not want me to be one, although at the same time I was also afraid of marriage.

At the end of my stay there, I had a greater inclination to be a nun. I did not choose that house on account of certain devotional practices which I understood prevailed there and which I thought were going a bit too far. Some of the younger ones encouraged me in the secret wish of mine to be a nun. If all had been of one mind, I might have profited by it.

**Juana Juarez in the Monastery of the Incarnation, Avila.**

Then I also had a great friend in another monastery. This made me resolve that if I was to become a nun it would be in the house where she was. In all this I looked more to the pleasure of natural sense and vanity than to the good of my soul. Even the good thoughts of being a nun only came to me from time to time. But they quickly left me. And I could not persuade myself to become one.

3

At this time, I was not careless about my own good. Our Lord was even more careful to dispose me for that state of life which was truly the best for me. Indeed, He sent me a serious illness so that I was obliged to return to my father's home.

4

**Maria, in Castellana de la Cañada; Don Martin Guzman of Barrientos**

When I became well again, they took me to see my sister in her house in the country village where she dwelt. Her love for me was so great that, if she had had her will, I should never have left her. Her husband also had a great affection for me; at least he showed me all kindness. This, too, I owe rather to our Lord, for I have received kindness everywhere. And all my service in return is that I am what I am.

5

**Pedro Sanchez de Cepeda at Hortigosa**

A brother of my father lived four leagues from Avila; he was a prudent and most excellent man. He was then a widower. Our Lord was also preparing him for Himself. In his old age, he left all his possessions and became a monk.

On the way home from Maria's, I visited this uncle. He insisted that I stay with him for some days. His practice was to read good books in Spanish. His ordinary conversation was always about God and the vanity of the world. He made me read these books to him.

Although I did not like doing this very much, I appeared as if I did. For in giving pleasure to others, I have always been anxious to please them. Though such service might be painful to myself, I was more concerned what others might think of me. This has always been a great fault in me because I was often extremely insincere.

O my God, in how many ways did His Majesty prepare me for His will and the state in which I should serve Him! Yet how against my own will did He constrain me! May He be blessed forever! Amen.

I remained with my uncle only a few days. Yet through  **6** the impressions that were made on my heart by the words of God both heard and read—as well as by Uncle Pedro's good conversation—I came to understand the truth that I had heard in my childhood. I learned that all things are as nothing, and the world is vanity passing rapidly away. I also began to be afraid that if I were to die, I would go straight to hell. Although I still could not bear the thought of becoming a nun, I saw that the religious state was perhaps the best and the safest. Thus, little by little, I resolved to force myself into this vocation (*Life*, III).

## V. SPIRITUAL DIRECTORS: WISE AND UNWISE

I was always fond of learned men, although confessors who were semi-literate did my soul much harm. I did not always find confidantes whose learning was as good as I could have wished. I know by experience that it is better, if spiritual directors are good men and of holy lives, that they should have no learning at all rather than just a little. For such men never trust themselves without consulting those who are learned, nor would I trust them myself.

Lax counsel is dangerous.

A really wise director never deceived me. Neither did the others willingly deceive me; they did not know better. I thought they were learned, and that I was not under any obligation to believe them. But their instructions to me were lax and left me more at liberty. At that time in my life, I was so wicked that if they had been strict with me I would have sought others instead. What in fact was sinful they assured me was no sin at all. Or that which was most grievously sinful they said was only a minor affair.

7

This did me so much harm that it is no wonder I speak of it here as a warning to others. May they avoid such a danger themselves. For I clearly see that, in the eyes of God, I was without excuse. The things that I did were, in themselves, not good; this should have been enough to keep me from them. I believe that God, by reason of my sins, allowed those counselors to deceive themselves and to deceive me. I myself deceived many others by saying to them what had been communicated to me.

Father Vincente Barron

I continued in this blindness more than seventeen years, until a most learned Dominican father exposed me. Then there were those of the Company of Jesus who also made me so afraid by strongly insisting on the error of these principles. I shall show this later.

9

Unwise affection with a foolish counsellor

I began by going to confide in a cleric of whom I have already spoken elsewhere. He took a strong liking to me, because I had then but little to confess in comparison with what I knew later. Also, I had little to tell him. There was no harm in liking me as he did, but it did cease to be good, because it was excessive. He clearly understood that I was determined on no account whatever to do anything that might seriously offend God. He gave me a like assurance about himself and his intentions, so our times together were very frequent. But at that time, because of the knowledge and the fear of the Lord which filled my soul, what gave me most pleasure in all my conversations with others was to speak about the Lord. As I was so young, this made him ashamed.

Then out of that good will that he bore me, he began to tell me of his own miserable condition. It was all very sad, for he had been nearly seven years in a most dangerous situation of morals due to his affection for and his communication with a woman of that place. Yet he continued to act as a priest.

The matter became so public that his honor and good name were lost, and no one ventured to speak to him about it. I was extremely sorry for him because I liked him so much. I was then so foolish and so blind as to think it a virtue to be grateful and loyal to one who liked me. Cursed be that loyalty which goes to such extremities as to go against the law of God. It is a madness that is common in the world and which now makes me mad to see it.

I began to discover more information about the affair [10] from members of his own household. I learned more about his disastrous condition, and I saw that the poor man's fault was not so serious because the miserable woman had attempted to entice him.

When I knew this, I began to show him greater affec- [12] tion. My intentions were good, but the act was wrong. For I ought not to do the least wrong for the sake of any good, however great the good may appear to be. I spoke to him very frequently about God. This must have done him some good, although I believe that what touched him most was his great affection for me.

In short, he broke off all relations with that woman completely and was never weary of giving God thanks for the light that He had given him. At the end of the year from when I first met him, he died.

As I said before, I would not then have done anything [13] wrong. I think that his observance of this resolve in me helped him to have affection for me. For I believe that all men have a greater affection for those women whom they see disposed to be good (*Life*, V).

## 14　A Life of Prayer

1
The later life
of Teresa
Until now my life was my own. But since I began to explain these methods of prayer, my life has been one in
which God has lived in me, or at least, so it seems to me.

2
The fear of being
deluded by mysti-
cal experiences
When I began to avoid the occasions of sin and to give
myself more unto prayer, our Lord also began to bestow
His graces upon me as one who desired to receive them.
His Majesty began to give me very frequently the grace of
the Prayer of Quiet, and very often also that of Union,
which lasted some time. But as in those days women had
fallen into greater delusions and deceits of Satan (for example, Magdalene of the Cross), I began to be afraid; I
feared because the joy and sweetness which I felt were so
great, and very often beyond my power to avoid. On the
other hand, I felt myself a very deep conviction that God
was with me, especially when I was in prayer. I saw, too,
that I grew better and stronger as a result.

3　But after some distractions, I began to be afraid and to
imagine that perhaps it was Satan who was suspending my
understanding of my experience of prayer. I believed he
was making me think that my experience was so good that
I withdrew from mental prayer. I believed Satan also was
hindering my meditation on the Passion and preventing
me from using my own understanding.

As I did not understand what was going on, I felt at a
great loss. Since the last thing I wanted to do was to offend
Him and to express how much I owed to Him, this fear obsessed me. It made me diligently seek out spiritual persons
with whom I might discuss my state of mind. I had already
heard of some.

The Fathers of the Society of Jesus had come into the
district, and although I did not know any of them, I was
greatly attracted to them. I had heard of their way of life
and their practice of prayer. But I did not feel worthy to
speak to them or strong enough to obey them. And this
made me all the more afraid. For it would have been a difficult thing for me to talk with them and yet continue to
be what I was.

I went around in this condition for some time, and after much inward distress and many tears, I made up my mind that I must confer with some spiritual person. I needed to ask him what was the nature of the kind of prayer that I was experiencing, and to show me if there was anything wrong in it. I was determined not to offend God. But for want of courage, I was so timid. What a terrible mistake to make, yet wanting to do good, I withdrew from the good! God help me!

4
Need of spiritual direction

Since I could not overcome this dilemma, I believe that the devil must lay much stress on this in the beginning of the way of devotion. He knows that the whole relief of the soul depends upon conferring with the friends of God. I did not have the strength to do this. I was waiting to amend my ways first, and when I abandoned prayer—which I should never have done—I began to fall into little bad habits which blinded me even from their evil. I so much needed the help of others, and they could have given me a hand to lift me up. Blessed be the Lord! For the first hand outstretched to me was Yours.

The temptation to stop praying

I was told of a learned cleric dwelling in Avila whose goodness and pious life our Lord was beginning to make known to the world. I contrived to meet him through a saintly nobleman. [Francisco de Salcedo became one of Teresa's closest friends. He was related to her by marriage, a cousin of the wife of Teresa's uncle.]

6
Gaspar Daza, a priest in Avila

This nobleman is married, but his life is so exemplary and virtuous, so prayerful and charitable, that the goodness and perfection of his life shines in all that he does. His reputation is well established because of the great good that has been such a blessing to many through him. Although he might consider himself handicapped in being a layman, nevertheless his life is always visibly involved in helping others. He is most wise, very sensitive with everyone, and his conversation is stimulating, charming, and sanctified; it is very attractive to those

Francisco de Salcedo, the nobleman

with whom he deals. Everything he does is toward the
good of those with whom he is in conversation. He does
not seem to have any other interest than to do good and
bless everyone he knows and meets.

7     Well, this blessed and holy man, with all the effort that
he made on my behalf, was really the beginning of deep
blessing to my soul. His humility in our relationship
amazes me, for he had spent somewhere between thirty-
seven and forty years in the practice of prayer. All his life
was oriented toward devotion.

**Mercia del Aquila**

His wife, too, was a great servant of God, and full of
lovingkindness, so that he was not in any way held back
by her. She was, indeed, the chosen wife of one whom
God knew would serve Him so well. Some of their relatives are married to some of mine. I also had a good deal of
association with another great servant of God who was
married to a cousin of mine.

**8**
**Alonso Alvarez**
**Davilá**

In this way, I arranged that the cleric I said was such a
servant of God would come to speak to me. But when the
nobleman brought the cleric to speak to me, I was most
embarrassed to be in the presence of someone so holy. So I
poured out to him an account of the condition of my soul
and the way I prayed.

At the same time, I did not want to confess to him. I
told him that I was too busy, and of course that was true.
But he began with a holy persistence to guide me, knowing I was a strong person. For he observed the kind of
prayer life I was exercising. I was doing this to avoid offending God in any way.

**Counsel can be
rushed too
quickly.**

When I saw that he was so determined to make me
break off the petty habits that I have spoken about, I did
not have the courage to give up at once. As a result, I was
miserable. I realize that he was trying to rush me to mortify
far too quickly my soul's attachments. There was need for
much more caution.

In short, I realized that the way he was trying to deal with me was not one that would really help my condition. These ways were more suited to those that were more mature in spiritual life. While I may have been advanced in receiving favors from God, I was still very much at the beginning stage with regard to discipline and self-mortification.

**9**

If I had had no one else to consult except this cleric, I believe that my soul would never have made any progress. For the discouragement that I felt in seeing that I did not do anything which he told me would have made me lose heart and give up everything. I wonder at times, how it was that he, being one who had a particular way with directing beginners in the things of God, was not allowed to understand my situation or to undertake the care of my soul. I see now that it was all for my greater good so that I might get to know and communicate with others as sanctified as the members of the Society of Jesus.

**Basic counsel is more often needed first.**

It was then that I arranged that the holy nobleman should come and see me now and again. It shows how great was his humility, for he consented to communicate with someone that was so bad as I was. He began to visit me, to encourage me, and to tell me not to give up. Little by little, I was assured that God would do the work little by little. For some years he himself had been unable to free himself from some minor deficiencies. O humility! What great blessings you bring to those in whom you dwell, and who draw near to those who possess you!

**10**

This holy man—for I think I may justly call him so—told me of his own weaknesses in order to help me. He, in his humility, thought that they were weaknesses. Considering his state of life, there was no fault or imperfection compared with the weaknesses which were so grievous in my state of life.

**Sharing our own weaknesses can encourage others.**

It may seem that I am going into great detail about

**11**

nothing very important, but I do say these things with some reason. For these things are so important at the beginning to encourage a soul and show it how to fly when it has not wings, as the expression goes. But because I hope in God that your Reverence will be able to help many other souls, I am mentioning it here.

Pedro Ibañez, to whom Teresa submitted her life, is named here as "your Reverence."

This gentleman was my complete saving. He knew how to cure me, and had the humility and love to stick with me. He also was patient when he saw that I was not reforming all at once. But, little by little, he went on discreetly showing me how to overcome Satan. My affection for him so grew that I was never more at ease than on the day when I was seeing him. However, I saw him very infrequently. If he was late, I used to be very distressed, thinking that he was not going to see me because I was so bad.

### 12
### Was it God or Satan in Teresa's experience?

When he began to learn about my great imperfections—they might well be called sins—and since I told him about the blessings God had granted me, he told me that my imperfections were quite incompatible with the favors. Indeed, these gifts were bestowed on those who were already spiritually advanced and mortified. So he could not help being afraid, because it seemed to him that I must have a bad spirit, although he did not come to a definite conclusion about the matter. He did, however, think well about my prayer life and told me so.

My difficulty was that I did not know how much to say about my experience of prayer. It is only recently that God has given me this gift of understanding what it is and knowing how I am to speak about it. This gentleman's remarks about this, and the fear that I was in, deeply distressed me, and I wept much about it. For certainly I was anxious to please God, and yet I could not persuade myself that Satan had anything to do with it. But I was afraid on account of my own sense of sin that God might lead me blind so that I could never understand the situation clearly.

I looked through a number of books in order to see if I could learn how to explain the prayer I was experiencing. I read one called *Ascent on the Mount* (by Bernardino de Laredo), which deals with the union of the soul with God, and touches upon the signs which I had experienced and thought nothing about.

It had been my experience that I could not reflect on the state I was in during prayer. I marked the passage and gave him the book that he and the other cleric might consider it and tell me what I should do. I decided that I would give up that method of prayer completely if they thought it right to do so. For why should I expose myself to moral danger, when at the end of nearly twenty years I should find that I had gained nothing except falling into a delusion of the devil? Would it not be better for me to give it up?

Yet giving this up seemed hard for me to do. I had already discovered what my soul would be like without prayer. So everything seemed so full of trouble. I was like a person in the middle of a river who, in whatever direction he may turn, fears a greater danger and a certain drowning. This was a very great trial to me, and I have suffered many of these as I shall show later on. Although the matter may seem trivial, it may help to show how one can be tested.

It is, I think, particularly important that women should not be told too emphatically that the devil is busy working with them. For our weaknesses are great. The whole matter should be considered very carefully, and we should be kept from any dangers that there might be. Certainly it is vital that our counseling should be kept secret.

I am speaking now about one who is suffering a bitter trial because my whole case was not kept secret; instead, this one, and then that one were consulted about it. All this did me great harm. There was talk that should have been kept confidential for this was not something for everybody to know about. And it seemed that I was the one who was publishing them abroad.

13
Teresa identifies her experience with Laredo's book.

14
Discretion is needed in speaking of the demonic world.

Spiritual counsel-
ing needs utmost
confidentiality.
Yet I believe the Lord allowed this whole matter without any fault on their part so that I might suffer. I am not
saying that they spoke about what I discussed with them in
confession. But since they were persons with whom I was
confiding my anxieties in order to help me, it does seem to
me that they should have held their mouths. Nonetheless, I never concealed anything from these people.

What I am saying is that one should counsel souls with
very great discretion, encouraging them and giving them
patience until the Lord helps them as He did me. For if the
Lord had not healed me, the greatest mischief could have
been done to me because I was scared and very anxious.
With the tension that I was suffering I am surprised that
much damage was not done to me.

16    Since I had given them both the book as well as told
them the story of my life and my sins, as best as I could
(though not officially through confession, since one of
them was a layman) I explained clearly how miserable I
was. Then the two servants of God with great charity and
affection considered what was best for me. I awaited their
answer in great dread having urged many people to pray
for me. I, too, had prayed much during those days.

Teresa is accused
of being possessed
by an evil spirit.
The nobleman came to me in great distress and told me
that, in their opinion, I was deluded by an evil spirit. He
advised that the best thing for me to do was to apply to a
certain father at the Society of Jesus who would come to
me if I sent for him saying that I needed his help. He also
said that I ought to generally confess to him an account of
my whole life and of the present state that I was in with as
much clarity as possible. Then God would, in virtue of my
confession, give him more light concerning me. Those
fathers were very experienced men in matters of spirituality. Further, I was not to swerve in a single point from the
counsels of that father. I was in great danger if I had no
one to direct me.

17    This so scared and pained me that I didn't know what

to do. So I could do nothing but cry. While I was in the oratory in such deep affliction, not knowing what would become of me, I read in a book—which it seems the Lord Himself placed in my hands—what the Apostle Paul said, that God is faithful (1 Corinthians 10:13). He would never let those who love Him be deceived by the devil. This gave me great comfort.

When I had made a clean breast of the state of my soul to that father servant of God, he understood all that I told him. He explained it to me and encouraged me greatly. He said it was obviously from God's Spirit and it was therefore necessary to return again to prayer. Clearly, I was not well grounded and had not really begun to understand what mortification meant for me.

**Juan de Padranos was the father to whom Teresa confessed.**

I was in no way to give up prayer. On the contrary, I was to strive very much more since God had blessed me with such special favors. He also wondered if the Lord did not intend to bless others through me. He went further, for he seemed to prophesy of what the Lord would do with me and said that I should be very much at fault if I did not respond to the favors that God was bestowing upon me.

**Advised to continue praying**

It seems to me that the Holy Spirit was speaking through him in order to heal my soul, so deep was the impression that he made upon me. He made me very much ashamed of myself and directed me by a way which seemed to change me completely. What a wonderful thing it is to understand a soul!

**Spiritual counsel reassures**

He told me that I should devote prayer each day to some aspect of the Passion and that I would benefit from this prayer in dwelling only on the humanity of our Lord. I was to resist indulging to the utmost on those experiences of recollections and consolation as much as I could until he gave me further directions in the matter.

He left me consoled and deeply encouraged, and the Lord helped me and him to understand my situation and how he might further direct me. I became firmly resolved

**19**

not to swerve from anything that he might tell me to do, and to this day I have kept his advice. Our Lord be praised, Who gave me grace to be obedient to my spiritual directors, even though imperfectly. They have nearly all been those wonderful men of the Society of Jesus. Although, as I say, I have followed them imperfectly (*Life*, XXIII).

**2**
**Teresa became deeply established in her prayer life.** I began with a renewed love of His most sacred humanity. My prayer began to take shape like a building that has a solid foundation.

I did everything because it seemed to me that the Lord commanded it. God gave the spiritual director the ability to command me in such a way as to make me obedient to him. My soul was very sensitive to feel any offense that I committed against God, however slight it might be. So I could not pray properly until I had rid myself of it.

I prayed earnestly that our Lord would hold me by the hand and not allow me to fall again, now that I was under the direction of His servants. For it now seemed to me that to turn my back on the way that I had been shown would be a great evil and that these men would lose their reputation on my account.

**Francis de Borja, Duke of Gandia** At this time Father Francis, Duke of Gandia, came to Avila. Some years before, he had given away all his possessions and had entered the Society of Jesus. My confessor, and the nobleman whom I mentioned before, arranged that Father Francis should visit me in order that I might speak to him and give him an account of my way of prayer. For they knew him to be much favored and comforted of God. He had given up much and was rewarded for it even in his life.

**Teresa advised to relax in her ways of praying.** When he had heard me, he told me it was the work of the Spirit of God and that he thought I was not right now to prolong any further resistance. Until now it had been safe to do so, since I had been meditating on some aspect of the Passion. So if our Lord should raise my spirit, I should not resist but allow His Majesty to raise it up since I was not seeking it. As one who had made great spiritual progress himself, he gave me both medicine and advice. He said that further resistance would be a mistake. I was left greatly comforted. So, too, was the nobleman, who greatly rejoiced when he was told that it was the work of God. He had always helped me and given me advice in matters where he could, which were great *(Life, XXIV).*

I now resume the story of my life. I was in much distress **1** and great pain. Many prayers, as I said, were made on my behalf that the Lord would lead me by another and a safer way. For they told me that I was under suspicion for the way that I was going. The truth is, that although I was praying to God before this, and wished that I could desire another way [to have her visions], yet when I saw the progress that I was making, I was unable to really desire any change even though I always prayed for it. But there were expectations when I was cast down by what people said to me and by the fears with which they filled me.

Yet I felt that I was completely changed. I could do **2** nothing but put myself in the hands of God. He knew **Teresa wholly** what was expedient for me. Let Him do with me as He **committed herself** willed in all things. I saw that, in this way, I was being di- **into God's hands.** rected heavenwards, whereas before I was going to hell. So I could not force myself to desire any change nor believe that I was under the influence of Satan.

At the end of two years that were spent in prayer by my- **3** self and by others for this end—namely, that our Lord **Teresa's vision** would either lead me by another way or show me the truth **of Christ** of this (for now appearances of our Lord were extremely frequent)—this happened to me. I was in prayer one day. It was the feast of the glorious St. Peter, and I saw Christ close to me; or to describe it more accurately, I felt Him. For I saw nothing with the eyes of the body, nor anything with the eyes of the soul. He seemed to me to be so close beside me. And I also believe I saw that He was speaking to me.

As I was completely ignorant that such a vision was

possible, I was very much afraid at first, and did nothing
but weep. However, He spoke to me with one word to assure me. I recovered myself, and was, as usual, calm and
comforted without any fear at all. Jesus Christ seemed to
be by my side continually. As the vision was not imaginary, I saw no form. But I had a most profound feeling that
He was always on my right hand, as a witness of all that I
did. Never at any time, unless I was too much distracted,
could I be unconscious of His near presence.

**4**
**How did Teresa
know it was
Christ she saw?**

In great distress, I went at once to see my confessor and
tell him about it. He asked in what form I saw our Lord. I
told him I saw no form. He then said: "How did you know
that it was Christ?" I replied that I did not know how I
knew it.

But I could not help knowing that Jesus Christ was
close beside me, and that I saw Him distinctly, and felt
His presence. The recollection of my soul was deeper in
the Prayer of Quiet and all the more continuous. So the
effects were very different from what I had previously experienced. This was absolutely certain. I could only make
a comparison in order to explain myself. But clearly there
were no comparisons in my view because of the kind of vision that can be described.

Afterwards, I learned from Friar Peter of Alcantara, a
godly man of great spirituality, and from others of great
learning, that this vision was among the most sublime,
the kind with which the devil can least interfere (*Life*,
XXVII).

**2**
**The encourage-
ment given
Teresa by Peter
of Alcantara**

Our Lord was pleased to succor me to a great extent by
bringing me to be with that blessed Friar, Peter of
Alcantara. I have spoken about him already, and said
something about his own ascetic life. Among other
things, I have been assured that he continually wore for
twenty years a girdle made of iron. He is the author of a
number of books in Spanish on prayer which are now in
common use. Because he was so much concerned about it,
his prayers are very profitable to those who are given to
prayer. He kept the first rule of the blessed St. Francis in

all its rigor, and did those things which I have already described.

Well, a widow, the servant of God and my friend, aware that such a wonderful man had come, knew exactly what to do. She had seen my great distress and was a real comfort to me. Her faith was so strong that she could not help believing that what others said was the work of the devil, she knew to be the work of the Spirit of God. As she is a person of much common sense and prudence, and one to whom our Lord is very bountiful in prayer, it pleased His Majesty to let her discern what learned men had failed to see.

So, when she knew that the blessed man of God (Peter of Alcantara) had come, she obtained leave for me to stay in her home without saying a word to me. Then I could more conveniently confer with him the first time he came. Afterwards, I had many conversations with him on various occasions.

3
Dona Guionar de Ulloa

For someone who has experienced the mystical events I have, there can be no pleasure or comfort that equals that of meeting someone else whom the Lord had raised in the same way. He was extremely sorry for me, telling me that one of the greatest trials in the world was what I had already put up with, namely the contradiction of good people. Indeed, he thought more was in store for me (*Life*, XXX).

6

May it please His Majesty that what I have written be of some use to you, my father! I have so little time, and therefore I have had great difficulty in finishing this. But it will all have been so worth while if I have succeeded in saying anything that will even cause a single act of praise to our Lord. In that case, I would think myself sufficiently rewarded (*Life*, XL).

32

# II

# ESSENTIALS FOR A LIFE OF PRAYER

### I. INTRODUCTION

 ou have asked me to say something to you on
the subject of prayer. In response to what I am
going to say to you I hope that you will read
these things often.

But before I say anything about the interior matters of
the soul, that is to say about prayer, I shall mention some
things that are necessary for those who seek to follow the
way of prayer. Indeed, they are so necessary that even if
such persons are not very contemplative in their disposition, nevertheless they can advance far in the service of
the Lord if they possess these qualities. And if they do not
possess them, then it is impossible for them to be very contemplative before God. And if they think they are already
contemplative without them, they are being highly deceived.

So may the Lord help me to speak of these things, and
may He teach me what I am about to say so that it may be
for His glory. Amen.

Do not think, my friends and sisters, that I shall burden  4
you with many things. May the Lord enable us to do those
things which our Holy Fathers established and observed;
for by walking the path that they themselves established,
they have merited the title that we give to them.

27

It would be wrong to seek any other way or try to learn about this path from anyone else. I shall only enlarge on three things which are from our very natures important in order to understand the path. It is highly important that we are concerned in observing these things if we wish to obtain—both within and without our hearts—that peace which our Lord has recommended to us so much.

The first of these is to have love one for the other. The second is to have detachment from all created things. The third is the exercise of true humility. Though I name this last, it is the most important of all. Indeed, it includes all the rest (*Way of Perfection*, IV 2, 4).

## II. LOVE ONE FOR THE OTHER

5    The first need is to love one another. It is important that we have this, for there is no annoyance which cannot be tolerated among those who mutually love each other. It must be a thing that would cause extreme annoyance before there should be such displeasure. If this commandment were observed in the world as it should be, then I think we would find that love would help us with the observance of all the other duties. But because of either excess or defect of love, we never reach the point of observing this commandment perfectly.

**Excessive love among ourselves can be wrong.**    Yet it may seem that having excessive love among ourselves can never be evil. But such excess carries with it so much evil and so many imperfections that I do not think anyone will believe this—except the one who has been an eyewitness of it.

It is in this context that the devil can lay many snares, for this excess is hardly noticed by those whose consciences deal only roughly with pleasing God. And the excess of such love may seem to them very virtuous. But those who are concerned about spiritual maturity have a deep understanding of the mischief this excess of love can cause.

Little by little, you see, excessive love among ourselves

can take away the strength of the will to be wholly occupied with loving God.

This, I think, happens to women oftener than to men, and it does very considerable injury to the community. It gives rise to the following: failing to love equally all the others; resentment to an injury done to one's friend; desiring to have possessions in order to give gifts; preoccupation with the need to speak to the person concerned; obsession with the need to communicate to the person loved how dear she is.

**6**

These and other trifling things distract one from a love for God. For these great friendships are seldom directed toward helping one to love God more. Rather, I believe, the devil is the cause of them in order to raise factions in the community. For when love is in the service of His Majesty, the will does not proceed with passion; it proceeds by seeking help to conquer the other passions.

I would prefer, therefore, that there would be many friendships within a large community. But in a house where there are no more than thirteen [which was the situation Teresa was talking about], then all must be friends of each other, all must be loved, all must be held dear, all must be helped mutually and equally.

**7**
**Many friendships are preferable in a large community.**

So watch out for those friendships which purport to love the Lord, however holy they may be. Even among brothers they can be poisonous. And I see no benefit in them. If the friends are relatives, the situation is much worse; it is a pestilence!

Believe me, sisters, that I speak the truth even though it may seem extreme. In such truth there lies maturity and real peace. Many occasions of sin are removed from those who are not overemphasizing some virtue. But if our will inclines more to one virtue than to another (and it is natural that it should do so), then we may often be induced to love in an unbalanced way. So let us stop this evil carefully and not suffer ourselves to be dominated by that affection. Let us love the virtues and the interior good, and let us use all care and diligence to prevent ourselves from making too much fuss of this exterior element.

8      Do not let us, therefore, become so submissive that we allow our wills to be slaves to anyone, save to the One Who bought it with His own blood (1 Peter 1:18-19).

9      To break away from these friendships involving a particular fondness, great care is necessary from the *outset* of the friendship. This breaking away should be done delicately and lovingly rather than harshly.

10      Return with me to our subject of loving one another. It is pointless to be recommending this love. For there are some who are so like brutes that they will not love each other, even though they are always dealing with and being in the company of each other.

Such people may have no dealings or recreation with persons outside the community. They believe that God loves them in a special way because, for His sake, they have left everything. But to those who think like this, I would like to say a little about how this love for one another must be practiced.

11
**Love is a great virtue.**      What is the nature of this virtuous love, which is the love I want to practice here? And how do we know if we have this love?

It is indeed a great virtue to have it, for our Lord Himself has so strongly recommended it to us (John 13:34). I can only express myself about it according to the dullness of my own mind. If in other books you can find a detailed explanation, do not take anything from me. Perhaps I do not really know what I am talking about.

12
**Two kinds of love**      There are two kinds of love with which I am dealing here. One kind is spiritual. This love does not seem to stir sensuality or affect the tenderness of our nature and take away our purity. The other kind of love is spiritual mixed with our sensuality and compassion. It is legitimate as the kind of love that we may have for our relatives and friends, for example.

I want therefore to speak especially about the love which is spiritual, that love which is not affected by any passion. For once passion creeps in, the harmony is destroyed quickly (*Way of Perfection*, Chapter 6).

Now it seems to me that those who know of His affection love others very differently from those who do not yet know God's love. This clear knowledge is about the nature of the world, yes, that there is indeed another world and a great difference between them. One is eternal and the other is only a dream.

Loving the Creator is also distinguished from loving the creature. This is seen through the eyes of experience, because experiencing the distinction is entirely different from merely conceiving of or believing about it.

People who know the distinctions between love of the creature and love of the Creator are much more indifferent to the love that others give to them or the love they desire from others. Sometimes these people may suddenly feel delighted in being loved; yet, when they think about it more soberly, they realize it is foolish to dwell on this love except as it causes them to do good to their souls by learning or by prayers. It is not that they cease to be thankful to those who love them and refrain from recommending them to God. But they consider our Lord to be the most concerned Person among those who love them. They know that love comes from God (*Way of Perfection*, Chapter 6).

This group of people leave it to His Majesty to repay those who love them, and they beg Him to do so. In this way they remain free. For it seems to them that the repayment of love is not really their business.

It will seem to you that such persons do not love or know anyone but God. I say, "Yes, they do love, with a much greater, more genuine, and more intense love. But it is a more beneficial love." Indeed, it is love. And these souls are more inclined to give than to receive. Even with respect to the Creator Himself, they are wont to give more than to receive. This, I say, is that attitude that truly merits the name of "love," for all other base attachments have usurped the name "love" in comparison.

**Spiritual love imitates the love of Jesus.**

Such spiritual love seems to be imitating the love which the good Lover Jesus has had for us. This spiritual love is the kind of love I would desire all to have. Even though its beginning is so imperfect, the Lord will gradually mature it.

**Be tenderhearted to all.**

So let us begin by using the suitable means, for even though love bears with it some natural tenderness, no harm will be done provided this tenderness is shown toward all. It is good and necessary sometimes in loving to show and also to have affection. It is good to feel some of the trials and sicknesses of our sisters, even though these may be small. For there are times when even trifles will cause as much suffering to one as a great trial will to another. Little things can bring much distress to persons who have sensitive natures. If you are not like these sensitive souls, do not fail to be compassionate toward them. Knowing then how to sympathize with your neighbor in his trials—however small they may be—is important.

**8**
**Spiritual love is selfless.**

How good and true is such love when a sister can help others by putting aside her own advantage for their sake. She will make much progress in all the virtues. Better friendship will in this way be fostered than all that tender words may utter, for tender words are not enough. If you do what lies within your power, the Lord will make you so strong that as a woman you will astonish men. And how easy this is for His Majesty since He made us from nothing.

**9**
**Spiritual love is practical.**

Another proof of such spiritual love is that you strive in your household duties to relieve others of work. You also rejoice and praise the Lord in these ways. All these things, not to mention the great good that they provide in themselves, will also help very much to further peace and unity among the sisters. May it please His Majesty that this love always continue *(Way of Perfection,* VII).

## III. Detachment

Now let us talk about the detachment that we ought to have in relation to created things. For if this detachment is practiced with perfection, it will include everything. I say that it will include "everything" because, when we embrace the Creator and heed not any creature at all, His Majesty will give us His virtues. Doing little by little what we can, we will hardly have anything else to fight against. It is the Lord Who is our defense and Who takes up the battle against the demons and the world on our behalf.

We think too much of ourselves and are dilatory in giving ourselves wholly to God. As His Majesty will not allow us to benefit from any attachment that is so precious yet also so costly, thus we should prepare ourselves for it. I see very plainly that only by self-detachment can such a good be procured in this life. If, however, we did not cling to anything in this world, but had all our thoughts and conversation in Heaven, then I believe that all this blessing would very quickly be given to us. It would be given provided we equip ourselves thoroughly for it at once, as some of the saints have done. We think that we are giving all to God. In fact, we are like tenant farmers who offer the produce while retaining the land, thinking the land is our own.

**2**
Hesitancy to be self-detached hinders our spiritual progress.

We decide to become poor. This is a decision of great merit. At the same time, we quietly make up our minds never to lack anything. We do this not just with the basic needs of life, but also with its luxuries. Moreover, we make friends with those who can supply us.

In these hidden ways of looking after ourselves, we do more harm to our integrity. We also place ourselves in greater moral danger than if we had—rather than becoming ascetic—simply held on to our own possessions.

**3**
We have difficulty in our self-detachment.

**4**
We still seek
self-significance.

We also thought that we had given up all desire and ambition for worldly honors when we took up the devout life and were seeking only godliness. Yet no sooner are we touched in some area of personal significance then we suddenly forget that we had surrendered that area to the Lord. So we grab it back again into our own hands, taking it out of His hands. We do this in spite of the feeling that we have surrendered our wills wholly up to God. So it is with everything else!

**5**
Self-detachment
requires self-
discipline.

This is a pleasant way of seeking the love of God! We will hold on to our own affections, and yet we want to grab in handfuls of the love of God! We make no efforts to bring our ideals to disciplined fruition or to lift them above the things of this world. Yet we still hope to receive spiritual consolations.

This attitude is not good enough! For we are seeking to hold together things which are incompatible. Because we do not give ourselves up wholly and immediately to God, this treasure is not given wholly and immediately to us. May it be the good pleasure of our Lord to give it to us bit by bit. In the meanwhile, it may cause us to endure all the trials in the world.

**6**
Persevere in
detachment.

God shows great mercy to whom He gives the grace and resolve to strive for this blessing. For God withholds Himself from no one who perseveres. He will little by little strengthen that soul so that it may come forth victorious. I say he who is given the "resolve" because of the multitude of things which Satan puts in our way. He tries to keep us from even beginning the pilgrimage of our souls toward God. Satan knows what he will lose; not only that soul, but a multitude of others inspired by such example.

Therefore, whoever enters on this road of detachment will, with the help of God, reach the end in safety. I believe such a one will never travel alone for he will also take many with him. God gives to such, as to a competent military officer, a good band who will be of his company (*Life*, XI).

Do you think, sisters, that it is a small blessing we receive in obtaining this grace to give ourselves to the Almighty entirely and without reserve? For in Him are all blessings. Let us praise Him very much, sisters, for having brought us together here, where the only concern is to give ourselves entirely to Him. Perhaps I can only speak properly about this matter by guessing from what I have experienced about the opposite of detachment.

People already see how disengaged we are from all things when they look in from the outside. It seems our Lord wishes that we, whom He has brought here, should separate ourselves from everything. Then His Majesty may draw us nearer to Himself without any obstacle.

**2**
**God's presence in us requires total self-abandonment.**

O, my Creator and Lord, how did I deserve so great an honor? It seems that You have sought out all the means necessary to approach nearer to us. May it please your Goodness that we lose not this favor by our own fault. O, my sisters! For the love of God, understand the great honor that our Lord has done for those whom He has brought here. How many there are who are better than myself and who would joyfully take this place. Yet our Lord bestowed this upon me, who so little deserves it (*Way of Perfection*, XIII).

Having abandoned the world and our kindred, and living under the rules which we have mentioned above, it now seems that we have done everything and have left nothing with which to contend. O, my sisters! Be not so smug nor allow yourself to get sleepy, or else you will be like to him who lies down very quietly in bed. Having bolted his door fast for fear of the thieves, at the same time he actually has them in the house. And you know that there is no thief worse than a domestic one.

**1**
**Never be sorry about your self-detachment.**

Since, therefore, our nature remains always the same, great care must be used, and everyone should constantly deny her own will. Yes, many things may wrench this holy liberty of the spirit from our grasp. But we must seek to fly to our Creator despite the burdens of earth and land.

2
Reflect on the
vanities of life.
The great remedy against the evil of self-will is to continually remember the vanity of all things and how soon they will come to an end. Thus we shall take off our affections from things that are so earthly and place them on that which shall never end.

This may seem a weak remedy, but it does strengthen the soul greatly. And with regard to trifles, it is useful to take great care when we have an affection for any object. We should turn our thoughts away from it and fix them on God. In this His Majesty assists us and does us a great favor, because in this house the greatest difficulty has already been overcome.

But this separating from ourselves, and this denying and renouncing of ourselves is so difficult. We are closely united to ourselves and love ourselves excessively, also. So here is where true humility must enter. For it is this virtue of humility and that other virtue of mortification which seem always to go together. They seem as two sisters who are inseparable. Indeed, they are.

## IV. Humility: True and False

The whole foundation of prayer must be laid in humility, and the more a soul humbles itself in prayer, the more God lifts it up (*Life*, XII, 5). The nearer we draw to God, the more this virtue should grow; if it does not, everything is lost (*Life*, XII, 5). The most elegant prayer is unacceptable to God unless it is accompanied by humility (*Way*, XXII, 4).

Remember
Who God is!
You must think and understand Whom you are speaking to. In a thousand lifetimes we shall never manage to understand how our Lord deserves to be addressed; before His presence, even the angels tremble (*Way*, XXII, 7). It is well if you remember to Whom you are talking and who you are yourself, if only so that you may speak with proper reverence. For how will you be able to call the King "Your Highness," or to know what ceremonies are used in ad-

dressing a nobleman, if you do not properly understand what is His estate and what is your own? (*Way*, XXII, 4).

Think about the certain kinds of humility which exist and of which I mean to speak. Some think it is humility not to believe that God is bestowing His gifts upon them.

*God's gifts are without merit on our part.*

Let us clearly understand this: It is perfectly clear that God bestows His gifts without any merit whatever on our part. Let us be grateful to His Majesty for them. If we do not recognize the gifts received at His hands, we shall never be moved to love Him. It is a most certain truth that, the richer we see ourselves to be—confessing at the same time our poverty—the greater will be our progress and the more real will be our humility.

An opposite course tends to take away all courage. We shall think ourselves incapable of great blessings if we begin to fear vainglory as our Lord begins to show His mercy upon us.

*5
God also strengthens us against the devil.*

So let us believe that He Who gives these gifts will also, when the devil begins to tempt us, give us the grace to detect Satan and the strength to resist him. That is to say, He will do so if we walk in simplicity before Him and aim to please only Him—not man. It is an obvious thing that our love for a person is greater the more distinctly we remember the good he has done to us.

If, then, it is lawful and commendable to remember that we have our being from God, that He has created us out of nothing, and that He preserves us, let us also remember all the benefits of His death and Passion. He suffered for us long before He made us. If this is so, should it not also be lawful for me to discern, confess, and consider often that I was once accustomed to speak only of vanities? And is it also not lawful now for me to consider that our Lord has given me the grace to speak only of Himself?

*6
Remember the benefits of Christ's Passion.*

Here is a precious pearl. When we remember that this precious knowledge is given to us and that we have it in our own possession, it powerfully invites us to love.

*7
Treasure the pearl of great price.*

In all this, the fruit of prayer is founded on humility. What will our thoughts be when we find pearls of greater price, such as contempt of the world and of ourselves, pearls which some servants of God have already received? Is it clear that these servants consider themselves greater debtors, and therefore are under greater obligation to serve Him?

We must acknowledge that we have nothing of ourselves. We must confess the great mercy of our Lord, Who on a soul so wretched and poor and so utterly undeserving as mine would bestow greater riches than I could deserve. He brings these riches even when the first of these pearls was enough for any soul.

**8**
**Be grateful.** We must renew our thanks to serve Him. We must strive not to be ungrateful, because it is on this condition that our Lord dispenses His treasures. For if we do not make good use of them and of the highest state to which He raises us, He will return and take them from us. Then we shall be poorer than ever.

His Majesty will give the pearls to him who shall bring them forth and employ them usefully for Himself and for others. For how shall one be useful—and how shall he spend liberally—who does not know that he is rich? It is not possible—our nature being what it is—that one can have the courage necessary for great things who does not know that God is on his side.

So miserable are we, and so inclined to the things of this world, that we can hardly have any real abhorrence or great detachment from all earthly things if we fail to cling dearly to those things listed above. It is by these gifts that our Lord gives us the strength which we through our sins have lost.

**9** A man will hardly wish to be held in contempt and abhorrence by others, nor will he seek after the other great virtues to which the spiritually mature attain, if he has not the pledge of God's personal love for him coupled together with a living faith. Our nature is so dead that we go after that which we see immediately before us.

It is these graces, therefore, that quicken and strengthen our faith. It may well be that I, one who is so wicked, measure others by myself; and that others require nothing more from themselves than the verities of the faith in order to render their words more perfectly. While I, wretched that I am, have need of everything! *(Life,* X, 4-9).

Keep yourselves, my daughters, from false humility which the devil suggests concerning the greatness of your sins. For in this way he tries to draw us away from Holy Communion and also away from prayer.

10
Guard against
false humility.

It is sometimes a great and a true humility to esteem ourselves as bad as we may be. But at other times it is a false and a spurious humility. I know it, for I have experienced it myself.

True humility, however great, does not disquiet or disorder the soul. It comes with great peace, and great serenity, and great delight. Although we should see our utter wickedness—how truly we deserve to be in hell, and how both God and man must despise and abhor us—yet true humility comes with a certain sweetness and satisfaction attending it. This humility does not stifle or crush the soul. Rather, it delights the soul and disposes the soul for the better service of God.

Humility
is serene.

While that other sorrow troubles all, and confounds all, and destroys all, it is the devil's humility when he gets us to distrust God. When you find yourselves in this state, lay aside all thinking on your own misery and meditate on the infinite mercy of God, and think on the inexhaustible merit and grace of Jesus Christ.

I was once considering what the reason was our Lord loved humility in us so much. I suddenly remembered that He is essentially the supreme truth and that humility is just our walking in the truth. For it is a very great truth that we have no good in us; we have only misery and nothingness. He who does not understand this walks in lies. But he who understands this the best is the most pleasing

Humility is
knowing God.

to the Supreme Truth. May God grant us this favor, sisters, never to be without the humbling knowledge of ourselves.

**Humility is the sovereign of the virtues.** O sovereign of all virtues! O lady of all the creatures! O empress of the whole world!

Whoever has you may go forth and fight boldly with all of hell at once. Let your soldiers not fear, for victory is already theirs. Your soldiers only fear to displease God. They constantly beseech Him to maintain all the virtues in them.

It is true that these virtues have this quality: They hide themselves from him who possesses them so that he never sees them in himself; nor does he think that he can ever possess a single one of them. Other men see all the virtues in him, but he so values them that he still pursues after them and seeks them as something never to be attained by such as he is.

Humility is one of these virtues. She is the queen and empress and sovereign over them all. In fact, one act of true humility in the sight of God is of more worth than all the knowledge, sacred and profane, in the whole world [Quoted in A. Whyte, *Saint Teresa, an Appreciation*, pp. 61-62].

8  Let us now return to our castle of many mansions (see chapter 5 of this book.)

You must not conceive of these rooms as one following behind another in sequence. Rather, turn your eye toward the center; it is the lodging or the palace where the King is. Think of it as a palmetto that has leaves surrounding and covering the tasty part that can be eaten. Here, surrounding this center room, are many other rooms.

**Humility is engendered by self-knowledge.** The same comparison holds true for those virtues listed above. The things of the soul must always be considered as abundant, spacious, and large. To do this is not to exaggerate. For the soul is capable of much more than we can ever conceive of, and the sun that is in this royal chamber shines in all parts.

It is very important for any soul that practices either little or much prayer not to hold itself back and stay in one corner. Let it walk through the dwelling places which are above, down below, and in all their length and breadth, since God has given the soul such great dignity. Do not force it to stay a long time in one room alone, unless it is in the room of self-knowledge.

How necessary this room of self-knowledge is—see that you understand me—even for those whom our Lord entertains in the same chamber in which He is Himself. For however favored they may be, they must know that only prayer and self-knowledge can mature them. They will not be able to become godly otherwise, even should they wish to do so. For humility must always be at work.

**Humility is the heart of prayer.**

Like a bee that flies abroad and sucks the flowers, so the soul, by this knowledge of herself, sometimes may soar above also to consider the greatness and majesty of her God. Here it will discover its true lowliness better than by thinking of itself, and it will be freer from the vermin that enter the first room which are those of introspective self-knowledge. For even though it is by the grace of God that a person practices self-knowledge, that which applies in lesser matters applies so much more in greater ones. And believe me, we shall practice much better virtue through God's help than by being tied down to our own misery.

**True loveliness is in considering God, not ourselves.**

I do not know whether I have expressed myself clearly enough. For knowing ourselves is something so very important that I would not want any complacency about this matter, however high you may ascend into the heavens. For while we are on this earth nothing is more important to us than humility.

**9**

I repeat that it is good to try to enter first into the mansions where self-knowledge is practiced rather than to fly to the others. This is the only way into all of them. Humility is the right road, and if we can journey along a safe and level path, why should we want wings with which to fly?

Let us therefore endeavor to advance more along this

way for, in my opinion, we shall never be able to know ourselves except as we endeavor to know God. By considering His greatness, we shall get in touch with our own lowliness. By looking at His purity, we shall see our own filth. By pondering His humility, we shall see how far we are from being humble ourselves.

11
Fears arise not from humility but from lack of self-understanding.

Many souls think that all their fears stem from humility. There are so many other sources that I could mention. These fears come from not understanding ourselves completely. For they distort self-knowledge. And I am not at all surprised if we never get free from ourselves, for this lack of freedom from ourselves is what should be feared.

So I say, daughters, that we should set our eyes only on Christ, Who is our Good and our Truth, and on His saints. For there we shall learn true humility. Then the intellect will be enhanced, and self-knowledge will not make us base and cowardly.

Even though this is the first mansion, it is so rich and so precious that, if the soul slips away from the vermin which are within it, nothing will hinder one from advancing. But terrible are the wiles and deceits which are used by the devil. He makes it so that souls may not know themselves or understand their own powers (*Interior Castle*, I, part 2).

An illustration.

[To illustrate the importance of self-knowledge, Teresa cites an example.]

I will give you some account of an individual with whom I conversed intimately not very long ago. She was a person who loved to communicate frequently. And she never did any harm to anyone.

This person was tender-hearted. She lived in continual solitude, dwelling in a house by herself. She was of such a sweet disposition that nothing could make her angry. She never uttered any unbecoming language. She had never married, neither was she now of an age to marry. She had suffered great afflictions and all with her usual peace and serenity.

When I noticed these good qualities, I thought they were signs of a soul that was far advanced in the ways of

God, and of a very high order of prayer. At first I esteemed her exceedingly, because I saw that she committed no offense against God. I heard from others also that she was careful not to commit any.

But when I conversed a little more with her, I began to perceive that all went on well with her until *her interest* or *self-love* were touched. Then her conscience was not so tender but was indeed very gross. For I discovered that although she suffered all things that were said to her with patience, yet she still adhered to points of honor or self-esteem. Thus she was immersed in this misery which really held her captive.

*Her spirituality was narcissistic.*

She was also so much addicted to listening and inquiring after what was said and done in the world, that I wondered how such a person could tolerate being alone one hour. For she was very fond of her own ease. She glided over all her actions and excused herself from sin. According to the reasons that she gave, I thought people had wronged her in some things. She quite took me in, and almost everyone considered her to be a saint.

After getting to know her, I had a different view respecting the persecutions that she said she had suffered. She ought not to have represented herself as being *free from all blame.* I could not envy her way of living nor indeed her sanctity. She and two more whom I have seen in my life—who were saints in their own opinions—have terrified me more than *all the sinners I ever saw.* May our Lord then give us light so that however much the devil labors, he will not delude you in the same way that he does those who live in their own houses (*Conceptions of Divine Love*, 11, 242-3).

*Fear meeting self-made saints!*

## V. TEMPTATION AND HUMILITY

It has occurred to me to speak about some temptations that beginners are liable to have. I myself have had some

[1]

of them. It may be helpful then to give advice about this matter.

**Have no confidence in self.**

Now strive in the beginning to walk in joy and freedom, for there are some persons who think that their devotion will go away if they live too spontaneously. It *is* right to be afraid of self, though. Having no confidence in ourselves, we will not place ourselves in those circumstances where men usually sin against God. For it is a most necessary fear to be afraid of trusting ourselves too much.

If, then, a temptation comes from our natural temperament, there are few who can consider themselves so strong as to be negligent about this danger. As long as we live, even for the sake of humility, it is good to be realistic about our own miserable nature.

But as I have just said, there are many reasons why it is permitted for us to relax. Then we are able to return with greater strength to prayer. Discretion is required in everything.

**2**
**Rather have confidence only in God.**

We need to have great confidence. It is necessary for us not to hold back our desires. Rather, we must put our trust in God. If we do violence to ourselves gradually we shall, though not all at once, reach that height which many saints by His grace have attained. If they have never resolved to desire, and have never little by little acted upon that resolve, they would never have ascended to so high a state.

**3**
**The humble advance quickly in the ways of God.**

His Majesty seeks and loves courageous souls. But they must be humble in all their ways and have no confidence in themselves. I never saw one of those lag behind on the road. And never does a cowardly soul make the progress in many years which the former can make in only a few. I never cease to marvel how important it is to be courageous in striving for great things along this path. The soul may not have the strength to be courageous and humble all at once. Nevertheless, it takes flight and ascends to great heights. And, like a little bird whose wings are also weak, it may grow weary and have to rest.

At one time I often used to think of those words of the Apostle Paul: "All things are possible with God" (Philippians 4:13). I saw clearly that I could do nothing of myself. This was of great help to me to see this. So also was the saying of Augustine: "Give me, Lord, what You command, and command what You desire." I often thought that the Apostle Peter did not lose anything when he threw himself into the sea, even though he was afraid afterward (Matthew 14:30).

**4**
**Humility is dependence upon God.**

These first acts of resolution are of great importance, even though in this initial stage it is necessary to hold back sometimes and be bound by discretion and the guidance of a spiritual director. But we must be careful that he is not one who will teach us to crawl like toads, nor one who will be satisfied when the soul shows itself set only to catch lizards. Humility must always go before us so that we may know that this strength comes not from our own.

But it is necessary that we should understand what this humility is like. For I believe Satan will try to do great harm. He hinders those who begin to pray from going forward by suggesting to them false notions of humility. He makes them think that it is pride to have spiritual ambitions, desires to imitate the saints, and longings to be like martyrs. He will tell us or cause us to think that since we are sinners, the deeds of the saints are only for our admiration and not for our imitation.

**5**
**Satan creates false notions of humility.**

I, too, say these same things. But we must see what are those actions which we admire and which are also those we can imitate without pride. It would be wrong for a person who is weak and sickly to undertake such fasting, intense asceticism, and an abode in the desert where he cannot sleep or find anything to eat.

Nevertheless we ought to think that we can, with God's help, strive to have great contempt for the world, to have no esteem of honor, and to be detached from our own possessions. We have such stingy hearts that it seems

**6**
**Why do we not progress faster in the spiritual life?**

we will lose the whole world if we neglect the body just a little for the sake of the spirit. Then we argue that it is a help to be secure in the possession of some necessities because concern about them is disturbing our prayer life.

It is painful to me that our confidence in God is so scanty, and our self-love so strong, such that any anxiety about our necessities should disturb us. But so it is, for when our spiritual progress is so slight, a mere nothing will give us as much trouble as great and important matters will give to others. And we think ourselves spiritual!

Enter, my daughters, enter into your interior, and pass beyond those miserable works of yours which you are required to perform as Christians. Let it be sufficient that you are God's subjects. Be not desirous of much more.

Consider the saints who have entered into the chamber of this King, and you will see by their lives what a difference there is between them and us. Do not demand that which you have not merited. For whatever service we do, we must not think we can merit it, *we* who have offended God!

O humility, humility! I know not what temptation has come upon me in this matter, or I cannot help believing that the one who is over-concerned about aridity in his soul is in some way lacking in this virtue of humility. Thus I do not wish to dwell upon those great interior afflictions of which I have spoken before, but I believe it evidences a great lack of humility (*Interior Castle*, III, part 1).

Consider well, my daughters, those points which I have marked out for you. For I do not know how to express them better. But our Lord will make you understand them in order that you may draw humility from your spiritual aridities and not restlessness. For it is this that the devil aims to do.

Let us then acquire humilities, sisters, for this is the ointment of our souls. If we possess this virtue, the Physician (who is God) will come and heal our wounds, although He may delay a little (*Interior Castle*, III, part 1, 1, and part 2, 2, 6).

## VI. HUMILITY AND SPIRITUAL IMPATIENCE

My aim in the foregoing section was to explain how much we may attain to ourselves. In these beginnings of devotion we are able in some degree to help ourselves. Thinking often and pondering on the sufferings of our Lord for our sakes moves us to compassion and the sorrow and tears which are sweet. The thought of the blessedness we hope for, the knowledge of the love that our Lord has borne us, and the understanding of His resurrection kindle within us a joy which is neither wholly spiritual nor wholly sensual. The joy is virtuous, and the sorrow is most effective.

All these help us to develop devotion through our understanding. But devotion is not merited or achieved by ourselves if God does not grant it.

Now it is best for the soul which God has not raised to a higher state not to try and seek to rise higher. Let this be well considered, because all the soul will gain in that manner will be but loss. In its present state, it can make many acts of good resolutions to do much for God and to enkindle its love for God. There are other acts which may help the growth of virtues according to what has been written in a book called *The Art of Serving God* (by Rodriguez de Solis). This is a most excellent work and profitable for those who do wish to understand.

**Wait on God.**

The soul also may place itself in the presence of Christ and accustom itself to many acts of love because of His sacred humanity. The soul may remain in His presence continually and speak to Him; it may pray to Him in its necessities and complain to Him of its troubles. It may be joyful with Him in all its joys and yet not forget Him because of its happiness. All this the soul may do without set prayers, but rather with words which are relevant to its desires and its needs.

3
**Place yourself in the presence of God.**

This is an excellent way in which to advance in maturity quickly. He that strives for this wonderful companion-

4

ship will make much of it and will sincerely love our Lord to whom we owe so much.

There is, therefore, no reason why we should trouble ourselves because we have no more external evidence of devotion. Rather let us give thanks to our Lord who allows us to have desires to please Him though our works be so poor. This practice of the presence of Christ is profitable in all states of prayer and is a safe way of advancing in spiritual progress.

**5**
**It is spiritual pride to be obsessed with self-involvement.**

He who would pass from this state and seek to advance further in order to satisfy spiritual ambitions that are denied him will, in my opinion, lose both the one and the next.* Since these spiritual blessings are supernatural, man is not capable of achieving them himself. He will thus be left desolate and in great aridity. It seems to be a kind of spiritual pride when we seek to ascend higher. Remember God descends so low He allows us, being what we are, to draw near unto Him.

**7**
**This does not mean that we do not seek higher things.**

It must not be understood that I am speaking of preventing our minds from considering the high things of heaven and of its glory; or of considering God and His great wisdom. I have never done this myself, because I did not have the capacity for it as I have said before. God gave me grace to understand truth about the things of this earth. Yet it is much more to think of heavenly things. Others may profit in this way, particularly those who are learned. But learning is a great treasure in exercising the thoughts of heavenly things only if it is accompanied by humility. I have observed this in some learned men who made their beginning and then made rapid progress. This is the reason I am so anxious that many learned men become spiritual. But I shall speak of this later on.

Let us not rise if God does not raise us. This is the lan-

---

*This is because he will lose the prayer of quiet dependence upon God since he is now seeking voluntarily to abandon it before he has been further blessed in it. And he will not attain to the next stage because he is attempting to do it in his own strength.

guage of true spirituality. He will understand me who has had any experience. And if I do not know how to explain it or if what I have said does not make sense, this one with experience understands.

In mystical theology, the understanding ceases from its acts because God suspends it. But we must not imagine that we can bring about this suspension. That must not be done. Nor must we allow the understanding to cease from its acts. In that case, we shall be stupid and cold and the result will be neither the one nor the other. But when our Lord suspends the understanding and makes it to cease from its acts, He puts before it that which astonishes and occupies it. Without making any reflections, then, the mind can comprehend in a moment more than we would comprehend in all our years with all the efforts of the world.

*True spiritual experience is not the suspension of the mind's activity.*

12

I repeat my advice. It is very important that we do not attempt to raise our spirits ourselves if God does not raise them for us. If He does, then there will be no mistaking it.

For women this is especially wrong, because the devil can delude them. I am certain, however, that our Lord will never allow us to hurt anyone when we labor to draw near to God in humility. On the contrary, we will derive more profit and advantage out of Satan's attempt to hurt us through humiliation. I have dwelt long upon this matter because of the importance of it *(Life,* XII).

# III

# Prayer, as Faith and Fervor for God Alone

 what utter ruin is the state of religious people today. I am not comparing men against women, as to whether or not the rules of the Order are kept more by one than the other. But I am speaking of the condition where two options are given, one of observance and virtue, and another of disregard and moral carelessness. Yet they are not equal options. For such is the sinfulness of our hearts that the latter option predominates. Because it is the broadest way, it is the more popular.

Since the way of religious observance is so little practiced, those who would do so find that they have to fear their own colleagues more than the devils themselves. They have to be very guarded how they speak of their friendship with God. It is so much easier to talk about those friendships which the devil himself might arrange in religious communities. So I wonder why we appear to be so astonished that the church is in so much trouble. For we see those who ought to be an example to others disfigure the work of the saints of God in times past. May it please His Majesty to apply a remedy to this, as He sees it to be needful! Amen (*Life,* VII).

## PRAYER AS AFFECTION AND DESIRE FOR GOD

**7
Prayer is
friendship
with God.**

For prayer is nothing else than being on terms of friendship with God. It is frequently conversing in secret with Him Who loves us.

Now true love and lasting friendship require certain affections; those of our Lord we know are absolutely perfect. Ours are vicious, sensual, and thankless. You cannot, therefore, bring yourselves to love Him as He loves you, because you do not have the same disposition to do so. If you do not love Him, you should be concerned with having His friendship and noticing how great His love is for you. Then you can rise above that pain of being much with Him Who is so different from you (*Life*, VIII).

**1
Teresa's
experience with
her Savior**

One day when I went into the oratory to pray, I saw a picture which had been hung there to celebrate a particular feast of the church. It was a representation of Christ so grievously wounded. The very sight of it deeply moved me. For it showed so graphically how much Jesus had loved us by His sufferings for us. So keenly did I feel my part in wounding Him that I thought my heart would break. So I threw myself upon the ground beside it, my tears flowing copiously. I implored Him to strengthen me once for all, that I might never grieve Him again.

**2**

I had a great affection for Mary Magdalene, and often I thought of her communion with our Lord, especially when I went to Holy Communion. As I then knew for certain that our Lord was within me, I used to place myself at His feet, thinking that my tears also would not be despised. I did not know what I was saying. What I do know was that He did great things for me.

The Lord seemed pleased that I should shed those tears. Looking often at that picture, I seemed to make greater progress in my devotions, for I was now distrustful of myself. I placed all my confidence in God. It seems to me that I said to Him that I would not rise up until He granted me my request. I certainly believe that this helped my worship, beause my prayer life became better after that.

This was then how I prayed. I pictured Christ as being inside me. I used to think about those times when He was most lonely. During those times He must have been most afflicted and alone, like someone in trouble. I then came close to Him.

I did many simple things like that. In particular, I used to find myself in the Garden of Gethsemane alongside of Him, keeping Him company. I thought of the bloody sweat, and of the affliction He suffered there. I wished, if it had been possible, to wipe away that painful sweat from His face. I remembered that I never dared to do that. For my sins stood too strongly before me. I used to remain with Him there as long as my thoughts could concentrate on Him.

But I had many other thoughts there to torment me. For many years before I went to sleep at night, I used to meditate a little upon the mystery of this scene of Christ's prayer in the Garden while I said my prayers. I believe I profited much from this practice. It led me often to pray without realizing that I was praying. Now it has become my constant habit (*Life*, IX).

As I have said, I used to have these pictures before me of throwing myself at the feet of Christ. Sometimes when I was reading, a feeling of the presence of Christ would come over me unexpectedly. I had not the shadow of a doubt that He was within me, or that I was wholly absorbed within Him. The soul at that moment is suspended in such a way that it seems to be utterly outside of itself. The will loves. The memory is completely absorbed, it seems to me. The understanding makes no reflections. Yet it is not lost. I do nothing but sit in amazement at the greatness of the things being experienced. For God makes it clear that all is ineffable of what His Majesty places before the soul.

Before I had this kind of experience, I had a certain kind of tenderness of soul which was very lasting. It was

54 A Life of Prayer

induced to some extent by my own efforts. It was a consolation of spirit that was not wholly of the senses nor yet completely in the spirit. All of it is clearly the gift of God.

However, I believe we help to experience this tenderness when we have contrition for all our vileness and ingratitude to God, when we consider all the great things He has done for us—His Passion with its grievous pains and His life, so full of sorrows. Also, such tenderness is induced within us as we rejoice in the contemplation of His works, His greatness, and the love that He bears us.

Many other meditations will fill the heart of the one who desires to make progress in the things of God. Progress takes place although we stumble over these meditations in ignorance. Where there is a little love, the heart will be softened, and the tears will begin to flow (*Life,* X).

**1**
**Prayer as abandonment to God**

Now I think it is for the soul's good that it abandons itself entirely into the arms of God. If He takes it to heaven, so let it be. If even to hell, no matter; it is going there with its sovereign Lord. If life is to come to an end for evermore, so let it be. If He wills it to last a thousand years, the soul wills that also.

His Majesty may do what He likes with the soul. It is His property. The soul no longer belongs to itself. It has been given over wholly to our Lord. Let it, therefore, cast its cares wholly aside for ever and ever.

**2**

In this state of prayer, the soul realizes that God is doing His work without any strain on the intellect. It is simply amazed that it can see the Lord act as such a good Gardener of the soul. It is then that, like the effortless wafting of the scent of flowers, the soul's fragrance is spread to all. When God raises a soul up to this state, it can do this and much, much more (*Life,* XVII).

**6**
**Guidance about friendships**

My soul was not strong, but rather weak, about giving up certain friendships, even though I was not offending God by them. There was much natural affection in them, and I thought it would be an act of ingratitude if I broke them off. So I asked my spiritual counselor about the mat-

ter. He told me to bring the matter before the Lord for a
few days and recite the hymn "Veni, Creator" so that God
might enlighten me as to the best course. One day, having
prayed for some time, and having implored the Lord to
help me to please Him in all things, I began to sing the
hymn. As I was singing it, I fell into a trance so suddenly
that I was, as it were, carried out of myself.

This was the first time that our Lord bestowed on me     7
the grace of ecstasy. I heard these words: "I will not have
you to converse with men, but with angels." This made
me wonder very much. For the confusion of my spirit was
very much and these words were uttered in the very depth
of my soul. They made me afraid, yet they also gave me
great comfort. So when the strangeness which caused my
fear had gone, I was left with deep comfort.

Those words have been fulfilled. For I have never been     8
able to form a friendship, or find comfort, or have any par-     **A definition of**
ticular love for persons except those who I believe love     **true friendships**
God; that is, those who strive to serve Him. It has not
been in my power to do so. It is nothing to me that they
are kindred or my friends if I do not know them to be lovers of God, or persons given to prayer. It is to me a painful
cross to bear to converse with any that do not really love
God. This is the truth as far as I can judge.
From that day forth, I have had courage so great as to
leave all things to God Who was pleased in one moment
to change His servant into another person. Accordingly,
there was no need to lay down any commands about the
matter. When my counselor saw how much I clung to
these friendships, he did not venture to ask me deliberately to give them up. He must have waited until our Lord
did the work, as He did indeed. Nor do I think I could
have succeeded in doing so alone, for I had tried in vain
before. The pain it gave me was so great that I abandoned
the attempt on the excuse that it was not wrong to have
such attachments. Now our Lord has set me free, and has
given me the strength to do so (*Life*, XXIV).

## SUFFERING FOR GOD

**26** I was in prayer one night when it was time to go to sleep. I was in very great pain, and my usual sickness was coming on. [This was her morning sickness which prevented her for over twenty years from eating any food until after midday (*Life*, VII, 18).] I saw myself so much a slave to my own weakness, and yet my spirit sought its own liberty to enjoy God. This distressed me so much that I wept copiously, feeling very sorry for myself. This happened to me, not just once, but very many times. It made me feel so weary with myself, so that I felt repugnance about myself. Habitually, I know, I do not have self-hate, for I seek to do what is good for myself. May the Lord grant that I do not indulge myself with doing more for myself than is necessary! But I am afraid I do.

**27**
**Teresa's thorn
in the flesh** When I was thus distressed, our Lord appeared to me. He comforted me greatly and told me I must accept this affliction for His sake, and bear it for love of Him. My thorn in the flesh now became relevant to me. And since then, I have not known any real pain, since I resolved to serve my Lord and my Comforter with all my strength.

Although God would permit me to suffer for a little, yet He would also console me in such a way that I now even long for troubles. Now it seems to me that there is nothing more worth living for than this, so now suffering is what I most heartily pray God may give me. Sometimes I say to God with all my heart, "O Lord, I ask of You nothing else than to die or to suffer! I ask for nothing else for myself." It is a comfort to hear the clock strike another hour, for it is an hour nearer when I shall have the vision of God, and another hour of this life has passed away (*Life*, XL).

**We need freedom
in our sufferings.** O my God, what unspeakable sufferings our souls have to endure. They have lost their liberty, and they are not their own masters. What tortures come on them through this condition. I sometimes wonder how I can live through such agony of soul as I myself suffer. God be praised who gives me His own life in my soul so that I may

escape from so deadly a death! My soul has indeed received great strength from His Divine Majesty. He has had compassion upon my great misery, and He has helped me.

Oh, what a distress it is for my soul to have to return to hold commerce with this world after having had its conversation with Heaven. To have to play a part in the sad farce of this earthly existence! And yet, I am in a strait between them (Philippians 1:23). I cannot run away from this life. I must remain in this world to discharge my duty.

**Suffering spiritual exile**

But meantime, how keen is my captivity. I am wretched in my soul. And one of my worst distresses is this, that I am alone in my exile. All around me people seem to have found their aim and end in life within this horrible prison house, and to have said, "Soul, take your ease" (Luke 12:19).

But the life of my soul is incessant trouble. The cross is always on my shoulder. At the same time, I surely make some progress. God is the Soul of my soul. He embraces my soul within Himself. He enlightens and strengthens my soul. He attends to my soul day and night. He gives my soul more and more grace. This has not come about because of myself. No effort of mine has brought this about. His Majesty does it all. And He has held me by the hand, that I might not go back.

It often happens to me that when I am not even thinking of the things of God—but am engaged in other matters, or when prayer seems to be beyond my power—the efforts I make to pray in this arid condition, though bodily pains hamper my spirituality, are rewarded by an elevation of spirit or recollection. It comes so suddenly that I cannot control it, but in an instant the fruits and joys of it are mine. This happens without having had any vision, or any locution, or knowing where I am, except that when the soul is in this state, it makes great progress. This I could not have made by myself in the whole year. The gain is so great.

**2
The experience of recollection**

**3**
**The experience of violent longings for God**

At other times, certain excessive impetuosities occur accompanied by a fainting away of the soul for God, so that I have no control over myself. It seems as if my life has come to an end. I have to cry out and call upon God for help. This comes upon me with great vehemence. Sometimes I cannot remain sitting, so great is the oppression of heart. This pain comes on without my doing anything to cause it. The nature of it is such that my soul never again wants to be without it as long as I live.

Yet the longings I have are not to go on living. These feelings come on because it seems as if I must live on without any relief, for relief comes only from having the vision of God which can only come by death. Yet death is what I can never take for myself. With all this, my soul thinks that everyone else is filled with consolation and finds help for their troubles; but not me! The distress that all this creates is so intense that, if our Lord did not relieve it by throwing me into a trance—where all becomes quieted and the soul rests in a great calmness and the satisfaction of hearing other things—it would be utterly intolerable to bear any longer.

**4**
**The experience of total desire for God**

At other times, there comes upon me certain desires to serve God with such intensity that the experience is indescribable. It is accompanied by certain kinds of pain at seeing how unprofitable I am.

On these occasions, it seems to me that there are no things in this work, neither death, nor martyrdom, that I could not easily endure. This conviction also comes in a flash and is the result of studied reflection. I am wholly changed and know not how I am given such great courage. It makes me feel as if I should shout from the house-tops how terribly important it is that no man should be satisfied with the *status quo,* when we see the marvelous things God is prepared to give us (1 John 3:1).

I repeat, these desires are so great that I seem to melt within me. For I desire what I cannot contain. The body then seems to be like a prison because of its inability to serve God and the condition I am in. Were it not for the body at this point, I would be able to do mighty things as far as my strength of desire would take me. But because I see myself without any strength whatever to serve God, I feel the pain of such frustration. It is intolerable. The issue is found only in the delight, recollection, and consolation of God.

At other times when these longings to serve God come over me, I just long to do penance to God. But I am incapable of doing so. This would be such a relief for me, but I am so weak that I am unable to do so. Because of my bodily weakness, I can do nothing. At the same time, I suspect that if I gave way to such desires, I would be unable to maintain any moderation.

**5**
**The experience of the longing to expiate before God**

Sometimes when I have to speak with others, I am so greatly distressed; I long just to be alone. It makes me weep abundantly within, for it is solitude before God that I long to have. At such times, however, I may not even read or pray; the drudgery of superficial conversation at such times seems oppressive to me. It makes me feel enslaved, except on those occasions when the conversation is turned to matters of prayer and the soul. In these I find comfort and joy. Yet even these are too much for me, and I would rather not see anyone; I want to go where I can be alone. However, this is not often the case, for I do appreciate those who are my spiritual directors.

**6**
**The desire for solitude with God**

At other times, it gives me much pain that I must even eat or sleep, for I recognize that I cannot forego these things. So I submit to their need so that I can serve God more effectively. Even these duties I offer up to God.

**7**
**The offering up to God of small concerns**

Time seems so short that I never have enough time in prayer, for I would never be tired of being alone with Him. I am always wishing I had more time for reading, for I have always been fond of books. I read very little, since I no sooner get into it than I become meditative over the pleasure it gives me, and thus I turn my reading into prayer. Yet it is but rarely that I can do this. For I have many duties which do not give me the same pleasure as reading does, yet they have to be done (*Relations*, I).

**16**
**The pain of longing for God**

Another kind of prayer that is commonly experienced [by Teresa] is a certain kind of wounding. It is as if an arrow were thrust through the heart or through the prayer itself. This causes the heart great pain so that the soul is forced to complain. Yet the suffering is also so ecstatic that the soul hopes it will never end.

The suffering is not that of sense, nor is the wound a physical one. For it is within the heart itself, without any outward symptoms of pain. I cannot compare it with other pains without appearing ridiculous. It is not something to write or to talk about, for it is quite impossible for anyone who has not experienced it personally to understand it.

It is enough, however, for one to appreciate that spiritual pains are infinitely more acute than physical pains. It makes one wonder, therefore, what must be the acuteness of the sufferings of hell.

**17**

At other times, this wound of love seems to have issued from the inmost depth of the soul. Great are its effects. When our Lord does not inflict it, there is no help for it, whatever we may try to induce. Nor can we avoid it when His Majesty decides to inflict it. But the effects of it are a longing after God, a loathing of sin, and a deep awareness of how man has been robbed by the fall of Adam from God's purpose for man in the image of God (*Relations*, VIII).

**21**
**The inner wounding of the heart**

During the Octave of All Saints, I had two or three days of intense anguish. This was the result of thinking about my great sins. I also dreaded being persecuted, which had no foundation except that malicious accusations were made against me. Then all my resolutions to suffer anything for God failed me. Although I sought to encourage myself and acted accordingly, it was futile; for the pain never left me. It was a sharp warfare.

Then I came across a letter in which my good father had written and quoted from the Apostle Paul. God will not suffer us to be tempted above what we are able to endure (1 Corinthians 10:13). This was a very great comfort to me.

But the following night, I came across another saying of St. Paul in my reading with which I began to be comforted. Being slightly recollected, I remained thinking how I had our Lord present within me so that I truly saw Him as the Living God. While meditating on this, He spoke to me, and I saw Him in my inmost being. He was right inside my heart. He spoke to me in a locution. His words were: "I am here, only I want you to see that without Me you can do nothing." I was immediately reassured and my fears left me (*Relations*, IX).

**22**
**The inner presence of God**

It happened to me on another occasion to be tested grievously [concerning the foundation of one of her houses]. Almost everybody in the place where I was living and the members of my own Order were involved against me. When I was in this distress, and afflicted by many occasions of anxiety within myself, our Lord spoke to me, saying: "What are you afraid of? Do you not know that I am the Almighty? I will do for you what I have promised you." And it was done, just as He promised. I found myself strong, and immediately I felt as if I could have endured even greater trials in His service (*Life*, XXVI).

**3**
**The comfort of God**

## THE VISION OF GOD

One day while I was in prayer, I experienced such sweetness in my soul that I began to think how little I deserved such blessing. So I began rather to think how I only deserved damnation in hell.

**1**

As I was thinking about this, I was carried away on fire in a way that I cannot describe. I seemed to be filled and absorbed with the grandeur of God. In that august majesty, I was given one truth to understand, which is the fullness of all truth. Yet I cannot explain how, for I saw nothing. I was told I saw not by whom the vision came,

**The vision of God's truth**

though I knew well enough by Whom it came, namely the Truth Himself: "What I am doing for you is no small thing. It is one of those things for which You owe Me so much. For all the evils in the world come from ignorance of the truths of the Holy Scripture in their clear simplicity of which not one iota will pass away" (Matthew 5:18).

I had thought all believers accepted this, and that I had believed it. Then He said: "Ah, my daughter, they are few who love Me in truth. For if men loved Me, I should not hide My secrets from them. Do you really know what it is to love Me in truth? It is to admit that everything is a lie that is not pleasing to Me. Now, you do not understand this clearly, but you will later, because of the benefit it will bring unto your soul."

2      Praise be the Lord, I found it to be so. For after this vision I have tended to look upon everything which does not tend to the service of God as vanity and lies. I cannot tell how much I am convinced of this, nor how sorry I am for those whom I see living in darkness, not knowing the truth. I derived other blessings also from this experience, some of which I can describe, and others which are indescribable.

3
**Submit to the authority of God's Word.**

Our Lord, at the same time, uttered a special word of deepest graciousness. I do not know how He did so, but I was filled in a way which I cannot describe. It came to me with exceeding conviction and earnest purpose to observe with all my might all that was contained in the Holy Scriptures. I thought I could transcend over any obstacles to do this.

4      Of this divine truth implanted within me, I know not how a truth remains which fills me with new reverence for God. It inspires me with a sense of His Majesty and power in a way I cannot begin to describe. I can appreciate that it is very exalted. I had a great desire not to speak about these deep truths to anyone; they far surpassed all that can be spoken about them here in this world. So the living of them instead began to be very painful to me.

The vision left me in great tenderness, joy, and humil- **5**
ity. It seemed to me that the Lord now gave me great
things. I had no suspicion whatever of any illusion. I understood now what it is for a soul to be walking in the
truth, in the presence of the Truth Himself. What I understood was simply this: our Lord Himself is very Truth
(*Life*, XL).

On one occasion when I was in prayer, I had a vision in   **13**
which I saw how all things are seen in God. I cannot ex-   A vision of
plain what I saw, but what I saw remains to this day,   the Godhead
deeply imprinted upon my soul. It was a great act of grace
in God to give me that vision. It puts me to unspeakable
confusion, shame, and horror whenever I recall that magnificent sight, and then think of my sin. I believe that had
the Lord been pleased to send me that great revelation of
Himself earlier in my life, it would have kept me back
from much sin.

The vision was so delicate, so subtle, and so spiritual,
that my hard understanding cannot even at this distance
of time close with it. To make use of an illustration, it was
something like what follows.

Suppose the Godhead to be like a vast globe of light, a   **14**
globe larger than the whole world, and that all our actions
are seen in that all-embracing globe. It was something like
that which I saw. For I saw all my most filthy actions
gathered up and reflected back upon me from that world of
light. I tell you it was the most pitiful and dreadful thing to
see. I did not know where to hide myself, for that shining
light, in which there was no darkness at all, held the
whole world within it, and all worlds.

15. You will see that I could not flee from its presence.   **15**
Oh that those who commit deeds of darkness could be
made to see this! Oh that they but saw there is no secret
place from God. That all they do is done before Him, and
in Him! Oh, the madness of committing sin in the immediate presence of a Majesty so great, unto Whose holi-

ness all our sin is so hateful. In this also I saw His great mercy, in that He suffers such a sinner as I am still to live (*Life*, XL).

O Thou Lord of my soul, and my Eternal Good, why is it that when a soul resolves to follow You, and does her best to forsake all for You, why is it that You do not instantly perfect Your love and Your peace within that soul?

But I have spoken foolishly and unwisely, for it is we who are at fault in prayer and never You. We are so long and so slow in giving up our hearts to You. And You will not permit our enjoyment of You without our paying well for so precious a possession.

There is nothing in all the world wherewith to buy the diffusion of Your love in our heart but our own heart's love. If, however, we did what we could, not clinging with our hearts to anything in this world, but only having our treasure and our conversation in heaven, then this blessedness would soon be ours, as all Your saints testify. For God never withholds Himself from him who pays this price and who perseveres in seeking Him. He will, little by little, now and then, strengthen and restore that soul until at last it is victorious.

If he who enters on this road only does violence enough to himself, he will not only go to heaven himself, but he will not go alone. For he will take others with him. God will give to him as to a good leader those who will go after him. Only let not any man of prayer ever expect to enjoy his full reward here. He must remain a man of faith and prayer to the end.

Let him resolve, then, whatever his aridity and sense of a lack of devotion may be, that he will never let himself sink utterly under his cross. The day will come when he will receive all his petitions in one great answer, and all of his wages in one great reward. For he serves a good Master Who stands over him watching him. And let him never give over because of evil thoughts, even if they are sprung upon him in the middle of his prayer, as the saintly Jerome was thus vexed in the wilderness.

But all these toils of soul have their sure reward, and

their just recompense set out for them. And I can assure
you, as one who knows what she is saying, that one single
drop of water out of God's living well will both sustain you
and reward you for another day and another night of your
life of life-long prayer.

## THE LORD'S PRAYER

I will now give you some meditations on the Lord's
Prayer. For in the multiplicity of books, it sometimes
seems that we lose all devotion for that prayer. Yet it is important that we should never forget it.

It is quite clear that when a master teaches anything,
he develops a love for his pupil so that what he teaches
will inspire and delight the pupil. It is helpful also to pay
attention to what is being taught. Our Heavenly Father
acts toward us in a similar way.

Take no notice, then, of the fears that men may represent to you [as to prayer, as some theologians argued in
Teresa's day], or of the dangers they put before you. Consider that these are not times when we should believe
everybody, but only those who you see are walking conformable with the life of Christ (*Way of Perfection*, XXI).

Mental and vocal prayer belong together. If some tell
you that you can recite the Lord's Prayer and yet still be
thinking of the world, here I am sadly silent. For if you
would conduct yourself before so great a Lord, it is proper
to realize Whom you are addressing—if you would pay
Him proper respect. For how can you address a king, and
call him "your majesty," or know the etiquette when addressing a noble, unless you are acquainted with his rank
and dignity?

*Mental and vocal prayer should be united.*

What, then, is this? O my Sovereign! How can it be
tolerated? For You are my God, the Eternal King, Whose
Kingdom is not a borrowed one! So I must meditate about
the greatness of God, even as I pray silently to Him (*Way
of Perfection*, XXII).

**Prayer needs real determination.**

In prayer, I also need to emphasize to you that much depends on strong resolution for beginners. There are many reasons for this, but I shall just mention a few.

The first is that since God has given us so much, and since He still continues to bless us, it is proper that we should be resolved to be serious with Him, and so give Him our prayers from the heart. If we give time to others, does the Lord deserve less than they? Do not let us think that time is our own, but give to Him all of it entirely.

The second reason for determination is that the devil has much less power to tempt us when we are in prayer. He is much afraid of resolute souls, for he knows from experience that these do him much mischief.

A third reason is that a resolute soul fights with greater courage. It knows that, come what may, he must not turn back (*Way of Perfection*, XXIII).

**Never forget Who God is.**

When we say the prayer of our Lord, then, God forbid that we should ever forget Who this Master really is who taught us this prayer. [See Matthew 6:13.] Let us also be mindful that we pray with love and desire also so that we benefit from such an attitude.

His Majesty also teaches us that such prayer should be made in solitude, for He also prayed like that. He did so, however, not for His own needs, but for our instruction. Remember what I have already said, that we cannot pray to God and to the world at the same time. Yet we do this if we are thinking all the time how others think of our prayers, or if we are distracted by and roam around in our scattered imaginations (*Way of Perfection*, XXVI).

Consider the words that His divine mouth utters, for by the very first words you will learn the very great love He has for you. It is no small blessing to realize that such a Master loves His pupils (*Way of Perfection*, XXVI).

**What a Father of such a Son!**

*"Our Father Who art in Heaven."* O my God! How justly do You seem to be the Father of such a Son, and how well does Your Son seem to be the Son of such a Father! May You be blessed for evermore! To conclude with this aware-

ness would be wonderful, but that is how You commence the prayer. At the very beginning You therefore fill our hands and endow us with such blessings. This is enough to occupy all our thoughts and will to such an extent that we could say nothing more.

Oh how well should contemplation now take over, my daughters! What higher reason can the soul have to enter within itself so that Christ may make it understood what a glorious place Heaven must be, where His Father dwells! So let us leave this earth, my daughters, since such a favor as this should be undervalued, were we to remain here.

O Son of God and my Lord! How is it that You give us so much in this first word? How is it, that not only did You humble yourself so much so as to unite Yourself with us in our petitions and make Yourself our Brother in spite of all our vileness, but You also gave us, in the name of the Father, all that can be given? You did so because You wanted Him to adopt us as sons. Your word can never fail. You oblige Him to keep His word which is no small task.

*What depth of meaning in "Our Father"!*

As a Father, God bears with us, however offensive our sins may be, if we return as the prodigal son returned. He has to pardon and to comfort us as such a Father would. He must, of course, be better than any earthly fathers, since there can be nothing in Him that is not perfect. In addition to all this, it is Your wish to make us partners and co-heirs with You! So now, daughters, do you not think He is a good Master, Who, in order to entice us to learn what He teaches, begins by giving us such a great favor? (*Way of Perfection*, XXVII).

Consider next what your Master has to say: "Who art in Heaven." Do you think it is of little concern to know about heaven, where your Most Holy Father is to be found? Yet it is very important to know this because of our wandering thoughts. To know this is to bind together our understanding and our recollection of soul. Already you know that God is everywhere. Now it is clear that where the court is, there also is the King. So where God is, there too is heaven. Without any doubt you can know that

*Heaven is wherever God is.*

where His Majesty is, there also is His glory.

**God is in the believer's soul**

But ponder also on the words of Augustine. He sought God in many places and came at last to find Him in himself. How vital is this truth to a distraught soul to realize this, that there is no need to go to heaven to speak with the Eternal Father. There is no need to speak aloud, for however low we speak He is close enough to hear. Neither do we need wings to fly and seek Him. For we can compose ourselves in solitude and behold Him within ourselves.

**The humility of God to confine Himself to the human heart**

Let us remember that there is within us an immense palace, whose magnificent building is of gold and precious stones. It is everything it ought to be for such a Lord. He sits there on a throne of immense value—your *heart.*

This may seem at first ridiculous! But what calls for such admiration is that He who could fill by His immensity a thousand worlds should be enclosed in such a small place! Yet He was pleased to confine Himself within the womb of the sacred virgin.

He, being Lord, brings us liberty; and in loving us much, He reduces Himself to our nature. When a soul begins to know Him, He does not reveal Himself fully all at once, lest the soul be overwhelmed by it being so small and yet containing so great a God. But by degrees, God enlarges one's heart according as He sees need. Therefore I say that He brings liberty with Him, for He has the power to enlarge this palace.

The point is that we give ourselves to Him as His own with a full and complete resolve so that He may do whatever He wants with our lives. This is His pleasure and His Majesty has His own reasons. Let us not refuse Him in any way. For since He will not force us, He only takes what we give to Him. But He does not give Himself entirely to us until we give ourselves entirely to Him (*Way of Perfection,* XXVIII).

**What are the consequences of saying "Our Father"?**

Let us now consider what else He says in His prayer. What does He ask Him? Even the dullest person will consider what he is going to ask beforehand of some great personage. Does he not also consider what he may need before asking? Could You not, Jesus, have asked in one word all that we might need? So could You not have asked, "Give us, Father, what is expedient for us," since to One Who understands all things so well, nothing seems so necessary?

O Eternal Wisdom! Between You and Your Father, this would have been sufficient, and so You prayed in the Garden. You revealed Your will and showed Your submission. You resigned Yourself to Your Father's will. And You know that we are not so resigned as You were to Your Father. For our nature is such that, unless we receive what we desire, we would not naturally accept what God would give us. Although this may be best in the long run, we never think we shall be rich unless we have money in our own pockets.

O Lord! Why is our faith so dormant and so benumbed? It is so vital, then, that we know what we are doing when we say, "Our Father." Take heed that when He grants you your request, you do not cast it back in His face. Be very careful what you say to God.

**What is God's Kingdom?**

Our good Jesus tells us to say these words in which we petition that such a Kingdom should come to us: "Hallowed be Thy name: Thy Kingdom come."

It is necessary that we should understand what we are asking for when we say "Thy Kingdom." Since His Majesty saw that we were incapable of either hallowing, praising, extolling, or glorifying this Holy Name of the Eternal Father in a fitting way, He provided for us His Kingdom here on earth. That is why Jesus placed these two petitions together [Teresa believes that contemplation, "the Prayer of Quiet," is the gift of the Kingdom.] (*Way of Perfection*, XXX).

**Is God's Kingdom in a meditative life of prayer?**

Our Lord begins to make known that He has heard our prayers, and that He has already begun to give us His Kingdom here in order that we may truly praise and sanctify His name and endeavor to help all men do likewise. Our Lord delivers His Kingdom into their hands [by the gift of the Prayer of Quiet]. Yet we make ourselves deaf because we love so much to hear ourselves speak, and we repeat so many vocal prayers in great haste—like the one who rushes to get the job done. We do this every day. So when our Lord delivers the Kingdom into our hands, we do not accept it, imagining we do better with these vocal prayers. As a result many may lose a great treasure.

So it is better to say one word of "Our Father" than to gabble it all without reflecting on its true meaning or really understanding it. He to Whom you pray is very near. He will not fail to hear you. Thus you may truly praise and sanctify His name, for now you glorify God as if you belonged to His household; and you praise Him with more ardent affections and desires. It seems you cannot help knowing Him better when you have tasted "how precious He is" (*Way of Perfection*, XXXI).

**His Kingdom is given in order to do God's will.**

Having bestowed upon us such a favor as to make us His brethren, let us now consider what the Son wishes us to give to His Father, what He offers to Him for us, and what He desires of us.

Since You have given us Your Kingdom, my Lord, You do not deprive us of anything. And we give all that we can when we say the next words: "Thy will be done on earth as they do in heaven." You have done well, O Lord, in asking this, so that we offer You what You have already provided for us to give. Were this not so, it would be impossible to do it. Since Your Father provides us with His Kingdom, I know we shall be able through faith to give Him what You offer for us. For when heaven shall become earth, it will be possible to accomplish Your will in me. Without this, in such barren soil as I am, I do not know how else it would be possible.

**What is God's will?**

I wish to remind you what His will is. Do not fear that it is to give you riches, pleasure, and honors, or any worldly advantage. Our Lord has greater love for you than to do this. He highly values what you give Him, and so He desires to reward you amply. Even when you are alive He gives you of His Kingdom.

Do you want to see what He does to those who pray "Thy will be done" in sincerity? Ask His glorious Son, Who said this when He prayed in the garden. As the Lord uttered it with strong resolve and an entire will, the answer was to give Him such an overflow of travail, pains, sufferings, and persecutions, that at the end He gave His life by the death of the cross. See here, then, what God gives to those who love Him most. This is how we know what it is to know His will.

So we pray, "Thy will be done. Be fulfilled in me, in whatever way You please. If You wish it to be fulfilled by afflictions, only grant me the strength and let them come. Whether they be persecutions, sickness, disgrace, and poverty, lo, here I am. I will not turn away my face, O my Father! Nor is it fit that I should turn my back on all this, for Your Son has offered on our behalf all of this. Why should I fail to do likewise? But grant me the favor to give Your Kingdom that I may be able to accomplish Your will. Dispose of me entirely as Your own, according as You will" (*Way of Perfection*, XXXII).

*Submission to God's will*

Knowing our weakness, and how often we make ourselves believe that we do not know the will of God—we are so weak, and He is so merciful—He realized that a remedy was necessary. So He asked on our behalf of His Eternal Father to have this heavenly bread. He realized that to accomplish the will of God without this provision was too difficult for us. For tell someone who lives richly and fares sumptuously that it is God's will to be moderate—so that others who are even dying with hunger may have some bread—and he will make a thousand excuses as to why he does not know the will of God. Or tell some cantankerous person to love his neighbor as he loves himself, and he will impatiently make every excuse why he does not know God's will.

*Our need of sustenance to do God's will*

Our good Jesus therefore saw our need and gave us this petition: "Give us this day our daily bread." He asked for more in this petition than in all the rest, because He knew the death they would make Him suffer and the disgraceful affronts He would have to endure. And how many affronts are now offered to Him in the most Holy Sacrament? So His Majesty gave us this nourishment, the manna of His humanity, so that we may never hunger and die of famine (*Way of Perfection*, XXXIV).

Our good Master, seeing that doing His will becomes easy for us by this celestial food, now beseeches Him that He would forgive our trespasses, as we forgive others. So proceeding in His prayer, He uses these words: "And forgive us our trespasses, as we forgive those that trespass against us." Notice He does not say, "as we shall forgive." Rather, having already been resigned to God's will, and having received the great gift of the previous petition, this one has *already* forgiven others.

Whoever has already said, "Thy will be done," should already have forgiven also. But whoever is resolved in prayer to forgive, and rises from praying without forgiving at all, this person does not think much of prayer. Indeed, the true test of our prayer is whether we do the will of God, including the spirit of forgiveness (*Way of Perfection*, XXXVII).

Those, however, who rise to spiritual heights need all the more to watch in case they fall all the more. So that they may not be deceived, without ever perceiving it, He adds this petition to those living in this land of exile: "And lead us not into temptation, but deliver us from evil." For the devil can do great mischief without us realizing it in making us believe we have virtues that we do not possess. This deceit is a terrible pestilence. For then we neglect to acquire that virtue which we think we already possess. And so we go on in a false security and fall into the ditch from which we cannot get out. This is a very dangerous temptation. The best remedy for it is to pray, beseeching our Eternal Father not to lead us into temptation (*Way of Perfection*, XXXIX).

[Teresa then speaks of other temptations, such as thinking we are really poor, or very humble, when we are really deceiving ourselves.]

Let not your soul hide in a corner. For instead of acquiring more sanctity, it will contract many imperfections by which the devil will acquire it in all of its ways. So here you see how these two virtues, the love of God and the fear of God, enable us to travel gently and quietly. As fear goes before, we must not travel carelessly. For while we live, we cannot enjoy security; it would be too dangerous. This our Instructor understood, because at the end of His prayer, He said to His Father: "But deliver us from evil." He well understood our need of this (*Way of Perfection*, XLI).

O my God and my Lord, deliver me now from all evil, and be pleased to conduct me there where all good things are. What can we expect of this world, those of us whom You have given some knowledge of what a mere nothing this world is, and those of us who have a lively faith in that glory which their Heavenly Father has reserved for them? Asking for this with intense desire and a firm resolve to enjoy God is a sure sign for devotees of prayer to know that the favors which they receive in prayer come from God. Hence, let those who have it also value it highly.

He has made me understand what great things we ask when we say this heavenly prayer. May He be blessed for ever, since it is certain I never imagined this prayer comprised such great mysteries. You have already seen how it includes in itself the way of perfection, from the very commencement until God takes the soul wholly unto Himself. He makes the soul drink abundantly of the fountain of living water in this prayer. So I am unable to go on further (*Way of Perfection*, XLII).

# IV

# THE PRAYER LIFE AS A GARDEN

## I. INTRODUCTION

n order to make great advance in prayer, and to be able to ascend to the mansions we desire, we must remember that the business of prayer does not consist in *thinking much,* but in *loving much.* Do, therefore, whatever may excite you most to love.

Perhaps we do not know what love is. I do not wonder at this, for it consists not in having greater delights, but in having greater resolutions and desires to please God in everything and endeavoring not to offend Him. It lies in beseeching Him that He would promote the honor and glory of His Son and extend the bounds of the church universal.

These are the signs of love. Do not imagine that it consists in not thinking on anything else, or that all is lost if you have a few distractions *(Interior Castle,* IV).

A beginner in prayer must look upon himself as making a garden. There our Lord may take His delight, but in a soil that is unfruitful and full of weeds. His Majesty roots up the weeds to replace them with good plants. Let us take for granted that this is already done when a soul is determined to give itself to prayer and has begun the practice of it.

As good gardeners, we have by the help of God to see that the plants grow. We should water them carefully so that they will not die, but rather produce blossoms. These will send forth much fragrance which is so refreshing to our Lord that He may come often for His delight into this garden and take pleasure Himself in the midst of these virtues.

**11**
**Four ways of watering the garden**

Let us now see how this garden is to be watered. How much trouble will it cost us? Will the gain be greater than the trouble, or how long a time will it take us?

It seems to me that the garden may be watered in four ways. The first is taking water out of the well, which is very laborious. The second is water raised by means of a water-wheel, which manner I myself have drawn water sometimes. It is a less troublesome way than the first, and it yields more water. The third is by a stream or a brook, whereby the garden is watered in a much better way. For the soil is more thoroughly saturated, and there is no necessity to water it so often. Moreover, the labor of the gardener is much less. And finally, by showers of rain, our Lord Himself waters the garden without any labor on our part. This way is incomparably the best of all those which I have spoken about.

**12**
**Four degrees of Prayer**

Let us now look at the application of these four ways of irrigation by which the garden is to be maintained. Without water it will fail. The comparison will help me to explain to some extent the four degrees of prayer to which our Lord, in His goodness, has occasionally raised my soul. May He graciously grant that I may so speak as to be of some service to one of those who has commanded me to write.

Our Lord has raised me in four months to a greater height than I have reached myself in seventeen years! He has prepared it Himself better than I did, and therefore it is His garden, without labor on His part, irrigated by these four means of watering, even though the last means is only drop by drop. But it is growing in such a way that soon, by the help of our Lord, He will be swallowed up therein. And it will be a pleasure to me if He finds my explanation so absurd that He should laugh at it.

## II. Watering from the Well

Those who are beginners in prayer are those who draw [13] the water up out of the well. This is a process which, as I have said, is very laborious. For they must be wearied in keeping the senses recollected. This is a great labor, because the senses have until now been accustomed to distraction.

It is necessary for beginners to accustom themselves in this regard to what they hear or see, and to put these things away from themselves during the time of prayer. They must be alone to think over their past life, although everyone must do this many times, beginners as well as those who are more advanced. All, however, must not do so equally, as I shall show.

Beginners at first suffer much because they are not convinced that they are penitent for their sins. Yet they are, because they are so sincerely resolved on serving God. They must try to meditate on the life of Christ, and the understanding is wearied in this. Thus far we can advance by ourselves by the grace of God. For without that, as everyone knows, we could never have even one good thought.

*Depend only upon Christ, not even upon your own contrition.*

This is beginning to draw water up out of the well. God [14] grant that there may be water in it! That, however, does not depend upon us. We are drawing it, doing what we can toward watering the flowers. So good is God that, for reasons known only to His Majesty—perhaps for our greater need—it is His will that the well should be dry. In that situation, He Himself preserves the flowers without water while we, like good gardeners doing all that lies within our power, find that our virtues grow. By water here I mean tears; and if there be none, then I mean tenderness and an inward feeling of devotion.

But what will one do here when he sees that after many [15] days there is nothing but dryness, disgust, distaste, and *Aridity of soul* very little inclination to go to the well to draw water?

He might give up gardening altogether if he did not remember that he has to please and serve the Lord of the garden. He would quit if he did not trust that his service was not in vain, and did not hope for some gain by a labor so great as that of lowering the bucket into the well so often, and drawing it up without water in it. It may happen that he is often unable to move his arms for that purpose or to have a single good thought. Working with the understanding, then, is like drawing water out of the well.

16    In this situation, what will the gardener do now?

He must rejoice and be comforted, and recognize that this is the greatest privilege that he could have to labor in the garden of so great an Emperor! Since he knows that this pleases the Lord, he will give the Lord much praise. For the Master has trusted him in the garden because he sees that, without any complaint, he is so diligent about what he is told to do. This gardener helps Christ to carry the cross and reflects that the Lord lives, all during his life. He does not desire the Lord's Kingdom here below or even abandon prayer. Instead he is determined that, even though this dryness may last for the whole of his life, he will not let Christ fall with the cross.

17    The time will come when he shall be paid once for all. Let him then have no fear that his labor is futile. For he serves a good Master whose eyes are upon him. So let him not be distracted by evil thoughts, but remember that Satan suggested them also to St. Jerome in the desert. These labors have their reward, as I know it. For I am one who underwent them for so many years. When I drew but one drop of water out of His blessed well, I considered indeed it was a mercy of God.

**Years of dryness compensated by one hour of God's presence.**

So I know how laborious these efforts are, and they require greater courage than many others in this world. But I have seen clearly that God does not need them without a great recompense, even in this life. For it is certain that in one hour, during which our Lord gave me to taste His sweetness, all the anxieties which I had to bear when persevering in prayer seemed afterwards to me to be ever perfectly rewarded.

It is my opinion that in the beginning and in that 18
which follows, the Lord often desires to give these torments and many other incidental temptations to test those who love Him and to find out if they will drink the chalice; He seeks those who will help Him carry the cross before He entrusts them with greater responsibilities.

I believe it is for our good that His Majesty leads us in   **Aridity may be given to test us.**
this way so that we may perfectly understand how worthless we really are. For the graces which He gives to us afterwards are of a great dignity. He wills us to know by experience our own worthlessness so that what happened to Lucifer will not happen to us.

O my Lord, what You do is always for the greater good 19
of the soul which You know is already yours and which desires to follow you wherever you go, even to the death of the cross. Your power is given to us to help bear that cross.
Whoever recognizes this resolve in Himself has nothing to fear. No, such spiritual people have nothing to fear. For there is no reason why he should then be distressed who has already been raised to such a plane as that of wishing to converse in solitude with God and to abandon the pleasures of the world. The greater part of the work has been done. So give praise to His Majesty for it, and trust in the goodness of Him Who has never failed those who love Him.

So close the eyes of your imagination and do not ask   **Let God do with us whatever He will.**
why He gives devotion to this person in such a short time
and none to me after so many years. Rather let us believe that all is for our greater good. Let His Majesty guide us wherever He will. We are not our own; we belong to Him.
He shows us mercy enough when it is His pleasure that we should be willing to dig in His garden and be nearer to the Lord of it. He certainly is near to us. If it is His will that some of these plants and flowers should be watered

and grow and others should receive none, what is that to me?

O Lord, accomplish Your will. And do not let my virtue be lost. If you have given me any, it is all from Your goodness. I desire to suffer because You, O Lord, have suffered. Fulfill in every way Your will in me. May it never be the pleasure of Your Majesty that a gift of something so precious as Your love will be given to anyone who serves You only for the sake of consolation.

20    It is to be carefully noted—and I say this because I know it from experience—that the soul which begins to walk along this path of resolute prayer, regardless of joy or affliction, in spite of great tenderness or a lack of consolation, this soul has traveled a great part of the way. However much it may stumble, it should not be afraid that it will turn back.

The building of this soul has been started on a solid foundation. This is true because the love of God does not consist in tears nor in the delight of tenderness, even though for the most part we certainly desire it and find comfort in it. Rather the will of God consists in serving with righteousness and fortitude of soul as well as with humility. Without certain service, it seems to me we will be receiving everything and giving nothing.

21
God comforts to
reinforce our for-
titude.

As for a poor woman such as myself who is weak and without much strength, it seems necessary that I should be led on to consolation as God is doing now so that I might be able to endure certain afflictions which it has pleased His Majesty I should have.

But it annoys me when servants of God, men of prominence, learning, and scholarship, make so much fuss because God does not give them devotion. I do not mean to say that they should not accept it if God gives it to them, and esteem it, because then His Majesty sees that this is appropriate. But when they do not have devotion, they should not get weary. They should understand that since His Majesty has not given it, it is not necessary. They should be masters of themselves. They should believe that their desire for consolation is false. This I have seen and experienced. They should believe that such fussing denotes imperfection, a lack of freedom of spirit, and the absence of courage to achieve something.

I am not saying this so much for beginners, although I do emphasize the importance that they should have freedom and determination in the beginning. I am saying it for others. For there are many who begin and yet who never reach the end. I believe that this is due largely to a failure to embrace the cross from the beginning. Thinking that they are doing nothing, they become upset. When the intellect ceases to work, they cannot tolerate it. But it is then, perhaps, that their will is in fact being strengthened and reinforced, although they may not be aware of what is happening.

**22**
**Embrace the cross at the very beginning of the Christian life.**

We must never think that the Lord is indifferent about these inabilities. Even though they may seem to us to be false, they are not. His Majesty already knows our distress and our fallen nature better than we do ourselves, and He knows that these souls always desire to think of Him and to love Him. It is this determination that He desires.

**23**

The other afflictions that we bring upon ourselves serve no other purpose than to disquiet the soul. And if it was incapable before of engaging in prayer for one hour, it will now continue for four. Most frequently this incapacity comes from some bodily disorder.

**Bodily affliction**

I have a great deal of experience in this matter of bodily affliction, and I know that what I say is true because I have carefully considered it and discussed it afterwards with spiritually-minded people. We are so miserable that our poor little imprisoned souls also share in the miseries of the body. So the changes in the weather and the cycles of the bodily condition often result in affecting the soul. Souls cannot do what they desire for they are constantly suffering. On these occasions, the more we force the soul, the greater will be the damage and the longer it will last. So discretion must be used in order to find out whether or not ill-health is the cause. The poor soul must not be stifled.

So let those who suffer in this way understand that they are physically ill. A change should be made in the hour of prayer, and often that change should be continued for some days afterwards. Let them suffer this desert experience as best they can. For it is a great misfortune to a soul that loves God to see that it lives in such misery. It is frustrated in its desires because it has a wretched guest as the body.

**24**

**Take care of your physical health.** I have already said that we should use discernment, because the devil is sometimes also the cause. So it is not always good to abandon prayer when there is great distraction and upset in the mind, just as it is not always good to torture the soul into doing what it cannot do. There are other things to be done outside one's life, such as charity and spiritual reading. However, at times it will not even be fit for these. Let us, then, look after the body out of a love for God, because many other times the body serves the soul. Engage in some physical exercises, such as a good chat with a friend or a walk in the country as your spiritual director may advise.

Experience is a great help in all of this, for it teaches what is suitable for us. And so God can be served in every situation. His yoke is easy (Matthew 11:30). Thus it is very helpful not to push the soul too much, but to lead it gently for the sake of making greater progress later.

**25**

I return to the advice I have already given. I need not repeat it many times since it is very important that no one be distressed or afflicted over dryness or restless and distracting thoughts.

**Do not be afraid of the cross.** If someone wishes to gain freedom of spirit and not always be troubled, let him begin by not being afraid of the cross. He will then see how the Lord helps him to carry. He will gain satisfaction and profit from everything. Clearly, if the world is dry, we cannot put water into it. Yes, it is true that we must not become negligent. When there is water we should draw it out; because then the Lord desires to multiply our virtues by this means (*Life*, XI).

Just as it requires effort to draw water from the well, so in these beginnings of devotion we are able to help ourselves somewhat. Thinking of and meditating upon the sufferings of our Lord for our sake moves us to compassion, and the sorrow and tears which result from such reflection are sweet. The thought of the blessedness we hope for, of the love our Lord has given us, and of His resurrection from the grave kindle within us a joy which is neither wholly spiritual nor wholly sensual. But the joy is elevating, and the sorrow is redemptive (*Life*, XII).

Why is it that we so desire to draw this water?

It is "the Fountain of Living Water" of which our Lord spoke to the Samaritan woman, "of which whoever drinks, shall not thirst again" (John 4:13). How true it is—since the word was spoken by the mouth of Truth Himself—one shall never thirst again in his life, that is with regard to the things of this world. Yet with regard to the things of this other life, this thirst is greatly increased. Indeed, it goes far beyond what we can imagine in regard to our natural thirst.

But with what a thirst is this thirst desired! For the soul understands its great value, and it is also a very painful thirst that afflicts us. Yet it brings with it a satisfaction whereby our other thirst is cooled. Thus it is a fiery thirst which only extinguishes a thirst for earthly things. It affects us also in such a way that when God satisfies it, one of the greatest favors that He can do to the soul is to leave it in this necessity. For the soul always has a greater desire to drink again of this water.

**True thirst is for God.**

Water has three properties which well illustrate my meaning. It may also have other properties.

**Water has three properties.**

The first property is that it cools. However hot we may be, when we take water, our heat goes away. If there is a great fire, water will put out all fires except for wildfire, which then burns all the more.

**1. Water cools.**

O my God! What wonders there are in this fire which burns all the more when water is poured on it; it is a strong and mighty fire, and it is not subject to the other elements! If I were a scientist I could explain this phenomenon. Knowing the properties of the elements, I should be able to express my meaning better. Instead I have to amuse myself with speaking of it, and I know not how to deal with it properly.

But when God brings you, sisters, to drink of this water, you delight in it as those who now drink of it. And you will experience how the true love of God is more than all the elements of the world.

Since water comes from the earth, fear not that it will quench this fire of the love of God. For this fire is not under an earthly jurisdiction. And although the two appear contrary to each other, this love is now the absolute master. It is not subject to the water.

Sisters, do not be surprised that I have said so much in this book about prayer. For I long for you to obtain this freedom. [Here Teresa writes in a rather confused way. But her point is that when this water of prayer is combined with the fire—God's love—then the combination produces a heavenly ardor that cannot be put out.] Thus I may indeed assure you that this water will leave no love for the sake of this world. Such a combination would inflame the whole world, were the soul not contained by these earthly things.

**2. Water cleanses.**   The second property of water is that it cleanses dirty things. If we had no water to wash with, what would become of the world? Do you know how well this "living water," this heavenly water, this pure water, cleanses, when it is clear and pure of sediment? If we drink of it only once, I am certain that it will leave the soul pure and cleansed from its sin. As I have said already, God will allow no soul to drink of this water except to cleanse and purify, leaving the soul free from dirt and misery.

Other consolations that come through understanding nevertheless are those which draw from water that flows over the ground. They are not drinking it at the fountain-head. Hence that water will always contain impurities.

I do not call this prayer, for however zealously we may desire to be clean, our souls always contract some impurities in spite of our will. This vile nature and body we each have contributes much to this state.

Let me explain myself a little more. Perhaps we are meditating on the character of the world and how all things will come to an end so that we do not wish to be tempted and excited by them. Then almost without our receiving it, our thoughts drift onto the things to which we are attached. Although we desire to be free from them for a time, we are distracted by thinking about the world around us, what it will be, what we have done, and what we want to do. As we think about things that might help to free us from such distractions, we fall into other dangers.

So we must fear, for it is our Lord Himself that takes this care upon Himself; for He does not wish us to trust it to ourselves. He values our soul so much that He will not allow the soul to engage in things which may damage it during the time when he wishes to favor it. He immediately places the soul near Himself and shows more truth and gives it a clearer knowledge of what all things are than we can obtain in this life after many years. Our sight is not free. The dust still blinds us as we walk along. So our Lord brings us to our journey's end, without our ever knowing *how*.

The third property of water is that it satisfies and quenches the thirst. But it seems to me that thirst implies the desire of something which we stand in need of, and which if not obtained will destroy us. What a strange thing which, if we want, fills us, and yet if taken to excess, will also destroy life. Just as we see this happening to those drowned in supplication.

**3. Water satisfies thirst.**

O my Lord! Who can be so blessed as he who finds himself so immersed in this "living water" as to end his life within it? Cannot this be effected? Yes! Indeed, for the love and desire of God may grow to such a height that nature cannot tolerate it. I know at least one person [probably Teresa herself] on whom this "living water" was poured so abundantly that, had God not come to her assistance, she might have taken leave of her senses.

Yet we must remember that since nothing can come imperfectly from our Surpreme God, all that He gives us is for *our* good. Therefore, however abundant this water may be, there is never an excess. There can be no superfluity found in anything belonging to God. If He bestows much, He will so dispose the soul as to make it capable of drinking much. This is comparable to a glassmaker who will make his glasses in whatever way he sees necessary to contain a certain quality. Desiring this water is never without some defect such as a desire that comes from ourselves. When it does have anything good, it is through our Lord's assistance.

But we are so unwise that, even though water is a sweet and delightful thing, we think we can never be satisfied with it. Yet we desire it without measure; and as we increase this desire, it sometimes kills us.

Yet blessed is such a death! And yet perhaps by living, such a person may help many others to die with a desire of such a debt. This I believe is what the devil does, because he knows the loss he will receive if such a one lives. And so he tempts us to make unwise penances which will destroy our health. Thereby Satan gains much.

**Be careful of your ardor.**

And so I say that whoever has this violent thirst should be very careful; may he know how to deal with these temptations. Although he may not die of thirst, he will lose his health and show it by external ways, even though he wills by all means to avoid bodily harm. Sometimes our diligence avails little, since we cannot conceal all that we so desire. But let us be careful when these great impetuous desires come to us.

This is an important thought because you may, for example, have to shorten the time that you spend in prayer, however delightful it may be. When bodily strength begins to fail or when it gives us a headache, we probably should cease. Discretion is necessary in everything.

Why do you think, my daughters, I have tried to explain all this? Why have I told you of the advantages we may derive from drinking of this heavenly fountain and this living water?

I have explained about prayer and its difficulties in order that you may not complain of the trials and the pains which you find in the way and so that you may also go on with courage and not be weary. For as I have said, it may be that when you have arrived at the well, all that you will want to do is to stoop down and go on drinking at this fountain. And yet you may leave all things and lose this advantage, thinking that you do not have strength to reach it and that you are not worthy of it.

Consider instead how our Lord invites us all. He being the Truth itself, there is no reason to doubt Him. If this banquet was an open invitation to everybody, our Lord would not call us at all. Even if He did, He would not say, "I will give you to drink." He might have said, "Come unto me all you that labor and are heavy laden and I will refresh you" or he might have said "if any man thirsts, let him come to me and drink" (Matthew 11:28). But he speaks to all without any condition, so I considered it certain that all those who do not loiter by the way shall not lack this living water. May our Lord, Who has promised us so much, give us in His mercy the grace to seek this water as it should be sought (*The Way of Perfection*, XIX).

## III. THE WATER WHEEL OR THE PRAYER OF RECOLLECTION

Having spoken of the toilsome efforts and of the [1] strength required for watering the garden when we have to draw water out of the well, let us now speak of a second way of obtaining water. This the Lord of the vineyard has ordained. It is like the *noria* or water wheel with buckets that enables the gardener to draw more water with less effort and so be able to take some rest without being continually at work. This is what I am now going to describe. I apply this metaphor to the prayer called the prayer of quiet or recollection.

2 Here the soul begins to be recollected. It is now touching on things which are divine, which it could never do by any effort of its own. True; it seems at times to be wearied at the wheel, as it labors with the understanding and as it fills the buckets. But in the second stage the water table is higher, and so the labor is much less needed to draw it up. What I mean is that the nearer the soul is to the water, the more "grace" reveals itself distinctly to the soul.

**In this level of prayer, the will is closer to the will of God.**

3 In this kind of prayer, the faculties of the soul are much more integrated so that they are able to enjoy that satisfaction with greater delight. But they are not lost, nor are they asleep. Only the will is occupied in such a way that, without knowing how, it has become subject to the will of God. It merely consents to allow God to capture it as one who knows well how to be captive of its lover.

O Jesus my Lord! How precious is Your love to us here! It holds our love so captive that it does not allow it the freedom during that time to love anything else except You.

4 The other two faculties [that is, the intellect and memory] help the will so that it may render itself capable of such a good fruitage. However, it occasionally happens that even when the will is in union, they hinder it very much. Then it should never heed them at all, but simply abide in its quiet and fruition. If it tried to make them recollect it, it would lose its way. It is like doves which are dissatisfied with the food that the master of the dovecote gives them, food that is there without their having to search for it. And so they go to look for food elsewhere, but they find it so scarce that they have to return. Thus these faculties go away and then come back to see if the will might give them what the soul enjoys.

5 If the Lord desires to throw them some food, they stop. If not, they return to their own search. They must think that they are benefiting the will.

Sometimes in desiring the memory or imagination to

represent the will in what these faculties are enjoying, they will do the will damage. Well, then, be warned to behave toward them as I shall explain.

Everything that takes place now in this state brings the very greatest consolation. The labor is so light that prayer, even if persevered in for some time, is never wearisome. The reason is that the understanding is now working very gently and is drawing very much more water than it drew out of the well. The tears which God now sends flow with joy. Although we feel them, they are not the results of any efforts of our own.

*Everything is consoling in this level of prayer.*

6

This water of great blessing and favors makes the virtues grow incomparably greater than in the previous stage of prayer. The soul is now ascending above its own sorrow and receiving a little knowledge of the delights of glory. This water makes the virtues grow better and also brings the soul much closer to the true Virtue, which is God Himself, from whence come all virtues. His Majesty is beginning to communicate Himself to the soul, as He wants it to experience how He is doing so.

7

Once the soul has reached this point, no wonder it begins to lose the desire for earthly things. For it sees clearly that even for a brief moment, this joy is not to be experienced on earth. There are no riches, no authority, no honors, no delights that can for one brief moment—even for the twinkling of an eye—provide such a joy. It is true satisfaction, and this soul sees that it is fully satisfied.

Now we who are on earth scarcely ever understand where our satisfaction lies, for it is always liable to be disappointed. But in this experience there is no disappointment. The disappointment only comes later when the soul sees that the time has passed and that it has no power to reproduce it; nor does it know how to reproduce it. Even if the soul were to be cut in pieces by penance and prayer, and to exercise every other kind of austerity, all would be useless if our Lord did not grant it. For God in His great mercy would have the soul understand that His

Majesty is so near to the soul that it does not need to send messages to Him; it may speak directly to Him. This can be done without loud crying, because He is already so near; and He understands even the movements of its lips.

8
This level of
prayer fills the
soul with delight.
It seems impertinent to say this since we know that God always understands us and is present with us. But our Emperor and Lord wishes to know that He understands us, that His presence is with us, and that He wants to begin to work in the soul in a special way. All that the Lord would desire to show us comes by a great interior, as well as exterior, satisfaction that He gives to the soul. He also shows us the difference between this delight and the happiness and delights of earth. For this delight seems to fill the void that we have caused in our soul through our sins.

9
This satisfaction lies in the most intimate part of the soul. The soul does not know from whence it has come, nor how it can wish or pray for it. The soul seems to find satisfaction all at once, and it does not know what it has found.

I cannot explain it, because for so many things, learning is essential. Here it would be helpful to explain clearly the difference between a general and a particular grace, for there are many who are ignorant of this difference. It would also be helpful to know how the Lord desires that the soul through prayer should see with its own eyes the reality of this particular grace.

Learning is also required to explain many other things, which perhaps I did not express accurately. But since what I say is going to be checked by people who will recognize any error, I am not worried about it. In matters of theology, as well as of those of the spirit, I know that I may be mistaken. Yet since this account will end in good hands, these learned men will understand and remove what is erroneous.

Let us now return to our orchard or flower garden, and see how well the trees begin to fill with sap for the bringing forth of the blossoms. Then there come the fruits, the flowers, and the plants also with their fragrance.

This illustration has its charm for me, for very often it is a great delight for me to consider my soul as a garden and to reflect that the Lord is taking a walk with me. I have begged Him to increase the fragrance of the small flowers of virtue that were beginning to bloom, and to preserve them so that they might be for His glory. For I have desired nothing for myself. I have asked Him to cut those that He wants, for already I know that better ones will flower.

I say "cut" because there are times when the soul has no thought about this garden. Everything seems to be dried up and there is no water to sustain it. Nor does it appear that there ever has been in the soul anything of virtue.

This, then, is a season of heavy trials. For our Lord would have the poor gardener suppose that all the trouble he took in maintaining and watering the garden appears to be for no purpose. This is a time really for weeding and for rooting out every plant—however small it is—that is worthless with the knowledge that no efforts of our own are sufficient if God withholds from us the waters of His grace. So in despising ourselves as being nothing, and even less than nothing, we gain great humility, and the flowers grow afresh (*Life*, XIV).

Let us now get back to the subject. This quietude and recollection of the soul makes itself felt through the satisfaction and peace which attends it with great joy and gentle repose of the faculties. It seems to the soul that since it has not gone further, there is nothing left to desire. So it would willingly say with the Apostle Peter that it will make its tabernacle there (Matthew 17:4). It dares not move or stir, because it thinks that this blessing it has received would then disappear from its hands. Now and then it would wish that it could even breathe. The poor

13
Our soul should be a garden for God (Genesis 2:15).

14

Rest and refreshment in a fruitful garden.

little soul is not aware that of itself it could do nothing to bring this blessing upon itself. So it is still less able to retain this blessing even for a moment longer than our Lord desires that it should remain.

2   I have already said that in recollection, the soul's faculties do not cease to function. But the soul is so satisfied with God that, as long as the recollection lasts, the quiet and peace are not lost since the will is united with God, even though the faculties may be distracted. In fact, little by little, the will brings the intellect and the memory back to recollection. Even though the will may not be totally absorbed, it is so preoccupied without knowing it that, no matter what efforts the two faculties of intellect and recognition may make, they cannot take away the will's contentment and joy. With hardly any effort, the will is helped gradually so that this little spark of the love of God may not be quenched.

3   Oh that it may please His Majesty to give grace to me to explain this state well enough! There are many, many souls who reach out for it but few who pass beyond it. I do not know whose fault this is. Most surely it is not God who fails, for once His Majesty has granted a soul the favor of reaching this stage, I do not believe that He will fail to grant it many more favors—unless it be through our own shortcomings.

**Realize how favored you are in this state.** It is very important that the soul which reaches this stage realizes the great dignity of its position and the great favor that the Lord has bestowed upon it. It is important also to see that it does not then belong to the earth, because it now seems that His goodness would make it a citizen of heaven. This is provided it does not stop through its own fault. Unhappy it will be, however, if it turns back. Indeed, I think turning back means falling back to the bottom, as I would have done had the mercy of the Lord not rescued me. For the most part, this turning back will come as a result of serious faults. Nor is it possible to leave so much good without the blindness caused by so much evil.

Therefore, for the love of our Lord, I implore those souls to whom His Majesty has given such a great grace to reach the attainment of this state. May they know and make much of themselves with a humble and holy presumption so that they will never return to the fleshpots of Egypt. If through weakness, sin, and a miserable nature they should fall as I did, let them always keep in mind the good that they have lost. May they be suspicious and walk with the fear of the Lord. They are right in doing this, because if they do not return to prayer, they will go from bad to worse. What I call a true fall from grace is when we develop an abhorrence of the pathway by which we have benefited from so much good. It is to such souls that I am speaking. For I am not saying that they should never offend God nor fall into sin, although it would be right for anyone who has begun to receive these favors to be very much on guard against sinning. But we are miserable creatures.

5
Be careful you
do not fall away.

What I strongly advise is not to abandon the habit of prayer, for it is in prayer that a person will understand what he is doing and so seek repentance from the Lord and fortitude to lift himself up. You must believe that when you are giving up prayer, you are in my opinion courting grave danger. I do not know if I understand what I am saying because, as I have said, I am judging by my own experience.

Do not stop
praying.

What the soul must do during these seasons of quiet amounts to no more than proceeding gently and noiselessly in prayer. What I mean by noise is running about with the intellect, looking for many words and meanings so as to give thanks for this gift, and piling up one's sins and faults in order to see that the gift is unmerited. Everything is in motion and rush. The intellect is thinking hard and the memory is hurrying about in the past.
Certainly these faculties will tire me out from time to

9
The mind
can be noisy.

time. Although I have a poor memory, I still cannot control it. Calmly and wisely the will has to understand that one is not dealing well with God by force; our efforts, then, are like the careless use of large pieces of wood which smother this little spark of fire. One should realize this and humbly say: "Lord, what am I capable of doing here? What has a servant to do with the Lord—or indeed earth with heaven?" Or he should use other words of love that suggest themselves to his mind which are well grounded in the knowledge that what is said is the truth. So do not pay attention to the intellect, for it is like a grinding mill.

10    If the will desires to communicate to the intellect a portion of that fruitage of which it has entered upon, or if it labors to make the intellect remember, it will not succeed. For it often happens that the will is in unison with the intellect and that it rests while the intellect is in extreme disorder.

It is better that the will should leave the intellect alone than to go after it, and that it remain like a wise bee in the recollection and enjoyment of that gift. If no bee were to enter into the beehive, and each were employed in going after the other, no honey would be made. As a result, the soul will lose a great deal if it is not careful in this matter, especially if the intellect is keen. When the soul begins to reflect and to search for reasons, it will think at once that it is doing something if its speeches and search for ideas appear to be good.

11    The only reason for the soul's reflection that ought to be acknowledged clearly is that there is no reason whatever, other than God's own sheer goodness. Why should God enable us to be aware that we are so near to Him and give us the ability to pray to His Majesty for His mercies? In His presence we can ask for His gifts, and pray for the church and for those who have asked for our prayers.

13
**Learning should
only serve Christ.**    Therefore, in such times of quietude, let the soul remain in its repose. Put aside learning. The time will come

when learning will be useful for the Lord. It should be esteemed so that it is not abandoned for any treasure, but it
should be used only to serve His Majesty. This alone is
helpful.

Believe me, in the presence of infinite Wisdom, a little
study of humility and one act of humility is worth more
than all the knowledge of the world. For here there is no
demand for reasoning, but simply for knowing what we are
and that we are humbly in God's presence. For He desires
the soul to become ignorant in His presence, as indeed it
is. Let us remember that His Majesty so humbles Himself
in order to allow us to be near Him—in spite of what we
are.

**14**

The intellect may well be stimulated to compose
prayers of thanksgiving. But the will calmly—and without
daring to raise its eyes like the publican (Luke 18:13)—
gives more efficacious thanks than the intellect can express with all its rhetorical devices.

Finally, at this stage, one does not have to renounce
completely discursive prayer or the use of some liturgy, or
even some spontaneous, vocal prayers if there should be
the desire or ability. But if the prayer required is great, it is
difficult to speak without a good deal of effort.

**15**
**Discerning**
**true quietude.**

I believe myself that we can discern whether this quiet
is from the Spirit of God or whether it is brought about by
our own efforts, once God begins to give us devotion. We
ourselves want to pass on to the prayer of quiet through
our own efforts. When we procure the quiet ourselves, it
will, however, produce no effect but will quickly go away
and leave behind nothing but aridity. If it comes from
Satan, the practiced soul, in my opinion, will detect it;
because it leaves trouble behind, with scant humility and
poor disposition—the opposite of what the prayer that
comes from God produces. It does not leave light in the
intellect nor constancy in truth.

**16**

Here Satan can do little or no harm if the soul directs to
God the delight and sweetness that it feels and fixes its

thoughts and desires upon Him as it was advised. Then Satan cannot gain anything. Rather, God will permit Satan by means of the very delight that he causes in the soul to lose much. For this delight will prompt the soul— since it thinks God gives the delight—to return frequently to prayer with a longing for the Lord.

If it is a humble soul and is not inquisitive or concerned about pleasures, but is above all a friend of the cross, it will pay little attention to the consolation that is offered by the devil. It will be unable to ignore the consolation coming from the Spirit of God; rather, it will highly esteem it. But anything that Satan gives is like himself; it is a total lie. When Satan sees that in this comfort and delight the soul humbles itself (for in this experience it must have much humility, and in all matters of prayer and consolation it must strive to come away humble), he will not return very often; because he sees that he loses by coming.

**17**    For this and for many other reasons, when I was speaking of the first method of drawing water, I insisted that it is very important for the soul to detach itself from every kind of joy when it begins to pray. It enters on the resolution only that it will carry the cross of Christ like a good soldier, that it is willing to serve his King without pay. For he is sure that at last his eyes will be directed to the true and everlasting Kingdom and His final victory.

**22**
**The Spirit of God**
**takes initiative in**
**our lives.**
When it is the work of the Spirit of God, there is no necessity for going about searching for the strength to elicit acts of humility and contrition, because it is our Lord Himself who supplies them in a way that is very different from what we could acquire by our own poor efforts.

So such false humility is nothing in comparison with that true humility which comes from the light which our Lord gives to us, and which really embarrasses us. It is well known that God gives a knowledge that makes us realize we have no good of ourselves. So the greater the favors, the greater this knowledge becomes.

It is God who bestows a strong desire to advance in prayer and not to give it up, no matter what trial may test us. The soul offers itself up in all things. It feels sure, while still being humble and fearing, that it will be saved. For God must cast out from it all servile fear and grant a more mature and trusting faith. The soul is thus made aware of the beginning of a love for God that has much less self-interest. It will desire periods of solitude in order to enjoy that good all the more.

In conclusion, this prayer of quiet is the beginning of all blessings. The flowers are already at the point in which hardly anything is lacking for them to burst out in bud. And this the soul sees most clearly so that it is impossible to persuade it now that God has not been with it. It is only when it looks again at the flaws and imperfections in itself that it begins to fear everything. It is good that the soul is fearful, although there are some souls that profit more by believing that this prayer comes from God than by experiencing all possible fears. For if by nature someone is loving and grateful, the memory of the favor that God has granted does much more to bring him back to God than all the threats of eternal punishment. At least this has happened in my case, even though I am still such a sinner (*Life*, XV).

23

## IV. THE WATER FROM AN IRRIGATED CHANNEL OR STREAM

Let us now speak of the third type of water supply wherewith this garden is irrigated. This is water running from a river or from a channel, whereby the garden is irrigated with very much less trouble even though there may be some guidance in directing the water.

In this state our Lord will help the gardener in such a way that the gardener himself does all the work. It is "a sleep of the faculties of the soul, which are not wholly unconscious, yet they do not understand how they are at work." The consolation, the sweetness, and the delight are now incomparably greater than those hitherto experi-

At the third level of prayer, God does everything.

enced in the previous prayer. The water of grace rises up to the mouth of the soul. It is so full it does not know what to do. It can only desire to enjoy this greatest glory.

I have no other words for describing it or how to explain it. The soul does not know whether to speak or to be silent, whether to laugh or to weep. This prayer is a glorious foolishness, a heavenly madness, where true wisdom is learned. It is for the soul a most delightful way of enjoyment.

2   In fact, it is now some five or six years since the Lord first gave me this state of prayer in its abundance. Nor did I know how to speak about it then. So it was originally my intention at this point to say very little or nothing about this. For I realized clearly that while it was not a complete union of all of the faculties, yet this prayer was far more excellent than the previous one. Yet I confess that I could not really discern or understand where the difference between them lay.

3   Yet I believe that it was the humility of your Reverence as you were willing to be helped by such a simple-minded person as myself which encouraged me. For the Lord today after communion granted me this request. Interrupting my thanksgiving, He put before me what the comparison between these two stages of prayer is and taught me how I could explain it and what the soul must do here. Of course, I was startled and yet I understood immediately.

Often I had been like one that was bewildered and indeed drunken in this love. But I never was able to understand its character. I understood clearly enough that it was God's work but I could not understand how He was working in this stage of prayer. For the truth of the matter is that the faculties are almost totally united with God and so absorbed with Him that they are not able to function. I am extremely pleased that I can now understand it. Blessed be the Lord Who has so favored me!

In this stage the faculties of the soul are so concentrated that they are only able to be occupied completely with God. It does not seem that any one of them dares to move, nor can we make them stir unless we strain to distract ourselves. Even then I do not think that we can do so entirely. So one utters many words here in praise to God without thinking them up, unless it is the Lord who thinks them up for us. Certainly the intellect has no role here. The soul might desire to cry out in praise as if it were beside itself in a delightful disquiet.

Now indeed are the flowers in blossom. They are beginning to spray their fragrance.

**4** Such prayer is preoccupation wholly with God.

In this state, the soul would have all men look upon it and learn of its bliss so that they will praise God and help it to praise Him more. He would have them to be partakers of its joy. For His joy is greater than it can stand. It seems to me that it is like the woman in the gospel who would call in all her neighbors (Luke 15:9). The admirable spirit of David, the royal prophet, must have experienced the same thing when he played on the harp and sang the praises of God. I have a very great regard for this wonderful king. I wish all had it, particularly those sinners like myself.

**5**

O my God, what must that soul be when it is in this state? It wishes that it were all tongue, in order that it all might be praise to our Lord. It speaks folly in a thousand holy ways, ever trying to find ways of pleasing the one who so possesses it.

I know someone [Teresa herself] who, although she was no poet, yet composed without any preparation certain stanzas that were full of meaning and most expressive of her pain. They were not the work of her own understanding. But in order to have a greater fruition of that bliss which so sweet a pain occasioned her, she complained of it in that way to God. She was willing to be cut up into pieces, soul and body, to show the delight that she felt in such pain. To what torments could she then be exposed

**6** Such prayer is utter praise to God.

that would not be delicious to endure for her Lord? She sees clearly that the martyrs did little or nothing so far as they were concerned when they endured their tortures, because the soul is so well aware that its strength is derived from Another Source.

7      But what will be its sufferings when it returns to live once more in the world by the use of its senses and goes back to the anxieties and the cares that it has? I do not think that I have exaggerated in any way, but rather I have fallen short in speaking of that joy which our Lord of His good pleasure gives to the soul in this, its exile. Blessed be You, O Lord! And may all created things praise You forever (Psalm 150:6, *Life*, XVI).

**1**
**God Himself is the Gardener of the soul.**

Enough has been said of this manner of prayer and of what the soul has to speak about what God is doing within it. For it is He who now takes upon Himself the gardener's work and who will have the soul take its ease. The exception is that the will is consenting to the graces. The graces are the fruition of that which it has and which it must resign itself to in order to do all that True Wisdom would accomplish in it. For that it is certain it has need of courage. Because this joy is so great, the soul now seems to be on the very point of going out of the body. What a blessed death that would be!

My meaning is that in a state of prayer that is so exalted as this, the soul understands that God is doing His work without any exhaustion of the intellect. The soul is, I think, only amazed at seeing how good a Gardener the Lord is, and how He does not desire it to do any of the work other than delight in the fragrance of the flowers which are beginning to send forth their perfume. For when God raises a soul to this state, it can do this and much more; for these are the effects upon it.

On one of these visits, however brief it is, the water is given without measure, because the gardener is Who He is—the Creator of the water. It is He who pours out the water without stint. So what the poor soul with all its own effort did perhaps over twenty years and could not bring

about, the heavenly Gardener now accomplishes in one
instant.

So the fruit grows and matures in such a way that the
soul can be sustained from its garden, if the Lord so desires. But He does not give it permission to distribute fruit
until it is very strong from what it has eaten. Otherwise it
would be giving to the others to taste without their receiving any profit or gain, and maintaining them and giving
them to eat at its own cost. Perhaps the soul will itself be
left dead from hunger. This possibility has been explained
well for those who are learned men, and they will know
how to make the application better than I know how to
explain it through my own efforts.

**Do not give
to others what
you have not
assimilated
yourself.**

Finally, the virtues are now stronger than in the previ-   **4**
ous prayer of quiet. The soul does not ignore them, because it sees that it is different and does not know how this
happened. It begins to perform great deeds by means of
the fragrance that the flowers give, for the Lord desires
that they so bloom that the soul may see it possesses virtue. Yet the soul is very clearly aware that it could not
have acquired them—nor was it able to—over many
years. It also sees in one moment that the Heavenly Gardener gave them.

Here then is that humility which remains in the soul
which is much greater and more profound than in the
past. For the soul sees more clearly that it did not do much
more than consent to the Lord's favors and embrace them
with its will.

This state of prayer seems to me to be a most distinct   **5**
union of the whole soul with God. But His Majesty desires
to give leeway to the faculties so that they may understand
and rejoice in the many things that He is now accomplishing. For He is the One doing them.

It happens often that the will is united, and the soul,
being aware of it, sees that the will is a captive and yet rejoices. I say it sees clearly that the will alone is in a deep
quiet. The intellect and the memory, on the other hand,

are so free that they can tend to business affairs and engage in works of charity.

This prayer differs from the prayer of quiet of which I have spoken, although it does seem as if they were all one with it. For in that prayer, the soul willingly neither stirs nor moves but delights in the holy repose of Mary who sat at the Master's feet. But in this third prayer the soul can be active like Martha, also.

So the soul is living both the active and the contemplative life at the same time; it is now able to apply itself to works of charity, attend to its business affairs, and do spiritual reading. Yet it is not master of itself completely. It clearly understands that the best part of the soul is somewhere else. It is as though we were speaking to someone at our side and from the other side there is another person speaking also to it. We cannot be fully attentive to one or to the other.

This prayer is something that is felt very clearly, and it gives deep satisfaction and happiness when it is experienced. It is an excellent preparation so that the soul may reach a profound quiet when it has time for solitude or leisure from business matters. It is like the life of a man who is full and requires no food because his appetite is satisfied. He will not eat of everything set before him, yet he is not so full as to refuse to eat if he sees anything that is a particularly desirable delicacy.

Thus the soul has no satisfaction in the world, and seeks no pleasure in it, because it has in itself that which gives it a far greater satisfaction, greater joys in God, and greater desires for the satisfaction of being with Him *(Life,* XVIII).

## V. WATER FROM THE FOUNTAIN

It may be that everything I say sounds confused. That is what I am afraid of. I think I was talking about spiritual consolations and trying to explain how they are sometimes bound up with our passions [just as water in a channel can be dirty]. They often cause fits of sobbing. Indeed I have heard of some persons who find themselves producing constrictions that cause chest pains which they cannot control, or others that have violent nosebleeds or produce similar disconcerting symptoms.

About all this I can say nothing, for I have not experienced it. But there must be some cause for comfort in it; it all leads to an intense desire to please God and to have fruition of His Majesty.

What I call "consolations from God" and which else-
where I have termed the "Prayer of Quiet" is something of a very different nature. Those of you who by the grace of God have experienced this will know.

**The Prayer of Quiet**

To understand this better, let us suppose that we are looking at two fountains, the basins of which can be filled with water. [Here Teresa is thinking of the two large, ornamental marble basins that were commonly found in the Moorish style courtyards of large Spanish houses in her day.] I find no comparison is more apt for explaining spiritual realities than this of water. This I account for because I have so little knowledge and my ability is of such little use. Yet because I am a great lover of this element which I have considered more deeply than other matters, let us use the analogy. I have observed it more attentively than anything else.

Now these two cisterns are supplied with water in differing ways. The one is supplied from a distance by several conduits and with human skill. But the other has been constructed at the very source of the water, that is over a spring; and so it fills without making any noise. If the latter spring is abundant, as is that of which we are speaking, it sends forth a great volume of water after it has filled the cistern. Here no skill is necessary, and no conduits had to be made, for the water flows all the time.

You see here the difference. For the water which comes through conduits resembles, in my opinion, the tenderness and pleasures spoken of in the third stage of prayer which we draw from our meditation. For these we draw from our thoughts by the help of meditating upon created

things. In short, the thoughts are obtained by our own diligence so that they make a noise when we fill them. So
this happens when we are filled with the benefits of these
thoughts.

The fourth<br/>level of prayer

The water now comes direct from the source to the
other fountain. This source is God. So when it is His
Majesty's will, and He is pleased to grant us some special
favor, His coming is accompanied by the greatest peace
and quiet and sweetness within ourselves. I cannot say
where it arises or how this happens. This contentment
and delight are not felt, like earthly delights are felt in the
heart. Not at the beginning, at least. Later the basin completely fills, and then this water begins to overflow all the
Mansions and faculties until it reaches the body. It is for
this reason that I have said it has its source in God and yet
ends in ourselves. For it is certain—and anyone will know
this who has experienced it—that the whole of the outer
man enjoys this consolation and sweetness as well.

While writing these words, I am thinking of this verse:
"You have enlarged my heart" (Psalm 119:32). This dila-
tion is not something which I think takes its rise within
the heart, but from some other more interior part that is
truly deep. I think it must be the center of the soul itself.
For I discover such wonderful secrets within me. They astonish me. But how many more there are!

O my Lord and my God! How wonderful is Your greatness! Yet here we live like so many silly shepherd boys,
imagining that we have attained some knowledge of You.
Yet when I say "amounts to nothing at all" I mean that
You are so surpassingly great. This is not because the signs
of greatness that we see in Your works are not very wonderful. But we have actually learned to know of them ourselves very little.

The affects of<br/>such prayer<br/>on the soul

Returning then to this verse, I think that what it says
about the enlargement of the heart may be of some help to
us. Apparently, as this heavenly water begins to flow from
the source of which I am speaking—from our very
depths—it proceeds to spread within us and to cause an

interior expansion. It produces an ineffable blessing so that the soul cannot understand all that it is receiving there. The fragrance that it experiences, we might say, is as if in those interior depths there were a brazier on which sweet perfumes were being burned. The light cannot be seen nor the place where it dwells, but the fragrant smoke and the heat penetrate the whole soul. Very often the effects will extend throughout the body.

See that you properly understand me here. For neither is any heat felt, nor smell perceived, since it is something more subtle than these sensory experiences. I speak plainly to help you understand me. But people who have not experienced this must realize that it really does happen. Its occurrence is capable of being seen, and the soul becomes aware of it more clearly than these words of mine can express. It is not something that we can imagine nor strive after nor acquire. For it is very clear that it is not something that is made of human metal; rather, it is made of the purest gold of divine wisdom. In this state the faculties are not in union, but they become absorbed and they are astonished at what they consider is happening to them.

It is possible that in writing about these interior experiences, I may in some way be contradicting what I have said before. It is no wonder, for it is about fifteen years since I wrote my book (*The Life*). Since then, the Lord has given me a clearer realization of these matters. Both then and now, of course, I may still be mistaken in all this, but I cannot lie about my experiences. By the mercy of God I would rather die a thousand deaths. So I am speaking exactly of it as I understand it myself.

The will certainly seems to me to be united in some way with the will of God. But it is by the effects of this prayer and the actions which follow it that the genuineness of the experience can really be tested. For there is no better test for doing so than this. If the person who receives such a grace recognizes it for what it is—that is to say that our Lord Himself is granting him a surpassingly great favor— the Lord will also give him another great favor if he does not turn back.

You will then desire, my daughters, to strive to attain to this way of praying, and you will be right to do so. As I have said, the soul cannot fully understand the favors which the Lord grants it. Nor can it know the love which draws it ever nearer to Himself. It is certainly desirable that we should know how to obtain such a favor. So I will tell you what I have found out about it.

The effects of this prayer are many, some of which I will now mention. There is another kind of prayer, however, which commences almost before this. So let me say a little about it here although I have spoken of it elsewhere.

This is the Prayer of Recollection which also seems to me to be divinely given. For it does not require the soul to be in the dark, nor to shut the eye, nor to do any external thing. It often happens that without our wishing it, our eyes close and we desire solitude. Then without any contrivance, it is like a building that seems to be erected for the prayer that I have just mentioned.

The senses and all external things then seem to lose their grip upon the soul so that the soul recovers what was lost. They say that the soul enters within itself, and that sometimes it ascends above itself. By these expressions I will not be able to explain anything. For I have this unhappiness in thinking that you will understand me best according to the way in which I can express my own experience. Perhaps then no one except myself will really understand (*Interior Castle*, IV, Ch. 3).

**2**
**Fruition of life**
**for others**
In this fourth stage there is no sense of anything; there is only fruition, without understanding what the fruition is that is given. It is understood that the fruitfulness is of a certain good containing in itself all good together at once. But this goodness is not comprehended. The senses are all occupied in this fruition in such a way that not one of them is at liberty to attend to anything else, whether outwardly or inwardly.

**3**
**Joy is intensified.**
The senses were permitted before to give some signs of the great joy that they feel. But now in this state, the joy of the soul is incomparably greater, and the power of

showing it is still less available. For there is no power in the body or the soul whereby this fruition can be made known. Anything of that kind would be a great hindrance, a torture, and a disturbance of its rest. And I say that if it really is a union of all the faculties, the soul, even if it wished, cannot make itself known. For if it can, then it is not a union at all.

How this which we call union is effected and what it is I **4** cannot tell. Mystical theology explains it, but I do not know the terms of that science. Nor can I understand what the mind is, nor how it differs from the soul or spirit either. For all three seem to me but the same thing, although I do know that the soul sometimes leaps forth out of itself like a fire that is burning and becomes like a flame. Occasionally this fire increases violently and the flame ascends high above the fire. But it is not therefore a different thing. It is the same flame of the same fire. Your learning, my fathers, will enable you to understand the matter; but I can go no further.

What I am undertaking to explain is what the soul feels **5** when it is in divine union. It is plain enough what that **Union with God** union is. It is that of two distinct things becoming one. O **becomes like a** my Lord, how good You are! Blessed be You forever, O my **fire.** God! Let all creatures praise You Who have so loved us that we can truly speak of this communication which You have with souls in this our exile! Yes, even if they be good souls, it is on Your part great munificence and kindness. In a word, it is Your lovingkindness, O my Lord (*Life*, XVIII).

In order to speak about the Prayer of Recollection, I **Any enlargement** have passed over the effects or signs to be observed in souls **of soul takes** to whom this prayer is granted by our Lord. It is clear that **place.** an enlargement of the soul does take place, as if the water proceeding from the spring had no means of running over. Instead, the fountain had such a device that the more the water flowed in, the larger the basin became. So it is with this kind of prayer. God works many more wonders in the soul, fitting it and gradually disposing it to retain all that He gives it.

**Service for God has freedom from fear.**

This gentle movement and the interior enlargement of the soul cause it to be less constrained in matters relating to the service of God than it was before; it has much more freedom, also. It is not distressed because of the fear of hell. Although it feels greater fear now for having offended God, yet it is freed from *servile* fear and has a great confidence that it will enjoy Him. The fear that the soul used to have of losing its health by ascetic practice has also ceased, and it thinks it can do all in God. It has more desires for using spiritual discipline than ever. The fear of afflictions which it used to have is also now moderated because it has a more living faith. It knows that if the soul bears them for God's sake, His Majesty will give it grace to bear them with patience. Indeed, sometimes the soul desires them since it has a great desire to do something for God. And as it now understands His greatness better, it accordingly esteems itself more vile.

Having also tried the delights of God, the soul finds those of the world to be in comparison as mere dirt (Philippians 3:8). So the soul separates itself from them little by little, and for doing this the soul has more control over itself. In a word, it has matured in all virtue and will not fail to go on increasingly, unless it should relapse and offend God once more. Then all would be lost, however highly raised a soul may have been in virtue and contemplation (*Interior Castle*, IV, Chapter 3).

**The soul despises the world's pleasures.**

I am now speaking of the water which comes down from heaven to fill and to saturate in its abundance the whole garden with water. If our Lord never ceased to pour it down whenever it was necessary, the gardener certainly would have plenty of rest. If there were no winter, but an equitable season throughout the year, the fruits and flowers would never fail. The gardener would have his delight always there. But in this life this is not possible. We must always be careful, when one water fails, to obtain another. This water from heaven comes down very often when the gardener least expects it.

The soul which seeks after God is conscious with an ex-   **14**
cessive and sweet joy that it is, as it were, utterly fainting
away in a kind of trance. The breathing and all bodily
strengths seem to fail it, so that it cannot even move the
hands without great pain. The eyes close involuntarily;
and if they are open, they are as if they see nothing at all.
Reading is impossible, for the very letters seem strained
and cannot be distinguished. The ears hear; but what is
heard is not comprehended. The senses have no function
except to hinder the soul's fruition. And so they rather
hurt it. It is useless to try to speak because it is not possible
to conceive a word. Nor if it were conceived is there any
strength sufficient to utter it. All bodily strength vanishes
while that of the soul increases to enable it to better have
the fruition of its joy. Great and most perceptible also is
the outward joy that is now felt.

However long it may last, this prayer does no harm. At   **15**
least it has never done any to me. Nor do I remember,
however ill I might have been to start with, that I ever felt
the worse for it. On the contrary; I was always better afterwards. By so great a blessing, what harm can it do? The
outward effects are so plain as to leave no doubt possible
that there must have been some great cause. It robs us of
our bodily faculties with much joy in order to leave the
faculties greater.

The truth is that it passes away so quickly in the begin-   **16**
ning that neither by the outward signs nor by the failure of   **This prayer**
the senses can it be perceived. But it is clear from the over-   **passes quickly.**
flowing abundance of grace that the brightness of the sun
which has shown there must have been great, since it has
thus made the soul melt away. It does seem to me that the
period of time—however long it may have been—during
which the faculties of the soul were entranced is really
short. Maybe half an hour, but that would be a long time.
I do not think that I have ever been in such a trance for so
long.

The truth of the matter is this. It is extremely difficult to know how long, because the senses are in suspense. But I think that at any time, it cannot be very long before one of the faculties recovers itself. It is the will that persists in the work. The other two faculties quickly begin to disturb it. As the will is calm, it surfaces them again. For a time they are quiet, and then they recover themselves once more.

17    In this way, some hours may have passed in prayer. When the two faculties begin to drink deep and to perceive the taste of this divine wine, they give themselves up with great readiness in order to be the more absorbed. They follow the will and the three rejoice together. But this state of complete absorption, together with the rest of the imagination—for I believe that even the imagination is then wholly at rest—lasts only for a short time. Although the faculties do not recover themselves so as to be the same for hours afterwards, yet God from time to time draws them to Himself.

18
Such prayer is     Let us now come to describe what the soul feels inter-
indescribable.   iorly. Let him describe it who knows it. For as it is impossible to understand it, much more it is impossible to describe it.

When I intended to write this, I had just communicated and risen from the very prayer of which I am speaking. I am thinking of what the soul was then doing. Our Lord said to me: "It undoes itself utterly, My daughter, in order that it may give itself more and more to Me. It is not itself that then lives, it is I" (Galatians 2:20). Since the soul cannot comprehend what it does not understand, it understands by ceasing to understand.

All I am able to say is that the soul is represented as being close to God. There abides a certain strong conviction that cannot possibly help believing this. Now all the faculties fail and are suspended in such a way that their workings cannot be traced. If the soul is making a meditation on any subject, the memory of it is lost at once, just as if it had not been thought of. If it reads, what is read is not remembered or dwelt upon. So it is with vocal prayer.

When I began to have these experiences, it happened [20] to me that I was ignorant of one thing. I did not realize that God was in all things. When He seemed to me to be so near, I thought this must be impossible. Not to believe that He was present was not in my power. For it seemed to me as if it were evident that I felt there His very presence. Some unlearned men used to say to me that He was present only by His grace. I could not believe that, because He seemed to me to be present Himself.

So I was distressed. It was a most learned man of the Dominican Order who delivered me from this doubt. For he told me that He was present and how He communed with us. This was a great comfort to me.

It is to be observed and understood that this water from [21] heaven—this greatest grace of our Lord—always leaves in the soul the best fruits (*Life*, XVIII).

When the prayer of union is over, there remains in the soul an exceeding great tenderness. This is so great that it could undo itself; not from pain, but through tears of joy. It finds itself bathed in them without being aware of it, and it does not know how or when it wept them. To behold the violence of the fire subdued by water—which makes it burn the more—gives the soul great delight. It seems as if I were speaking an unknown language. So it is, however.

**Great tenderness of heart results.**

It has happened to me occasionally when this prayer [2] was over to be so beside myself as not to know whether I had been dreaming or whether the bliss I felt had really been mine. I found myself in a flood of tears which had painlessly flowed with such violence and rapidity that it seemed as if a cloud from heaven had shed them. This was no dream. Thus it was with me in the beginning when it passed quickly away. The soul remains possessed of so much courage that if it were now hewn in pieces for God, there would be great consolation in it.

**There is heroic determinism.**

This, then, is a time of resolution, of heroic determination, of the living energy of good desires, of the beginning of hatred to the world, and of a clear perception of its vanity. The soul makes greater and higher progress than it has ever made before in previous states of prayer. It grows in humility more and more, because it sees clearly that neither obtaining nor retaining this grace will ever enable it to do anything of itself. It looks upon itself as most unworthy. It is like the sunlight that enters strongly into a room where not a cobweb can be hid. It sees its own misery so clearly. Self-conceit is so remote that it seems as if it never could have had any. For now the soul's own eyes behold how very little it could ever do, or rather that it ever did anything.

The soul abides alone with Him. What has it to do but to love Him? It neither sees nor hears unless on compulsion. It is no thanks to the soul. Its past life stands before it, then, together with the great mercy of God in sharp distinctiveness. It is no longer necessary for the soul to go and hunt for food with its understanding because it now can eat and ruminate upon what is already prepared. So far as itself is concerned, it sees that the soul deserves hell and that its punishment is due.

4    The good effects of this prayer abide in the soul for some time. Now it clearly apprehends that the fruit is not its own. The soul can then begin to share it with others without any loss to itself. It begins to show signs of its being a soul that is guarding the treasures of heaven, and it is desirous of communicating them to others. It desires to pray to God that it may not itself be the only soul that is rich in them.

The soul begins to benefit its neighbor as it were, without being aware of it or of doing anything consciously. Its neighbors understand the matter because the fragrance of the flowers has grown so strong as to make them eager to approach them. They see that this soul is full of virtue. They see the fruit and how delicious it is and they wish to help that soul to eat it.

If this ground is well dug by troubles, by persecutions, 5
by infirmities, and by other detractions, they are few who
ascend so high without it. If it be well broken up by a great
detachment from all self-interest, it will drink in so much
more water that it can hardly ever be parched again.

But if the ground which is mere waste and covered with
thorns (as I was when I began) does not avoid sin, then it
will be an ungrateful soil that is unfit for so great a grace. It
will dry up again. If the gardener becomes careless, and if
our Lord out of His goodness will not send down rain upon
it, then the garden is ruined. Thus it has been with me
more than once so that I am amazed at it all. If I had not
found this to be so by experience, I really could not have
believed it possible.

I write this for the comfort of souls which are weak as I   6
am. May they never despair nor cease to trust in the power
of God. Even if they should fall after our Lord has raised
them to this high degree of prayer, they must not be discouraged unless they lose themselves utterly. Tears of
repentance gain everything, and one drop of water at-
tracts another.

# V

# THE INTERIOR CASTLE:
# THE INTERIOR LIFE AS MANY
# MANSIONS FOR GOD'S PRESENCE
# PART 1

### Letter VII: To the Most Illustrious
### Don Alonso Velasquez, Bishop of Osuna

h that I could make your Reverence understand the quiet and tranquility which my soul
now enjoys! For I am so certain that I enjoy
God. He seems to have given my soul the possession, although not the enjoyment, of Him. It is as if
someone had, by a legal deed, settled a great estate upon
someone else, so that he should have possession of it after
a certain period and receive the rents. But until then, he
can only enjoy the promise of the title that is made over to
him.

But through gratitude that he feels for the donor, he
does not wish to enjoy the estate now. He thinks that he
does not deserve it. Instead his only desire is to serve Him,
even though it is in much suffering. Sometimes he even
thinks that this is very little, although his afflictions
should last until the end of the world, provided he could
be of service to the Giver of this possession. For in truth,
such a person is not subject to the miseries of the world as
he used to be formerly. Although he endures more, it
seems to be only outwardly so. For the soul is as it were a
castle with sovereign power; and thus the soul does not

have any anxiety.

And yet this security does not preclude the soul from having a great fear of offending God and of removing everything which might prevent it from serving Him. Indeed, it increases its fear and carefulness. But so mindful is the soul of its own interest that it seems in part to have lost its very being, so unconsciously self-forgetful has it become. In everything it looks to God's glory and how to accomplish His will the best. It looks to glorify Him.

An interior peace, as well as the presence of the Three Persons, continues. They do so in such a way that I clearly seem to experience what the Apostle John says: "that He will dwell within you" (John 14:23). This He does, not only by grace, but He also makes the soul perceive this presence. This brings so many good things, it cannot adequately be described, especially since there is no occasion to seek consideration for knowing that God is in the soul.

This presence occurs nearly all the time, except when the soul is oppressed by severe sickness. Sometimes it seems as if God wished it to suffer without any inner consolation. But never, not even through any first inclination, does this turn the will from desiring that God's will should not be accomplished in it. The soul's resignation to this will has such strength that it desires neither death, nor life, except for a short time when it desires to see God.

But the presence of these Three Persons is immediately represented to the soul with such power, that even my grief at being distant from my Spouse is diminished. A desire to live continues, if such be His will, in order to serve Him the more. My desire is only to be instrumental in causing at least one soul to love Him more, and to praise Him through all my means. Although this should be for a very short time, I think it will be more profitable than to enjoy eternal glory.

Your Lordship's unworthy servant and daughter,

Teresa de Jesus

## THE FIRST MANSIONS: PRAYER FOR
## SELF-REALIZATION BEFORE GOD

### Part One: The Beauty and Dignity of the Soul

Today, while I was interceding with our Lord to speak through me, I could not think of anything to say and had no idea how I could fulfill the obligation laid upon me by my obedience. There came to my mind what I should talk about and set down in writing in order to have a basis on which to build.

The thought occurred to me that each of our souls is like a castle that is made entirely out of one diamond or at least a very clear crystal. In it there are many rooms, just as in heaven there are many dwelling places (John 14:2). Now in reflecting upon this very carefully, sisters, we realize that the soul of the righteous is nothing but a paradise. In it God reminds us that He takes His delight (Proverbs 8:31). If He is a King so mighty, so wise, so holy, and so full of goodness, what do you think a room will be like in which He delights? There can be nothing comparable to the greatness or the beauty and the capacity of the soul. This is a mystery which even the sharpest intellect can hardly comprehend, just as it cannot comprehend God. But He Himself tells us that He has created us "in His own image and after His own likeness" (Genesis 1:26).

*Each of our souls is like a castle.*

Well then, if this is true there is no point in exhausting ourselves by trying to understand the beauty of this castle. For although it is but His creature—and there is as much difference between it as there is between God the Creator and any creature—the very fact that His Majesty says that He made it in His own image means that we can hardly form any conception of the sublime dignity and the beauty of the soul.

It is too bad and really unfortunate that, through our own fault, we do not understand ourselves or really know who we are. Yet would we not think it really absurd for somebody to be so ignorant that, when he was asked who he was, he would reply that he had no idea who he, or who his father, or his mother was, or indeed what country he even came from?

**The need to know ourselves before God**

If this then is so absurdly stupid, is our own state not much worse if we make no attempt to discover what we are and only vaguely know that we are living in these bodies? We just assume that, because our faith tells us so, we possess our souls but have no real way of knowing this is true. Seldom do we consider what the quality is of our interior life, or Who dwells there, or how precious it really is. As a result, we make little effort to preserve the beauty of the soul. Instead, all our interest is focused on the externals like the rough setting of a diamond, or upon the outer wall of the castle; that is to say we focus upon these bodies of ours.

Well then, let us imagine that this castle—my soul—has many Mansions. Some of these are above, others are down below, others are to the sides. But in the center is the main dwelling place where the most intimate exchanges take place between God and the soul.

It is necessary that you keep this comparison in mind. For perhaps God will be pleased to use it to demonstrate to you something of the favors which He is pleased to grant to souls and to note the difference between these favors.

**God bestows His favors to reveal His greatness.**

But I am sure that if anyone thinks that he will be harmed by believing God bestows such favors, then such a person is really standing in great need of humility and love for his neighbor. For how can we otherwise help rejoicing that God bestows these favors on a brother of ours when we see that this does not hinder Him from bestowing the same upon us? His Majesty sometimes bestows them only in order to show them, as He said concerning the blind man to whom He restored sight (John 9:2). He grants these favors, then, not because those who receive them are holier than those who do not, but that His greatness might be made manifest. This we see in the case of the Apostle Paul and Mary Magdalene. Thus we may praise Him in His creatures.

Some may say, "These things seem impossible, so it is

no good scandalizing the weak." My reply is that the loss is *less* to believe such wonders than to forego doing good to those on whom God bestows them. The result will be to be more stimulated to love Him Who shows such mercy and Whose power and majesty are so great.

In any case, I do not believe that I am speaking to anyone who will run into this danger, because they all know and believe that God gives to us still greater evidences of His love. But if any one of you does not believe this, you will never find it in your own experience. For our Lord is exceedingly desirous not to have His works limited. Thus, sisters, never let this happen to any of you.

Let us get back to our beautiful and delightful castle. **Enter into yourself** For we now have to examine how we are going to get into it. It may seem that I am talking ridiculously now, because if this castle is the soul, it is obvious that there is no need to enter into it since the soul is the castle itself. This is as ridiculous as telling a person to go into a room when he is already there. However, you must understand that there is a mighty difference between one room and another. For many souls dwell near the walls of the castle, namely where the guards are, and yet never care about going further into it. Neither do they wish to know what is within that precious place, nor who dwells there, nor what rooms are there. You must have heard or read in many books of devotion that "a soul is advised to enter into itself." This is exactly the same as I am saying here.

A very learned man once told me that souls without the exercise of prayer are like a body that is paralyzed or crippled. Although it has hands and feet, it cannot use them. In the same way there are some souls that are so weak, and so caught up in external affairs, that they have no idea how they can enter into themselves. In fact, they have got so used to dealing with the insects and vermin that are in the wall that surrounds the castle that they become almost like them. Although they have been given a nature which is so richly endowed that they are able to hold communion even with God Himself, yet there is no remedy for them. Like Lot's wife, who looked back and was turned into a pillar of salt, so these souls that do not strive to understand and to amend their miserable condition will likewise be changed into pillars of salt (Genesis 19:26).

As I understand it, the door of entry into this castle is prayer and meditation. I am speaking here of both silent and vocal prayer. For if a person does not think about Whom he is addressing, and what he is asking for, I really cannot believe that he is praying at all. He may be constantly moving his lips, but that is all. True, it is sometimes possible to pray without paying heed to these things, but that is only because they have been thought of previously. If a man is in the habit of speaking to the Majesty of God as if he were speaking to his own slave or utters vain repetitions, and never ponders to think if he is expressing himself properly, then he really does not pray at all.

May God grant that no Christian ever speaks to Him in this way! My sisters, I hope to God none of you ever will, for we are accustomed here to talk about interior matters. This is a good way of keeping oneself from falling into such abominable manners.

Let us think of those who eventually will enter the castle. At the moment they are very much absorbed in worldly affairs. Their intentions are good. Sometimes, although infrequently, they do commit themselves to our Lord. But they think rather carelessly about the state of their souls. They are full of a thousand preoccupations, and so they only pray a few times a month. As a rule, they are thinking all the time about their own worldly preoccupations, for they are much attached to them. We are reminded, "where their treasure is, there will also be their heart" (Matthew 6:21). Sometimes they do put these things aside, and the self-knowledge and awareness that they are not progressing spiritually in order to get to the door is important for them.

At least, these people do enter the first or lower rooms. But there are so many reptiles which get in their way that they are prevented from seeing the beauties of the castle and from having the inner quiet. They feel that they have done quite enough simply to have entered it at all.

Now, my daughters, you may think that because of the goodness of the Lord, you are not one of these, and that I am speaking irrelevantly to you. But you must be patient, for there is no other way in which I can explain to you some of the ideas that I have had about the interior matters that concern prayer. To explain to you what I would like to say is very difficult unless you have also had that same personal experience. But anyone with such experience, as you will see, cannot help touching upon these subjects.

## Part Two: The Ugliness of Sin in the Soul

Before I proceed further, I wish you to consider what a spectacle it is to behold this castle. It is brilliantly shining and has the beauty of a pearl from the Orient; it is a tree of life that is planted in the midst of the living waters of life (Psalm 1:3).

What a tragedy it is then when it is plunged back into sin. There can be no darker darkness, nothing more obscure and black, when this happens. But you need know only one thing about it and that is that, although the Sun Himself has given it all its splendor and beauty, He is still there in the center of the soul. Yet if sin occurs, it is as if He were not there for any participation which the soul has in Him; this is so although the soul is as capable of enjoying Him as the crystal is of reflecting the sunshine.

*Only God's presence in our lives makes our souls authentic.*

When the soul is in a state like this, it will profit nothing. Hence when it is fallen into sin, none of the good works that it may do will be of any use to win it glory. For sin does not have its origin in the principle of grace, which is that God, Who is the cause of our virtue, is alone virtuous. To be separated from Him means that we cannot please Him in any way. Indeed, the purpose of anyone who commits sin is to please the devil, who is darkness incarnate, and not God. So the poor soul becomes darkness itself.

I know someone our Lord wanted to show what it was like for a soul to be in sin [again, Teresa herself]. This person says that if people really understood the sinful state, she thinks that they would find it impossible to sin at all; at least it would be impossible to sin willfully, even though the soul would have to be tested in the most severe fashion. The Lord gave her a strong desire that all might realize this. May He give you, daughters, the desire to beseech Him earnestly for all who are in this state, and who have become total darkness, and whose works have also become darkness.

**God's presence within is like a spring.** Just as all the streams are clear which issue from a clear spring, so is a soul in a state of grace. Because the streams proceed from this fount of life, a fount in which the soul is planted like a tree (Psalm 1:3), they are most pleasing in the eyes of both God and man. But there would be no refreshment, no fruitage, if it were not for this fount sustaining the tree of the righteous man. This fount keeps the soul from drying up, and helps it to produce good fruit.

In contrast, the soul that deliberately separates itself from this fount can only be planted in a pool of foul and stagnant water from which flow equally foul and fetid streams. But we should clearly understand that this fountain and this resplendent sun—the very center of the soul—do not lose their brightness and glory; these always remain and nothing can take away this beauty. But if anyone should cover the crystal with a black cloth when it is exposed to the sun, it will be obvious that, even though the sun may shine upon it, it will have no effect on the crystal.

Souls, redeemed by the blood of Jesus Christ—know and pity yourselves! For how is it possible that, knowing this truth as you do, you do not try to take away the pitch from this crystal? Consider how when once your life is ended, you will never return anymore to enjoy this light.

O Jesus! What a misery is it to behold a soul that is separated from and deprived of this light! What miserable objects are the poor mansions of such a soul! How disordered are their senses! How wretched are the people who live in them! With what blindness and bad government do the faculties rule, which are their governors and bucklers and stewards! In short, when a tree is planted where the devil is, what fruit can it bear?

I once heard a godly man say, "I wonder not so much at the evil which a person committed in sin, as that which he did not commit." So may God in His mercy deliver us from so great an evil. For while we live in this life, sin only deserves the name of evil since it only brings upon us eternal evils. This, my daughters, is what you ought to fear, and from which we must beseech God in our prayers to free us. For "unless He keeps the city, they labor in vain who keep it" (Psalm 127:1). We in ourselves are vanity itself.

I have referred to a person above who said, "I have received two benefits from the favor God has bestowed upon me in showing me the miserable state of my soul in sin." The first was an exceedingly great fear of offending Him, and therefore she was constantly beseeching Him not to let her fall. She could see the dreadful evil that would ensue.

*May God reveal to us our sinfulness against Him.*

The second benefit was that she obtained a looking glass in order to promote humility in her, for she knew that the good which we do is not originally from ourselves but from the fountain in which this tree of our souls is planted. It is this Sun which gives heat to our actions. She said this was represented so clearly to her that when she did any good deed, or saw one done by another, she always referred again to this principle that God alone is the source of all our goodness. She saw that without Him "we can do nothing" (John 15:5). It was this that prompted her to praise God. As a rule, whenever she did any good action, she never gave a thought to herself at all.

*God alone is the source of our goodness.*

So sisters, if you can remember these two things, then the time that you have spent in reading all this, and the time that I have spent in writing it, will not have been lost.

**How has prayer affected us?**

I know very well that it is important for you that I should explain to you these interior things as well as I can, since we always hear it said: "What a good thing prayer is." We are bound by our rule to exercise prayer so many hours each day, and yet this is not explained to us. Little is mentioned to us regarding what we ourselves can do in prayer, and in respect to those things about how our Lord operates within the soul, doing His supernatural work.

As this is so little explained to us, it will be a great comfort for us to take a view of this heavenly, internal building. Mortals understand it so little, although many walk through it.

**God is in the center of our lives.**

Let us now return to our castle of many Mansions. Do not imagine that these Mansions are all arranged in a single row, one behind the other. Instead, fix your attention on the center, the room or the palace which is occupied by the King Himself. Think of it as like a palmetto [a shrub that is common in the south and east of Spain]. It has many outer rinds that surround the delicate savory part within, all of which must be taken away before the heart can be eaten. Likewise, around the central room are many more beautiful Mansions, as there are also above it.

In speaking of the soul, we must always think of it as an ample, spacious, and lofty sphere. This can be done without the least exaggeration, for the soul's capacity is far greater than we can ever appreciate. The Sun which is in this palace radiates its influence to every part of it.

**The Mansion of self-knowledge**

Now it is very important for a soul which makes use of prayer not to feel confined or restricted within the palace. Let the soul walk freely through all the Mansions, above, below, and on every side, since God has bestowed upon you so great a dignity. Do not feel forced to remain too long in any one Mansion, not, at least, unless it is the Mansion of self-knowledge. For this is the right floor from whence to begin. And if we can journey along at a safe and level progress, why should we want wings to fly? Rather, let us make every effort to progress in self-knowledge. But it is my opinion that we should never completely know ourselves unless we seek to know God. It is by gazing at His Majesty that we get in touch with our own lowliness. It is by looking at His purity that we shall see our own filth. It is by pondering His humility, that we shall see how far we are from being humble.

You may have noticed that in these First Mansions, hardly any light comes from the King's royal chamber. Even though they are not dark and black—as when the soul is in sin—they nevertheless are in some way darkened so that the soul is not enlightened in these rooms. This is not through any fault of the Mansions, but because there are so many bad things like serpents, lizards, vipers, and other poisonous creatures which enter within the soul and do not allow it to be aware of the light. It is as if a person were to enter into a place where the sun is shining, but his eyes were so covered with mud that he could hardly open them. Actually, the floor is bright, but he does not enjoy it because of the impediment of things like these wild animals or crawling beasts that make him close his eyes to everything except them.

*The soul is darkened by carnal things.*

So I think it must be the condition of the soul itself. Even though it may not be in a bad state, it is so caught up in worldly things and so absorbed with its possessions, its honor, or its business affairs that even though the soul wants to see and enjoy its beauty, these things do not allow it to do so. Nor does it seem capable of escaping these many impediments.

It is very important that if the soul is desirous of entering into the Second Mansions, he should strive to give up every business which is not necessary. Unless he does this, he will never be able to enter into the inner mansions of the castle. Instead he will remain in the first series of rooms where he is already and where he will be exposed to danger. There among so many poisonous creatures it is impossible not to be bitten at some time or another.

*Conditions of entry into the Second Mansions*

Think also, my daughters, of the possibility that we who are already free from these snares—as we are—and have entered much further into the castle to other secret dwelling places can return through our own fault to the place where there is such tumult. Because of our sins, there are many persons to whom God may have granted favors who have fallen back into this state of misery.

Here in our convent we are free with respect to external dangers. But in the internal matters of the heart, may it please the Lord that we are also free and that He may free us. So guard yourselves, my daughters, from all extraneous cares. Remember that there are few dwelling places in this castle in which the devils are not prepared to wage battle.

Yes, it is true that there are some rooms where the guards (that is, our faculties) have the strength to fight. But it is essential that we do not become careless in recognizing the wiles of the devil and that he does deceive us by changing himself into an angel of light. There are a host of things that he can do to cause us damage. For he can enter little by little until he has done all the damage and we have not recognized him.

Indeed, he is like a noiseless file; so we need to recognize him at the beginning. Let me now say something that will explain this better to you.

Deceptions of Satan

For example, Satan may give a sister various desires to do penance. It may seem to her that she can have no rest except when she is tormenting herself. This may be a good start. But if the Superior has ordered that no penance should be done without permission and the devil makes the sister think that the practice is so good that one can do so daringly, she may secretly give herself up to it to such an extent that she loses her health and does not even observe the rule that has been commanded. Then you will see clearly that this good only ends up as an evil.

Or the devil may imbue another with a great zeal to seek holiness. Such zeal is good in itself. But it can be done in such a way that every little fault the sisters commit will seem to her as a very serious breach. She will be critical in observing whether they commit these things and then inform the Superior. It could even happen at times that she does not see her own faults because of her intense zeal for her own religious observance. Since the other sisters do not understand what is going on within her and yet see all this concern, they may not accept her zeal quite so enthusiastically.

What the devil is aiming after in all this is not a small matter. It is, in fact, the cooling of our love for each other and of our charity. This causes great harm in the community. Let us remember, daughters, that true perfection consists in the love of God and of our neighbor. The more we are able to observe these two precepts consistently, the more perfect we shall be. Our whole rule and constitutions serve for nothing else but that we should be enabled to do these two things with more perfection. Let us, then, avoid such indiscreet zeal that may injure us as a community and let each one look at herself.

*The destruction of love in the community*

This mutual love is so very important that I hope you will never forget it. For it is by the obsession with trifling matters about others—with little knowledge of the interior of the soul of the other person—that such a critical person may lose her own peace of mind and also disturb the peace of others. Consider, then, the cost of what you are doing in striving for holiness.

The devil can also raise this temptation against the Superior, and it may prove in that case even more dangerous.

So great discretion is necessary. If faults are committed against "the rules and constitutions," they cannot be passed over lightly; but the Superior, not others, should be informed of them. If they are not corrected, the Superior must be told of the matter, for this is charity. Again, if any very serious faults are found among the sisters and allowed to pass by—even if this allowance is through fear that it might only be a temptation—this itself is a temptation.

*Much discretion is required in the desire to be a holy person.*

So great care should be taken, lest the devil deceive us and keep us from mentioning this matter to another person. In that way the devil may gain much and introduce a habit of gossiping in the community. But speak of it to those who can and should remedy the evil. For in this house, which is to the glory of God, there should be no occasion for gossip; instead, continual silence should be kept. But we must be kept on our guard, as this is good.

## THE SECOND MANSIONS: PRAYER OF RECOLLECTIONS CONCERNING THE CHARACTER OF GOD AND THE NEED FOR SELF-SURRENDER

### The Importance of Perseverance

Let us now consider the kind of souls that enter into the Second Mansions and what such a soul does there.

This section has to do with those who have already begun to practice prayer and who realize the importance of not remaining in the "First Mansions." At the same time, these do not have sufficient determination to remain in this second stage without on occasion turning back, for they do not avoid occasions of sin. The failure to avoid these occasions can be quite dangerous. But these persons have received a good deal of mercy in that they contrive to escape from the snakes and other poisonous creatures, if only for short periods. They realize that it is good to flee from them.

In some ways, these souls have a much harder time than those in the First Mansions. But they are in less peril, for they seem now to understand their situation, and there is great hope that they will enter further into the castle.

**Dwelling in the Second Mansions requires much more effort.** I say that dwelling in these rooms involves more effort, because those who are in the first dwelling places are like deaf mutes. Thus the difficulty of not speaking is more easily tolerated by deaf mutes than it is by those who hear but who cannot speak, that is, those in the Second Mansions. These persons are able to hear the Lord when He calls them. Since they are getting closer to where His Majesty dwells, He is a very good neighbor. So great are His mercy and goodness that although we continue to be addicted to our previous pastimes, our business affairs, our pleasures and worldly buying and selling, and though we still fall into sin and rise again, nevertheless our Lord is so anxious for our companionship that He calls us ceaselessly to come to Him. His voice is so sweet that our poor soul is consumed with grief at being unable to do His bidding at once. That is why I say that such a soul suffers more than if it could not hear Him.

I do not mean to say that He speaks to us and calls us in any prescribed way. His appeals rather come through the conversations of good people, or from sermons, or by reading devotional books, or indeed in many other ways by which we have often heard God call us. They may come through sickness and adversity. His appeals may also be by a special truth which He has taught us during our times of prayer. However remiss these times of prayer may be, yet they are greatly esteemed by God.

So do not, my sisters, make light of this favor, nor be discouraged, although you may not immediately correspond with our Lord. His Majesty knows how to wait many days and even years, especially when He sees that we are persevering with earnest desire. This is what is most necessary to do here, because by perseverence we shall never fail to gain a great deal.

But the attack which the devil makes here can be more terrible in a thousand different ways and can cause more grief to the soul than in the former Mansions. There the soul was dumb and deaf; or at least it heard little and resisted less often, giving up all hope of victory. But in these Mansions the understanding is much more vigilant and the faculties are keener, even though the clash of arms and the noise of cannon are so loud that the soul cannot help hearing them.

*Evil attacks are more intense.*

Here the devils again show the soul the vipers, that is to say, the things of this world. But now they pretend that these earthly pleasures are almost eternal in their value. They constantly remind the soul of the esteem which men have had for us. They remind us of our friends and relatives. They bid us remember that our health will be ruined by the austerities of our self-discipline, for a soul which desires to enter these Mansions always begins to desire self-mortification. In this, and a thousand other ways, they will present obstacles to us.

**The assistance of reason, faith, and memory**

O Jesus! What confusion the devils bring into our poor soul. And how distressing it is not knowing if we can proceed further or whether we have to return to the Mansions where we were before!

On the other hand, reason does tell the soul how mistaken it is in thinking that all these earthly things are of the slightest value by comparison with what it is seeking. Faith teaches the soul what is sufficient for it. Memory reveals how all these things will come to an end, and reminds it that those who have derived so much enjoyment from such things have died. Sometimes they have died suddenly and have become quickly forgotten. People whom we once knew to be very prosperous are now beneath the ground. When we trample upon their graves, we reflect that their bodies are now full of worms. Of these and many other things the soul is reminded by memory.

**The assistance of the will and of understanding**

The will inclines to love One in Whom it has seen so many acts and signs of love. It would like to return to this One. It is particularly impressive to the soul how this true Lover never leaves it but always waits upon the soul and gives it life and being. The faculty of understanding comes in, then, and helps the soul to know that, though it should live many years, it will never find a better friend than God. The world is full of deceit. Those pleasures which the devil proposes to it are full of troubles, cares, and contradictions. So understanding gives the soul confidence that out of this castle it will never find safety or peace. It reminds the soul not to go to other Mansions, since this Mansion is so well provided with good things—if only the soul will enjoy them.

How fortunate, then, is the soul that it can find all that it needs at home, especially when it has a Host Who will put all good things into its possession. So why wander from home like the prodigal son and be forced to eat the food of the swine!

It is reflections like these which help to conquer the devils. But oh my Lord and my God, how everything is ruined by the foolish habits that we fall into and the way everyone follows them! Our faith is so dead that we desire what we see more than what faith tells us about. And indeed, we see only misfortune overtaking those people who pursue these visible follies.

But these poisonous things that we are dealing with are the cause of this misfortune. For if a man is bitten by a viper, his whole body becomes swollen and poisoned. And so it is in this case, and yet we do not take care and watch ourselves. Clearly, there are many remedies necessary to cure us, and God favors us a great deal when we do not die from the bite. Obviously this soul will suffer great trials at such a time, especially if the devil sees that its character and habits are such that it is ready to make further spiritual progress. Then all the powers of hell will combine to drive it back again.

Ah, my Lord! Your help is so vitally needed here, for without it we can do nothing! So in Your mercy, do not permit this soul to be deceived by being led astray when its journey has just begun. Give it light to see that all its welfare consists in the avoidance of bad company. It is, therefore, very important to converse with those who are walking in the right way, not only with those who are in the same rooms where the soul is, but with those also who it knows have entered further into the Mansions that are nearer the King. For this will be of great help to the soul to be able to converse with them in such a way that they might take him with them further. **We need God's assistance.**

So let the soul have a fixed purpose not to allow himself to be beaten, for if the devil sees that he is firmly resolved to lose his life and peace and everything rather than return to the First Mansions, he will very soon cease bothering him. Let the soul always be on its guard, lest in this attack it is conquered by yielding.

So be mindful, and do not be like those who went down on their knees in order to drink when they went to battle **Be resolute in your intent.**

(Judges 7:5, that is, with Gideon). But let him be resolute since he is going forth to fight with all the devils; there are no better weapons than the cross. Although I have mentioned this on other occasions, yet I repeat it once more here. For it is at the beginning that one must not think of such things as spiritual favors. That is a very poor way of commencing to build such a noble and costly erection. If we should begin to build it upon such sand, it will all collapse and we shall always be having annoyances and temptations. It is not in these Mansions, but in those that are further on where manna comes down from heaven. Once there, the soul will have all that it longs to have, because it desires only what is the will of God and what is pleasing to God.

**Suffer for Christ's sake.**   It is, indeed, very strange that although we are full of a thousand imperfections and hindrances, and our virtues are so immature that we have scarcely learned how to walk, yet in spite of all this we find that we are not ashamed to desire the delights of prayer and to complain of periods of aridity. Never allow this to happen to you, my sisters. Instead, embrace the cross, which your Spouse has borne on His shoulders, and realize that this cross is also yours to carry. Let the one who is capable of the greatest suffering, suffer most for Him. And he will have the most perfect freedom. Indeed, all other things are of quite secondary importance. If our Lord should happen to grant them to you, then give Him heartfelt thanks for them.

**Conform to His will.**   You may think that you are fully resolved to resist all exterior trials, if God will only grant you inward favors. But His Majesty knows best what is sufficient for us. He needs no advice as to what He should give us, since He may justly say to us, "You know not what you ask" (Matthew 20:22). Never forget that the beginner in prayer is, above all, to labor and to be resolute and prepare himself with all possible diligence to make his will conformable with the will of God.

It is in God's will that all true spirituality lies. It is in this that we make our spiritual progress. The more perfectly that we practice this, the more we shall receive from our Lord, and the further shall we advance in His way. But do not think that we have to use strange jargon or dabble in things of which we have no knowledge or understanding. For our entire well being is to be found in what I have just described, namely, doing God's will.

But if we err in the beginning, and desire that God would immediately do *our* will, and lead us according to our fancies, what strength can this edifice ever have? Let us rather endeavor to do all that we can and to be aware of those poisonous creatures which often our Lord allows to trouble us. Indeed, they afflict us without our being able to drive them away. There are times when He allows these beasts to bite us, and to leave us with spiritual aridity, so that we may afterwards learn how to avoid them. He thus wishes to test whether we are repentant for having grieved Him.

**Do not be discouraged.**

But be not discouraged if sometimes you fall. What is more important is not to neglect to go forward; for from such falls God may draw out good on our behalf, just as He provides the antidote for those who have taken poison. This proves His antidote is really effective.

Even if we did not see our miserable condition or the great harm that a distracted life does to us by any other means than this assault, this would surely be enough. For can there be any greater evil than that which we find dwelling in our own home? What hope can we have of being able to rest in other people's homes, if we cannot rest within our own? But it seems that those most intimate and sincere friends and relatives (I mean the faculties of the soul) with whom we must always live sometimes make war upon us, as if sensing the rebellion which our vices have raised against them. "Peace, peace be with you," my sisters, as our Lord said (John 20:21). But believe me, that if we neither have peace, nor endeavor to find it in our own home, we shall not find it in another person's home.

So by the blood which Christ shed for us, let this war now cease within us. I beg you who have not begun to

**Be at peace in Christ's sufferings.**

enter within your own souls; and you who have begun to do so must not allow such warfare to turn you back. You must realize that to fall a second time is worse than to fall once. You can see that it will lead ultimately to ruin.

Let these dwellers, therefore, place their trust not in themselves, but in the mercy of God, and they will see how His Majesty will lead them from one mansion to yet another, and to place them in a country where these beasts cannot touch or attack them, but where they can subdue them all and laugh them to scorn. Then they themselves, even in this life, will be able to enjoy many more good things than they could ever imagine.

*Meditate gently.*    Recollection can only come gently. Afterwards you will be able to practice it for longer and longer periods of time. So I will say no more about this here, except to declare my conviction that it is very important for you to consult people of more maturity and experience. Otherwise you will be thinking that you are seriously failing to do some necessary thing. Provided we do not abandon our prayer life, the Lord will turn everything that we do to our benefit, even though we may not find anyone to teach us. There is no other remedy for this evil of giving up prayer than to begin again. Otherwise the soul will gradually keep on losing a little more each day. May it please God that you come to realize this.

Some of you may be tempted to think that it is dangerous to go backwards. Would it not be better never to have entered but always to remain outside the castle? I have already told you in the beginning, and our Lord has also said so, "He who walks in danger, perishes in it" (Ecclesiastes 3:27). But the door by which we can enter this castle is prayer.

*A Christian life without prayer is useless.*    To think that we can enter heaven without praying, and that we can enter into ourselves without the knowledge of ourselves and the awareness of our own misery and of that we owe to God, is mere foolishness. For our Lord Himself has said, "No one can come to the Father, but by Me" (John 14:6). I am not sure if these are the exact words, but I think they are. He also adds, "He that sees Me sees my Father" (John 14:9).

Now, if we never look at Christ, nor consider how much we owe to Him, I do not see how we will ever know Him, or perform works on His behalf. For what value can faith have without these, and what worth can these have, if they are not united with the merits of Christ? Nor can we know who can excite us to love this Lord. So may His Majesty be pleased to make us know how dearly we have cost Him, and that "the servant is not greater than his Lord" (Matthew 10:24). We must *work* in order to enjoy His glory, and for this reason we must also pray, so that we may not fall into temptation (Matthew 26:41).

## THE THIRD MANSIONS: THE DECEPTION OF A GOOD AND EXEMPLARY LIFE THAT IS STILL SELF-CENTERED

### Part One: The Moral Precariousness of Life

To those who, through the goodness of God, have won these battles, and by perseverance have reached the Third Mansions, what shall we say? Surely these words: "Blessed is the man that feareth the Lord" (Psalm 112:1).

His Majesty has conferred no small favor upon me by making me now understand the meaning of these words upon my own tongue. With reason do we truly call such a man "blessed," since as far as we can understand, unless he turns back, he is now secure in his salvation.

Here you see, sisters, how important it is to have conquered in the former battles. For I consider it certain that our Lord will not fail to place the soul which has arrived so far in security of conscience. This is no small blessing. I say "security of conscience," but I was wrong; for there is no security in this life. So always understand that I mean "unless he strays from the way on which he has set out."

It is really a great misery to have to live a life in which we are going about like men whose enemies lie at their

*Security of conscience*

gates, and who cannot, therefore, lay aside their arms even when they are sleeping or eating. Instead, they are always afraid of being surprised by a breaching of their fortress at some weak spot.

O, my Lord and my God! How is it that You want us to live such a miserable life, for it is impossible for us to avoid wishing and requesting to be taken out of it. We would request such were it not for the hope of losing it for Your sake, or spending it entirely in Your service, and above all, because we know it is Your pleasure that we should live in it. If this is so, my God, let us die with You, as Thomas said (John 11:16). For to live without You, and in the fear of it being possible to lose You forever, is nothing else than to die many times over.

So I think, daughters, that the blessing we should pray for is to enjoy the complete security of the blessed. For what pleasure can anyone have when he is beset by these fears, if his only pleasure consists in pleasing God? Consider that all this, and much more, could be said of some saintly souls who fell into grave sins; and yet we cannot be certain that God will give us His hand and help us to abandon such evil.

**Without the indwelling Christ we have no security.** Certainly I can assure you, my daughters, that while I am writing these words I am so gripped with fear that I neither know how to write nor how to live when I reflect upon this subject. This I very often do. So pray, my daughters, that His Majesty may ever live within me. For otherwise, what security can such a life as mine have, which has been so wicked? But do not be upset on hearing that it has been so. But what can I do, if I lose this holiness through my own fault? I cannot complain that God has ceased to help me fulfill His desires for me. I cannot help saying this without tears and great confusion when I realize that I am writing for those who are themselves capable of instructing me.

This is hard obedience. But may our Lord grant that, as it has been performed for His sake, so it may in some way prove beneficial to you. If for nothing else, may it help you to beg pardon of our Lord for this miserable sinner who is so presumptuous. But His Majesty knows that I can only presume upon His mercy. Since I cannot help having been what I was, I have no other remedy but to have recourse to His mercy, and to trust in the merits of His Son. Even my sins and my being what I am have not been sufficient to bring any kind of tarnish upon this sacred Order.

But I do wish to warn you against one thing, namely, not to be too smug. Remember that although David was a very holy man, yet you remember what Solomon became. Nor should you set much store by the fact that you are cloistered and lead lives of penitence. Nor must you become overconfident because you are always talking about God, continually engaging in prayer, or withdrawing yourselves completely from the things of this world and, to the best of your knowledge, abhorring them. All these practices are very good, but they are not a sufficient reason, as I have said, for us to stop being afraid. Rather repeat this verse often and bear it constantly in mind: "Blessed is the man who fears the Lord" (Psalm 112:1).

*Do not be complacent.*

Returning to what I began to say respecting souls who have entered into the Third Mansions, I could consider this to be no small favor which our Lord has bestowed upon them. Indeed, it is a very special favor; namely, that they have overcome the first difficulties. For I believe that there are many such souls in the world who, through the goodness of our Lord, are extremely desirous of not offending His Majesty. They guard themselves from falling into sin; they are lovers of spiritual discipline; they spend hours in meditation and prayer. In doing so they occupy themselves well, and they are exercised in works of charity toward their neighbor. They are very regular in all their actions and in the government of their own homes, at least such as have families.

This is a very desirable state, and there seems to be no reason why these should not be denied entrance into the very last of the Mansions. Nor will our Lord deny it to them, if they are willing to go forward. For this is an excel-

*Exercises in the Third Mansions*

lent disposition to induce Him to show them all kinds of favors.

Causes of spiritual stability

O Jesus! Who will not exclaim that He is desirous of so great a blessing, especially as He has overcome the greatest trials? Everyone must desire it. Indeed, we all say that we desire it. But if something more is required in order that our Lord may take complete possession of the soul, it is not enough to say these words, just as it was not sufficient for that young ruler who asked our Lord how to be perfect (Matthew 19:16-22). Indeed, ever since I began to speak of these Mansions I have had that young man in my mind, for we are exactly like him. This as a rule is the origin of our long periods of sterility in prayer, although these periods may have other causes as well. I am not talking here of interior trials, which may vex many good souls to an intense degree and through no fault of their own. From these trials our Lord always rescues the godly for their great benefit. He does so also to those who suffer from depression and from other emotional infirmities. Indeed, in all such things we have to let God be the Judge.

But personally I believe that what I have said is what usually happens. Since such souls realize that nothing should induce them to commit a sin, many of them would not intentionally commit even a small peccadillo [petty sin]. And so they conduct their lives and households well. With such an attitude they cannot accept patiently that the door of entry to the place where our King dwells should be closed to them when they consider themselves to be His servants. But even though a king here on earth has many vassals, not all enter into his bedchamber.

## Part Two: Aridity in Prayer Life

Experienced and yet depressed Christians

I have known some souls—and I believe I can say even many souls—who have reached this stage and have lived many years in this upright and well-ordered way both in body and soul, as far as can be known. Yet after all these years when it looked as if they had gained complete mastery over the world or were now completely detached from it, His Majesty has sent them trials which have been by no means minor affairs. In the process they have become so restless and depressed in spirit that they have been exasperated. Indeed, they have made me thoroughly afraid for them. It seems useless to give them any advice, for they have been so long engaged in the practice of the spiritual life that they actually can teach others; at this same time, they feel the more justified in feeling as depressed as they do.

Well, with such people I cannot find—nor have I ever found—any way of encouraging them, except to express great sorrow at their trouble. Then when I see I am making them more miserable, I really do feel sad for them. It is useless to argue with them, for they persist in brooding over their woes and have made up their minds that they are suffering for God's sake.

Thus, they never really understand that all the time it is due to their own imperfection. We should not be at all surprised at what they are experiencing. However, I do think that the feelings stirred up should pass away quickly. For it is often God's purpose that His elect should be conscious of their misery and so He withdraws His help from them for a time; but no more than is needed to make us recognize our own limitations very quickly. They should gain the reality that they are still grieving after earthly things, and not very important things at that. So it is, I think, a great mercy on the part of our God that, even though they are at fault, they can gain a great deal in humility.

Unfortunately, this is not the case with the people that I am talking about. For while they will admire these ideals theoretically, and wish others to admire them likewise, they are not really experiencing it themselves. So let us mention some of these feelings that we may be able to understand and to test ourselves before the Lord tests us. For it is very important to be prepared and to have some understanding of ourselves beforehand.

*Such do not really experience humility before God.*

**Such is not really trust in God.**

Let us suppose there is a rich person without children or anyone to whom he might want to leave his possessions who happens to lose his wealth. However, he has not lost everything; he does not lack necessities for himself or for the management of his household. He may even have something to spare. Now if he should go about looking worried and disturbed as if he did not have a crust of bread left to eat, how can our Lord ask him to leave all for his sake? It may be, of course, that he is suffering because he wants to give the money to the poor. But I think that God would rather I were resigned to what His Majesty does, and kept my own peace of soul, than that I should do such acts of charity as these.

So this person cannot resign himself, because the Lord has not led him thus far. Well and good. But he should understand that he is lacking this spirit of freedom. And because the Lord will ask him for it, he should prepare himself for the Lord to be able to give it to him.

**They are not truly sacrificial.**

Or suppose another person has an abundance to live on and something to spare. Supposing an opportunity presents itself to obtain more property. Let him take such an opportunity certainly, if it comes his way. But if he strives after obtaining it, and strives after more and more, however good his intention may be such an individual may well be assured that he will never enter into the Mansions that are closest to the King.

**They want to hold on to their own preconceived reputations.**

It is much the same thing, if such people are despised in any way or if they lose their reputation. God often grants them the grace to bear such trials well, for He loves to help people to be virtuous for others. This He does so that the virtue itself which they possess may be not thought less of. Or perhaps He will assist them because they have served Him, for this our God is good indeed. Yet they become restless, for they cannot do what they would like to or control their feelings.

Dear me! Are not these the very same people who before were meditating upon how the Lord suffered and thinking what a good thing it was to be able to suffer, and who were even desiring to suffer? They would like others to live a regimented life as they did themselves. God forbid that they should now imagine that the anxieties they are suffering are only the faults of others, for in their own thoughts they imagine themselves to be virtuous indeed.

You may think, sisters, that I am wandering from the subject and that what I am saying does not relate to you. Here in this house there are no such things, since we have neither the desire for nor seek after wealth, nor does anyone do us the least injury. You may say these comparisons have nothing at all to do with us.

It is true that these examples are not directly applicable to us, but many deductions and applications are relevant to us. For it is by these comparisons that you discover yourself, whether you are completely disengaged from all attachments to that which you have abandoned. For trifling incidents arise, which though not precisely the same as this, still give you the opportunity to test yourselves and to discover if you really have obtained control over your own passions.

Comparing yourself with such will help you see when you really are greedy.

Believe me, the matter does not center around wearing this or that religious habit, but in trying to practice virtue, and in subjecting our own will in everything to that of God. It also consists in regulating our lives, conforming to whatever His Majesty shall so order and appoint, and desiring not our own will but only His. Since we may not have reached this stage of humility, let us practice it, for it is the ointment for our wounds. If we are truly humble, God our Physician will come in due course, even though He may linger in order to heal us.

The ascetic practices which such should perform are well-balanced just as their lives are. They have a great desire for such disciplines in order to serve our Lord by them. There is nothing wrong with this, and thus they are very discreet in doing it in a way that will not harm their health. Have no fear that they will kill themselves. For

The progress of some is slow because they take good care of themselves.

they are eminently sensible people! Their love is not yet ardent enough to overwhelm their reason.

How I wish we would be so dissatisfied with this habit of always serving God at the pace of a snail! And as we seem to be walking along and getting fatigued all the time—it is an exhausting journey—we shall be fortunate if we escape getting lost. Do you not think, daughters, that if we could get from one country to another in a week, that it would be advisable with all the winds and snow and floods and bad roads to take a year over it? Or would it not be better to get the journey over and done with quickly? For there are all these obstacles for us to meet and there is also the danger of serpents. What a lot I could tell you about all that! I would to God that I had gotten further than this myself, although I am often afraid that I have not!

**Some stumble along because of this timidity.**

When we proceed along timidly and cautiously, we will find stumbling blocks everywhere. For we are afraid of everything and so we dare not go further. We have no courage to venture forward and believe we could arrive at these Mansions, leaving *others* to endure the difficulties of the way. But this is not possible.

So let us, sisters, for the love of God, encourage ourselves to go on, and leave our reasons and our fears in His hands. Let us forget this natural weakness which occupies us so readily. Let our Superiors look after the care of our bodies, for that is their concern. Our only task is to journey on with good speed so that we may see the Lord. Although we may get few or no comforts here, we shall be making a big mistake if we worry about our health, especially as it will not be improved by further anxiety over it. That I know from my own experience. I also know that our progress has nothing to do with the body, which is the thing that matters least of all.

The journey about which I am referring demands great humility and it is the lack of it that will prevent us from making progress. We may think we have advanced only a few steps and consider that our sisters' progress is so much more rapid. Moreover, we should strive that they should consider us much worse than others.

When humility is present, this state will be a most excellent one. But if humility is lacking, we shall remain in this state all our lives and suffer a thousand troubles and afflictions. Without complete self-renunciation, this state is very arduous and oppressive. We should be walking weighed down with this mud of our own human misery, which is not so with those who have reached the later Mansions.

In these present Mansions the Lord does not fail to reward us righteously and even generously, for He always gives us much more than we deserve by granting us a spiritual serenity. This serenity is much greater than we could obtain from the pleasures and distractions of this life. But I do not think that He gives many spiritual blessings, except when He occasionally invites us to see what is happening in the remaining Mansions so that we may prepare to enter them also.

**Without humility our spiritual lives remain static.**

It may seem to you that consolations and spiritual delights are the same thing, so why should I make this distinction? To me it seems there is a great difference between the two. Now, I could be wrong. But I will speak about this when I come to speak of the Fourth Mansions. For then I will have something to say about the consolations that the Lord gives to those dwelling in those Mansions.

Great comfort comes to the souls that God brings to the Fourth Mansions. And confusion comes to those who think that they have everything already. If souls are humble, then they will be moved to give thanks. But if there is a lack of humility, then they will feel an inner distaste for which they will find no reason. Spiritual maturity and its reward do not consist in spiritual delights, but rather in the increase of love. Upon this do the righteousness and truth of our actions depend.

**The consolations of God are explained in humility.**

Of what use is it to speak of these inner blessings, and how can we discover how they are to be known? This I do not know, so ask him who has commanded me to write on

**How are we to experience inner blessings?**

the subject. For I would not dispute with my Superiors since this would be unseemly, but simply obey them. What I can tell you truly is that, when I had none of these blessings, and knew nothing of them by experience, and never indeed expected to know about them all my life long, nevertheless, when I write in books of these blessings and consolations which the Lord grants to souls that serve Him, it gives me much consolation and moves me to give great praise to God. Well, if He did this to me whose soul is so wretched, then those souls that are good and humble will praise Him so much more! And if only one person is so led to praise Him even once, it is very good that the subject be mentioned. Then we can learn more about the joy and happiness that we lose through our own fault.

But do not imagine that it is of no importance whether we work or not to obtain them. For if the fault is not our own, then the Lord is just and what His Majesty denies you in this way He will give you in other ways, as His Majesty knows best. But the secrets are hidden deep. All that He does will be the best for us, without the slightest shadow of a doubt.

**Be obedient to God.**

It is by the goodness of the Lord that we are brought to this state. He shows so much mercy in bringing us to it. But it is of the greatest profit to those of us who are on the point of rising still higher to realize that we should be more attentive to give Him ready obedience.

**Do this through the wise counsel of a spiritual director.**

Even though such persons are not in a religious order, it is of great importance for them to have someone to whom they can go as many people do. Then they will not be following their own prescription in anything, for it is in this way that we usually do ourselves spiritual harm and deceive ourselves. They should not look for anyone who is cast in the same mold as themselves, who may only flatter instead of striving to detach them from the things of this world. But they should seek to procure someone who knows well the deceits of the world, because by conversing with one who already knows them, they shall then be better enabled to discover these deceits themselves. Because some things which at first appear impossible become possible when we see that others can easily perform them and are sanctified in them, choosing someone to tell who has succeeded will encourage us exceedingly. By his flying, we may venture to fly, just as young birds do. Although they cannot at first take a high flight, yet they do it by little in imitation of the older ones.

However determined such persons may be not to offend God, yet it is best they do not run any risk of offending Him. For they are so close to the First Mansions that they might easily return there if their courage does not rest on a solid foundation. So they need the guidance of those who are already practiced in suffering. These latter people are familiar with the storms of the world and they realize how little need there is to fear them or to desire worldly pleasures. For if those of whom I am speaking about had to suffer great persecutions, they might well return to such pleasures. And the devil knows well how to raise such storms in order to do us harm. These persons, intending through a laudable zeal to prevent the sins of others, prove unable to resist that which may happen to themselves upon such occasions.

So let us mind our own faults, and not trouble ourselves about those of other people. For those who live carefully regulated lives are apt to be shocked at everything, yet we might well learn very important lessons from those who shock us. True, our outward demeanor and behavior may appear better than theirs, but this, although good, is not the most important thing. We should not expect everyone else to travel along our own road, and we should not attempt to point out to them the spiritual path when perhaps we do not know it ourselves.

**Mind your own business spiritually.**

Even with these desires that God may give to us to help others, sisters, we may make many mistakes. Hence the best course is to follow the directions of our Rule; that is, always endeavor to live in silence and in hope since our Lord will take care of the souls that He loves. And if we do not neglect to pray to His Majesty, we shall by His assistance advance greatly. May He be blessed forever.

# VI

# THE INTERIOR CASTLE
# PART 2

## THE FOURTH MANSIONS: THE PRAYER OF QUIET, THE BEGINNING OF A PERSONAL ENCOUNTER WITH THE LIVING GOD

### Part One: The Benefits of Contemplative Prayer

ow that I am about to speak of the Fourth Mansions, it is necessary, as I said, that I should commend myself to the Holy Spirit, beseeching Him to speak for me. This is necessary that I may say something of these Mansions that yet remain which you can understand. For here I am beginning to touch upon supernatural subjects. This is most difficult to explain unless His Majesty takes it in hand, as He did when I described as much as I understood of the subject about fourteen years ago. Although I had then learned and experienced these things, it is a different matter trying to explain the favors which the Lord grants to some souls. So may His Majesty undertake this if there is any advantage to be gained from its being done. But if not, then I do not wish it.

As these Mansions are getting nearer to the chamber where the King dwells, great is their beauty. There are exquisite things to be seen and appreciated so that the understanding is incapable of finding words to explain them. But for anyone who has experience, he will understand what I am saying very well.

In order to reach these Mansions, it may be necessary to live a long time in the previous ones. As a rule, one must have dwelt in those which we have already described, although there is no infallible rule about this. For our Lord bestows His favors *when* and *how* and to *whom* He pleases; and as the gifts are His own, this is doing no injustice to anyone.

Poisonous reptiles seldom enter into these Mansions. If they do, they will do no harm; in fact, they may do the soul some good. Indeed, I think that in this state of prayer, it is much better for them to enter and to make war upon the soul. For if it had no temptations, the devil might mislead the soul with regard to the consolations which God gives. These vipers do much more harm than he can when the soul is being tempted. I do not consider it safe, then, if the soul always remains in the one state. Nor does it seem to me possible that the Spirit of God should, during this exile, continue always in the same state.

**The nature of "consolations"**    I need to discuss the differences between consolations and spiritual delights. The term "consolations" can be given to those experiences that we acquire ourselves through our own meditation and petitions to the Lord. This proceeds from our own nature although, of course, God plays a part in the process. (In everything I say you must understand His part, for we can do nothing without Him.)

These "consolations" arise from the good works which we perform, and which we think we have acquired by our own efforts. We are quite right to feel satisfaction at having worked in this way. But when we come to think about it, the same satisfaction can be derived from numerous things that may happen to us here in the world.

For example, a person may suddenly acquire some valuable property; or equally suddenly may meet a person whom he dearly loves; or he may bring an important piece of business or some other significant matter to a successful conclusion, so that everyone speaks well of him; or a woman may be told that her husband or brother or son is dead and then comes back to her alive. In such experiences I have seen people shed tears of great joy; in fact, sometimes I have done this myself. I think then that, just as these joyful consolations are natural to us, so they are also afforded us by the things of God, although we may think of the latter as a nobler kind. However, the others are not bad. In some persons, joyful consolations in prayer have their beginning in the human nature, although they end in God.

We can sum this up by saying that while spiritual delights begin in God, yet human nature may feel and enjoy them as much as it does those that I have mentioned above—indeed, much more. O Jesus! How I long to be able to explain myself in this! For I think I discern a very recognizable difference, and yet I do not have the knowledge to be able to explain myself. May the Lord do so in assisting me.

Now I have just remembered a verse which we say at the end of the last Psalm at Prime. The last words of the verse are: "I have run the way of Your commandments, when You did enlarge my heart" (Psalm 119:32). For anyone who has had much spiritual experience, these words are sufficient to see the difference between consolations and spiritual delights. For anyone who has not had this experience more explanation is needed. The psalmist indicates that the consolations that are mentioned do not expand the heart. Rather, they seem to constrain it, although there is the greatest consolation at seeing what is done for God's sake. But it sheds a few bitter tears which seem somehow to be the result of the passions. I do not know much about these passions of the soul. If I knew more, perhaps, then I could make the thing clearer and explain what proceeds from sensuality and what from our own nature. But I am very dull. If only I knew how to explain myself, as I have experienced it. Knowledge and learning are such a help in everything.

But my own experience of this condition (I mean of this joy and consolation that comes through meditation) is that if I began to weep over the passion, then I could not stop until I got a severe headache. If I did so over my sins,

*The nature of spiritual delights.*

the same thing would happen. Then our Lord granted me a great favor. I do not want to enter into the subject as to the difference between the one and the other or to examine whether the one is better than the other. For tears sometimes flow in consideration of these things and the desires arise aided by our own nature and temperament. But as I have said, they at last end in God regardless of their nature. They are to be esteemed if there is humility to understand that one is no better because of the experience of them, for it cannot be known whether they are all the effects of love. But when they are, it is the gift of God.

For the most part, the souls that dwell in the proceeding Mansions are those who have these devout feelings, for these souls work almost continually with the understanding and make use of it in their meditations. They are right to do this, because nothing more has been experienced by them. Yet it would be also good sometimes to employ themselves in performing acts of love and praise to God, to rejoice in His goodness and His other attributes, and also to desire His honor and glory. Doing all this in the best way we can, these acts will powerfully excite the will. But let them take care, however, when our Lord bestows such affections upon them, not to forsake them in order to finish their usual meditation.

## Part Two: Confusing Experiences in the Contemplative Life

**Why are thoughts so often confused?**     Sometimes I have been terribly confused and oppressed by the turmoil of thought. Indeed, it is only four years ago that I began to understand by experience that "thought" (or to put it more clearly, imagination) is not the same thing as understanding. I asked a learned man about this, and he said I was quite right. This gave me encouragement. For as understanding is one of the faculties of the soul, I found it very hard to see why it was sometimes so irresolute; whereas thoughts, as a rule, fly so fast that only God can restrain them. This He sometimes does by uniting us in such a way that we seem in some sense to be loosened from this body. But it frustrated me to see how the faculties of the soul, as I thought, were occupied with God and recollected in Him, and yet imagination (thought) seemed on the other hand so confused and excited.

O Lord, take into account the many things that we suffer as a result of a lack of knowledge! The worst of it is that we do not realize we need to know more when we think about You, and so we cannot ask those who know. Indeed, we have not even any idea what there is for us to ask. That is why we have to suffer terrible trials, because we do not understand ourselves. Many times we worry over what is not bad at all but good, and sometimes think it very wrong.

*Many sufferings come because of grievances about our interior lives.*

This is how the afflictions of many people who practice prayer occur, and their complaints of interior trial—especially if they are unlearned people—create depression. Their health declines and they even abandon praying altogether, because they fail to realize that there is an interior world here within us. We can no more stop the revolution of the heavens, moving as they do with such speed, than we can restrain our own thoughts. Then the faculties of the soul accompany it, and we think we are lost and we have wasted the time spent before God.

Meanwhile the soul may be perhaps wholly united with Him in the Mansions which are very near to His presence while the mind is on the outskirts of the castle, suffering from a thousand wild and poisonous beasts, and meriting favor by this suffering. So this should not upset us, nor should we be tempted to give up the struggle, as the devil tries to make us do. Most of these trials and times of unrest come from the fact that we do not understand ourselves.

Even as I am writing this, I am thinking about what is going on in my head with the great noise there that I mentioned at the beginning. It makes it almost impossible for me to write what I have been ordered to write. It seems as if there were in my head many rushing rivers and that these waters are dashing downward. A host of little birds

*Teresa's experience of migraine headaches*

seem to be whistling, not in my ears, but in the upper part
of the head where the most elevated part of the soul is said
to be. I was in that upper part of my being a long time, for
it seemed that this powerful movement of the spirit is a
swift upturning one.

Please God, that I may remember to mention the cause
of this elevation in discussing the dwelling places that
come further on; but this is not the right place to do so. Indeed, I would not be surprised if the Lord has given me this
headache so that I can understand these things better. For
all this turmoil in my head does not hinder prayer or what
I am saying, but the soul is completely taken up in its quiet
while love in my soul is quite unaffected. So are also its desires and clarity of mind.

But if the superior part of the soul is in the upper part of
the head, then why is not the soul disturbed? I do not
know the answer to this. But I do know that what I say is
truthful. I suffer when my prayer is not accompanied by a
suspension of the faculties; but when the faculties are suspended, no pain is felt until the suspension passes. It
would be a terrible thing if this experience forces me to
give up praying all together.

## Part Three: The Prayer of Recollection in Attentiveness to God

The call of the
Shepherd to those
who know His
voice

Let us imagine that the senses and the faculties, which I
have called the guards of the castle, have gone out of the
castle, and for days and years have been consorting with
strangers, to whom all the good things in the castle are
abhorrent. Then, realizing how much they have lost, they
come back to it, although they do not actually reenter the
castle, because the habits they have formed are now hard
to conquer. But they can no longer be considered traitors,
and so they walk about in the vicinity of the castle. The
great King, Who dwells in the Mansions within this
castle, perceives their good inclination, and in His great
mercy He desires to bring them back to Him. Like a good
Shepherd, He makes His sheep know His voice by such a
melody that they can scarcely hear (John 10:4). This He

does that they may not wander and be lost but return to their Mansions. This call of the Shepherd has such power that they immediately abandon all those external things which deceive them and hasten back into the castle. I do not think that I have ever explained this before so clearly as here.

Seeking God within ourselves is to find Him more effectively and more profitably than other creatures. I refer to St. Augustine who, having sought Him in many places, did find Him within (*Confessions*, X, 27). So it is a great help if God grants us such a favor. Do not suppose that the understanding can reach to Him merely by trying to think of Him as existing within the soul, or even by the imagination picturing Him as there. This is a good habit, and an excellent method of meditation; for it is founded upon this truth: namely, that God is within us. But this is not what I mean here, because everyone may do this by the assistance of our Lord.

The prayer I am speaking about is of a very different nature. These people are sometimes in the castle before they have begun to think about God at all. I cannot say when they have entered it or how they heard their Shepherd's call. It certainly did not come by the ear, for outwardly there was no audible call. Instead, a sweet recollection in their interior was experienced, as those who go along this way will find out. I do not know how to express my meaning better.

I think I have heard this compared to a tortoise that retreats within itself. Whoever made use of this comparison no doubt understood it well, for these creatures would draw into themselves whenever they will. Here, however, is not the case for the recollection of which I am speaking. It is only in our power when God is pleased to bestow this favor upon us. I think that whenever His Majesty bestows it, He gives it to such only as are already disengaged from the things of this world. I do not say that they are actually so, for perhaps their state will not allow it. But they are so in their affections and in their desires, since He so especially invites them to attend to interior matters.

> God gives the prayer of quiet to those who are unattached to the world.

Hence I believe that were we to give ourselves up entirely to His Majesty, He would bestow not only this but many other gifts upon those whom He begins to call to higher things. Let him praise God greatly, whoever shall experience this in himself. For it is very proper that he should understand the favor and give thanks for it. Then he may dispose himself for other favors which are greater still.

**Listen to God in your interior life.** The disposition which will prepare us for this is to listen attentively to whatever our Lord shall speak to us interiorly. In this we should contrive not to use our reasoning powers, but to be intent upon discovering what the Lord is working within the soul. For unless His Majesty begins to give us ecstasies, I cannot understand how the mind can be restrained. This is likely to do us more harm than good, although this is a question frequently discussed among some spiritual persons.

One person mentioned to me a certain book of the saintly Friar Peter of Alcantara, for I really believe he is a saint. He is convincing, for I know how much he knew about these interior things. On reading the book, we found that he said the same as I did, although not in the same words. But we may gather from what he said that our love is still to be kept awake. (See "Eighth Counsel" of the *Treatise of Prayer and Meditation*, II, pp. 113-114.)

**Being and doing** It is possible that I am mistaken, but I base my opinion about interior matters on the following reasons. First, in such spiritual activity as this, the person who does most is he who thinks least and desires to do least. All we have to do is to ask, like some poor persons before some great and rich emperor, and immediately let us cast down our eyes and wait with humility. When by His secret ways it seems that He hears us, then it is good to be silent, since He permits us to stand nearer to Him. It will not be amiss to forebear working with the understanding if we can.

But if we are not quite sure if the King has heard us, or that He is paying any attention to us, we must not then act like fools. For the soul becomes quite a fool when it tries to induce this prayer on its own. As a result, it is left much drier. Then the imagination becomes more restless through the effort that is made not to think at all. Rather, the Lord desires that we should beseech Him and call to mind that we are in His presence. He knows what is suitable for us.

At the same time, I cannot persuade myself to believe that human effort is of any avail in such matters because of the bounds that His Majesty has placed and which He wishes to reserve for Himself. This He has not done in many other things that are within our own power, provided that He assists us. Examples would be in ascetic discipline, in prayer, and other good works where our wretchedness cannot do these things alone.

The second reason is that these interior works are all gentle and peaceful. Doing something arduous would cause more harm than good. By anything "arduous" I mean anything that we may try to force ourselves to do. For example, it is arduous to hold our breath. Leave, then, the soul in God's hands entirely to do with it whatever He pleases, without taking any concern about your own interest. Be resigned totally to the will of God.

**Be at peace.**

The third reason is that every effort which the soul makes in order to cease from thinking will perhaps awaken thought and cause it to think all the more.

**Relax the mind.**

The fourth reason is that the most important and pleasing thing in God's eyes is to have only His honor and glory in view, and to forget ourselves, our own benefits, our delights, and our pleasures. But how can such a person be unconscious in self-forgetfulness when he is taking such great care about his actions that he dare not even stir or allow his understanding and desires to be stirred up?

**Seek out God's glory.**

When His Majesty wishes the working of the understanding to cease, He employs it in another way, and illumines the soul's knowledge to so much higher a degree than any we can attain ourselves that He leads it into a

**Let God absorb our thought.**

state of absorption. In this state, the soul is much better instructed than it could ever be as a result of its own efforts, which would only spoil everything. For as God has given us faculties that we may work with, we need not try to cast a spell over them, but rather let them do their work until God gives them something better.

**Let God's presence lessen the load of the mind.**

As I understand it, the soul that the Lord has been pleased to lead into these Mansions will do best to act as I have said. We should likewise endeavor, without violence or effort, to keep the understanding from all discursive reasoning. Yet we should not suspend the understanding, nor cease from all thoughts. It is well for the soul to remember that it is in God's presence and to realize Who this God is. If what it feels is the cause of suspending it, well and good. But let it not try to understand what this is. For as it is bestowed on the will, let it enjoy it without using an effort. Let the soul do nothing, except only utter a few loving words. For although we strive here not to be without cessation of thoughts, yet often we are so, although it may be only for a short time.

**Be careful not to offend God**

Be extremely careful not to expose oneself to any occasions of offending God. For as yet the soul is not even weaned, but is like a child that is beginning to suck her mother's breast. So if it be taken from its mother, what else can be expected to happen but that it will die? That, I am very much afraid, will be the lot of anyone to whom God has granted this favor, if he gives up prayer. Unless he does so for some very exceptional reason, or unless he returns to it quickly, he will go from bad to worse.

**The devil will attack in such circumstances.**

I know that there is great reason to fear in this case, and I know some whom I pity very much. For I have seen this happen to them about which I am speaking when they forsook Him Who so ardently desired to become their Friend and prove Himself by such actions. I warned them beforehand to avoid the occasions, because the devil will labor much more against such souls than against many others on whom our Lord does not bestow such favors. For he knows that such a soul may do him much more harm by drawing others after them who may bring great advantage to the church of God. The devil may see nothing else in them except that His Majesty is showing a particular affection toward them, but this is enough to induce him to do his utmost to destroy them. That is why Satan so furiously attacks them. If once conquered, they will more deeply ruin many others.

As far as we know, sisters, you are free from these perils. But may God free you from pride and vainglory, and grant that the devil may not counterfeit these favors. Such counterfeits, however, will be recognizable, because they do not produce these spiritual effects; they produce quite contrary ones.

However, I wish to warn you about a danger which I have spoken of elsewhere. I have seen people who live the meditative life—especially women—who are weaker in their constitution, or those who are naturally fragile, or those weakened by a severe ascetic life. These swoon away on receiving some of these mystic consolations. Then their constitution fails them. As soon as they feel any interior joy there comes over them a physical weakness and languor, and, falling asleep, they become confused about their feelings and judge they should be absorbed in this situation. The more they relax, the more absorbed they become, because in fact their physical condition continues to deteriorate. So they get it into their heads that it is rapture which they are experiencing. I call this plain stupidity, for it is nothing else but wasting our time and destroying our health.

*Do not take the meditative life to extremes.*

I can think of someone who continued for eight hours in this way, having neither sense nor any real perception of divine things. It was only when she was made to eat properly and to sleep and to eliminate all her indiscreet penances that she was cured. She had misled both her confessor and other people, although she did this quite unconsciously and with no intent to deceive. I believe that the devil used these circumstances for his own gain.

Indeed, he was beginning to make good progress with this individual.

**Be guided by wise counsel.** We must, therefore, realize that when an experience really comes from God, although there may be both an interior as well as an exterior languor, there will never be any languor in the soul. For the soul will have strong emotions on seeing itself so near to God. Moreover, this continues only for a very short time. Although the soul may become absorbed again, yet in this kind of prayer, except in cases of physical weakness, the body will not be overcome or have produced in it any exterior sensation. So be sure that when you experience this kind of thing, let your spiritual director know about it.

**Take care of yourself physically.** Take, then, as much recreation as is possible, and do not have such prolonged hours of prayer. You should be made to sleep and eat enough until your normal strength is restored in case you have lost it in this prayer exercise. But if someone's physical constitution is so weak that this is not sufficient, then he should be certain that God is not calling him to anything other than the act of life.

**Accept, sometimes, the absence of God.** For there is room in convents for all sorts of people. Let anyone that is of this kind be kept busy with duties, and be sure that she is not left alone very much or else her health may be completely destroyed. This would then be a very great mortification to her. The Lord may be testing her love for Him by seeing how she reacts to His prolonged absence, and after a time He may be pleased to restore her strength. But if not, then her vocal prayers and obedience will do just as much for her as she would have obtained in other ways; indeed, perhaps more.

**Do not be naive.** There may also be some who are weak in intelligence and imagination. They can be so naive that they believe they actually see all that they imagine. This is a highly dangerous state to be in, and perhaps we should talk about this later. I have already said enough about this dwelling place, because it is the one where more souls enter. However, since it is the sphere where both the natural and the supernatural intersect, the devil can do much more harm here. But in those dwelling places which are still to be discussed, the Lord does not allow him so much elbow room. May His Majesty be forever praised. Amen.

## THE FIFTH MANSIONS: THE PRAYER OF SIMPLE UNION WITH GOD

### Part One: Experience of the Presence of God

My dear sisters, how am I able to explain to you the riches, treasures, and delights which are found in the Fifth Mansions? I am tempted to think that it would be better not to say anything about these remaining mansions, for there is no way that I can describe them. The intellect is incapable of understanding them, and no comparisons can help explain them. Earthly things are too crude for such a purpose.

*Teresa's inability to distinguish the mystical experience and her response*

O my Lord! Send light from heaven that I may be able to enlighten these, Your servants, since You have been pleased that some of them should enjoy these delights. Illuminate some of them that they may not be deceived by the devil, who transforms himself into an angel of light; for their whole desire is to please You.

Although I have said "some," there are only a very few who enter into the Mansions about which I am now going to speak. There are various degrees, and for that reason I say that most will enter the previous Mansions. But I believe that only a few will go on to experience the Fifth Mansions. However, even if they only reach the outer gate, God still shows them a great favor. Although many are called, yet few are chosen (Matthew 22:14).

*Very few have such mystical experiences.*

And so I say now, that although we all wear this sacred habit of Carmel, and are all called to prayer and contemplation (because this was our rule in the beginning, which those holy fathers of Mt. Carmel drew up; they would purchase this treasure and this precious jewel which we now speak of by great solitude and contempt of the world), yet few of us dispose ourselves so that our Lord may discover that this jewel of contemplation is characteristic of us. Externally we may present ourselves in all things necessary. But in practice of the virtues that are necessary for arriving at this state, we need so much. So we cannot afford to be negligent in the slightest detail.

**Seek the great treasure of God's own presence.**

So let us, my sisters, earnestly beseech our Lord that we may in some degree enjoy heaven upon earth; that He would grant us His grace and show us the way, lest through our own fault, we miss it. May He give the strength to our soul to enable us to dig until we find this hidden treasure which is certainly within us. This I would like to explain, if our Lord is pleased to enable me to do so. I said "strength to the soul" in order that you may know that, as regards bodily strength, there is no obstacle to one on whom our Lord does not bestow it. No one is prevented from purchasing His wealth. If one gives what he has, God is content. Blessed be so great a God!

**God wants all from us.**

Reflect however, my daughters, that in order to obtain this object of which we are speaking, He does not wish you to keep anything back, whether it be small or great. He wants our all, and in proportion to what you know you have given, He bestows greater or lesser benefits upon you. There is no greater proof than this, than discovering whether we have arrived at the prayer which attains to union. Do not think of it as a state, like the last one, in which we dream. I say "dream" for the soul seems to be, as it were, in a languor; it neither seems asleep nor does it feel awake. However, in this dream it is thoroughly awake to God, although fast asleep to worldly things and to ourselves. For in truth, during the short time that this lasts, the soul is almost senseless and unable to think on anything even if it wished.

Oh, wonderful secrets of God! I shall never tire of trying to explain them, but I know I shall never succeed. So I will say a thousand foolish things, provided that I may just happen to speak to an important point. But I did say it was not a dream. For in the preceeding Mansions, until the soul's experience is great, it remains doubtful what has actually happened to it, whether it has had desire, whether it was asleep, whether it came from God, or whether the devil transformed himself into an angel of light. In a word, the soul has a thousand suspicions; and it is just as well that it does have since our nature itself may deceive us at times.

In these Mansions there is not much room for poisonous things to enter, although tiny lizards may do so. Being so small, they can insinuate themselves everywhere, although they do not do harm, especially if they be despised. They represent the little fancies which come from the imagination, and from what has been mentioned above. Yet they can be often very troublesome. But these lizards, however small, cannot enter into these Mansions; because here there is no imagination nor is there memory nor understanding that can hinder this good.

*No worldly intrusions can enter here.*

I also dare to say that if the union truly comes from God, then the devil cannot enter or do any harm. His Majesty is so joined and united with the soul that the devil dare not approach. Nor can he understand this secret, for it is clear that he does not know our thoughts, much less can he understand so profound a secret as this union. This applies to the acts of the understanding and the will, for the devil clearly sees the thoughts of the imagination unless our Lord blinds him at that moment.

*The devil cannot intrude or harm.*

Oh, blessed state, in which this cursed one cannot hurt us! Thus the soul gains much blessing because God works in it without anyone, even the soul itself, being able to hinder Him. And what then will he not give, who is so willing and desiring of giving, and who can do whatever God wills?

It seems to me that you are not yet satisfied, for you will think you may consider these interior matters very difficult to examine. Although what has been said may be sufficient for someone who has experienced them, yet I want to give you a clear proof by which you may be *certain* whether it comes from God. For His Majesty has today brought the proof to my mind and it seems to me a sure one.

In difficult matters—although I think I undertand them, and speak the truth—I always use these words: "It seems to me." For I may be mistaken, although I would be the more willing and ready to believe what learned men communicated to me. They themselves have not experienced these matters, yet they have great weight because they are great scholars. As God considers them so many lights in His church, He uncovers the truth of things to them in order that they may recognize them. If they are not immoral persons, but true servants of God, they will never be astonished at His greatness, because they know that His power is able to do exceeding abundantly above all that we can ask or think (Ephesians 3:20).

**Fruitfulness in God keeps us from most intimate experiences.**

I have had much experience with scholarly men, and have also had some experience with half-learned, timid men, whose shortcomings have cost me a great deal. From this I have learned that whoever does not believe that God can do so much more, and that He has been pleased and is sometimes still pleased to reveal Himself to His creature men, such a person will keep the gate closely shut against receiving any favors for himself.

So may this never happen to you, my sisters, but believe that God can do so much more. Nor consider whether those to whom He communicates His favors are good or bad. His Majesty knows all about this, so any intervention on our part is unnecessary, but rather with humility and simplicity of heart, let us serve His Majesty, and praise Him for His works and wonders.

Let us now turn to the indication which I have described as a decisive one. For now you see that God has made this soul a fool with regard to all so as to more readily have impressed upon it the reality of true wisdom. For as long as such a soul is in this state, it can neither see nor hear nor understand. The period of this state is always short, and it seems to the soul even shorter than it really is. God implants Himself in the interior of that soul in such a way that, when it comes to itself, it cannot but help believing that it was in God and that God was in it. This truth becomes so deeply rooted in it, that although many years may pass away before God bestows a similar favor upon it, the soul will never forget it. Yet this is quite apart from the effects which remain within it and of which I shall speak later. What matters now is this certitude.

How does the soul see this truth or understand it? My answer is that the soul did not see it then, but afterward it saw it clearly. For this was not so much a vision as a certitude which remains in the soul, and which only God can implant within it. I knew someone who did not know that God was in all things by His presence, power, and essence. But by an experience of this kind that was received from God, she came to believe it firmly, and one of the half-learned men of whom I have just spoken answered that God was *only* there by His grace. Yet the truth was so imprinted within her that she did not believe him. Afterward she asked others, and they told her the truth which comforted her exceedingly!

But do not be mistaken by thinking that this certitude has anything to do with a corporeal form. God is not present in that way, but only by His divinity. Yet again you ask, how can I have certainty when we do not see it? I do not know, for it is His work. But I do know that what I say is true. Whoever has not this certainty, all I can say is he has not experienced this union of the soul with God.

In all these matters we must not seek to know the reasons for seeing how they are done, since our understanding cannot comprehend them. Why then should we desire to labor in vain, and to trouble ourselves about it? Surely it is enough to know that He Who is all powerful has done it. With regard to what I was saying about our inability to do anything, I remember what I have heard the bride say in the Song of Solomon: "The King brought me into the cellar of wine" (Song of Solomon 1:4; 2:4). It does not say that she actually *went*. It also tells us that she was wandering about in all directions, seeking for her Be-

*Accept these things. Do not afterwards analyze such experiences.*

loved (Song of Solomon 3:2). By the wine cellar I take it to mean the place where our Lord is pleased to put us, when He wills, and as He wills. But we cannot enter it by any efforts of our own. His Majesty must place us there and enter Himself into the center of our soul.

So that He may show His marvels clearly, He does not want our will to have any part to play; for the will has been already entirely surrendered to Him. Nor does He wish the door of our faculties and senses which are all asleep to be opened to Him. For He will come into the center of the soul without using a door, as He once did when He came unto His disciples, and said, "Peace be unto you" (John 20:19). Further on in the last Mansions, you will see how His Majesty desires that the soul should enjoy Him in its own center, even more so than here.

O my daughters! What great things shall we see, if we wish to look upon nothing else but our own baseness and wretchedness and to understand that we are not worthy to be the handmaidens of so great a Lord. For His wonders exceed all comprehension. May He be eternally praised! Amen.

### Part Two: Growth of the Soul to Receive More from God

You may think that I have already mentioned what is to be seen in these Mansions. Yet much more remains to be said, for as I have mentioned, there is more still to come. As regards mystical union, I think I can add nothing more. But when a soul on whom God bestows these favors prepares itself for them, there are many things to be said about what the Lord does in it. In order to better explain the soul's state, I will make use of a comparison which is suitable for this purpose. May we see how, although this work which our Lord does Himself is something we can do nothing about, yet our own disposition can contribute much to induce His Majesty to bestow this favor upon us.

**Parable of the silk worm**    You already know of the wonderful way in which silk is made, a way which no one but God could invent. It comes from a seed that is no bigger than small pepper-corns. I have never seen this, but only heard about it, so if it is incorrect in any way the fault is not mine. When the warm weather comes and the leaves first begin to appear on the mulberry tree, the seeds start to become alive; until then they were dead. The silkworms feed on the mulberry leaves until they are full grown, and it is then that twigs are placed so that with their tiny mouths, the worms can start spinning silk, making themselves tight little cocoons in which they enclose themselves. The silk worm which is fat and ugly then dies, and in its place a beautiful white butterfly comes right out of the cocoon.

However, who could believe this, since we ourselves have not seen it? But it has been related to us as being the case in many times and in different countries. Without this evidence, could our reason ever comprehend that such a creature so void of reason as a silkworm or a bee should be so diligent and so industrious in toiling for our benefit? Indeed, the poor little worm loses its life in this work. Yet this may serve you, sisters, as a meditation over a period of time, without my having to say any more about it to you. For it is by means of this illustration that you may have some idea of the wonders and the wisdom of our God.

What then should we do, if we were to understand the property of every created thing? It is very profitable for us to be occupied in meditating on these wonders, and in rejoicing that we are the spouses of so wise and powerful a King.

But let us now return to what I was saying, and apply the comparison that I have mentioned to ourselves. This worm begins to have life when, by the warmth of the Holy Spirit, it begins to make use of that general help which our Lord gives to everyone and to take advantage of the remedies which God has left in His church. Such remedies include frequenting the sacraments and reading good books, as well as hearing sermons. For these are powerful remedies for a soul that is dead by negligence and sin, and is plunged into the occasions of sin. Then this worm begins

God's help to us

to live and supports itself with good meditations until it has fully grown. This is what concerns me now, for the rest is of little importance.

**Our life in Christ**

When it is full grown, then it starts to spin its silk, and to build the house in which it is to live. By this house I mean you to understand Christ. I think I read or heard somewhere that our life "is hid" in Christ in God (Colossians 3:3), so that Christ *is* our life.

**How God enlarges our efforts**

Here then, daughters, we can learn by God's help to do what we can, since His Majesty Himself is our Mansion as He is in this Prayer of Union; this Mansion we spin ourselves. By saying this I may be misunderstood to say that we are able to take from or to add to God in saying that He is our Mansion, and that we are able to erect it for our own abode. But the truth is, we can neither subtract nor add to God. But we can take from and add to *ourselves,* as these little worms do. For no sooner have we done all we can about it, than God will unite our insignificant labors, which are nothing, with His own greatness. He will then give them so high a value that our Lord Himself, for Whom this has cost so much, unites our small trials with the great trials which He suffered, and makes of them all one.

**Renounce self-love**

Oh, then, my daughters, let us quickly perform this work and spin this cocoon, casting aside all self-love and our own will; and let us not adhere to any earthly thing. Let us practice penance, prayer, mortification, obedience, and all the other good works that you so value. May God grant that we act according to our knowledge, and to the instructions we have received concerning our duty. Let this worm die; let it die when it has performed that for which it was created. And you will then perceive how we see God. Then we behold ourselves immersed in His greatness just as the worm is in its cocoon. Notice how I say, "We shall see God." This is in proportion to how He allows Himself to be apprehended in this kind of union.

And now let us consider what becomes of this silkworm. For all that I have been saying about it is leading to this purpose. As soon as in this prayer it becomes sufficiently dead to the world, then it comes forth as a white butterfly.

*A transformed life through death to self*

Oh, wonderful greatness of God! How transformed does the soul come forth, by having been only for a short time—a half hour at most—immersed in the greatness of God, and united closely in Him! Truly I tell you, the soul does not know itself. For you must remember that there is the same difference here as there was between the ugly silkworm and the beautiful butterfly. The soul cannot think how it could have merited such a blessing, or how it came about.

Now the soul finds itself longing to praise God, so that it would gladly be consumed and die a thousand deaths for His sake. Then it finds itself longing to suffer and endure great afflictions and unable to do otherwise. Its desires of penance, solitude, and of all men knowing God are all excessive, and on this account it is deeply distressed whenever it sees God being offended. In the next Mansions, we shall deal with these things further in more detail, for although the experiences of these Mansions and of the next are almost the same, yet their effects come to have much greater power.

*Freed to worship God*

But now see the restlessness of this little butterfly. While it has never been quieter and calmer in its life, yet at the same time it does not know where to alight and rest. Will it return from whence it came? It cannot, for it is not in our power, until God be pleased again to bestow this favor upon us.

*Earnest longings for God are devotion to Him*

O Lord! What fresh struggles now begin for this soul! Who could imagine this, after receiving such sublime blessings? For in a word, one way or the other we must bear the cross as long as we live. Should anyone say that, having reached those Mansions, he will now always rest and delight? My answer is that to think like this is evidence that he has never reached these Mansions. Perhaps he had experienced some other spiritual delight if he had entered into the previous Mansions and then his experience has been helped along by a natural weakness or perhaps even by the devil. The devil gives him peace so that subsequently he can wage a much greater war against him.

**Spiritual discontent causes prayerful suffering in the soul.**

I do not mean to say that those who arrive here will not have peace. Of course they do have it and it is very deep indeed. For the afflictions which they have had are so valuable and have such good roots that, although they appear very excessive, they do give rise to peace and contentment. The very discontent which is caused by the things of the world arouses the desire to leave it. Yet this is not enough to comfort it, for despite all that it has profited, the soul is not yet wholly resigned to the will of God. Yet it does not fail to act in conformity with God's will, though it does so with many tears and with great sorrow at being unable to do more becuase it has been given no more ability. Every time the soul prays, its grief is accompanied with many tears. This pain seems, perhaps, to arise in some degree from being exceedingly troubled on beholding God offended and esteemed so little in this world. Moreover, the soul is distressed at the damnation of so many souls, heretics as well as enemies.

Yet it is so-called Christians that excite its compassion the most. For although the soul sees that the mercy of God is great, and that however wickedly they may live, they can still repent and be saved, yet it is afraid that many are lost.

**The transformed self**

Oh, the greatness of God! It was only a few years ago, perhaps even only a few days ago, that I was thinking of nothing but myself. Now my soul has been plunged into grievous anxiety on behalf of others. Even if we tried to meditate for years on end, we could not feel this as keenly as the soul now does.

God help me! If I could spend many days and years simply trying to realize how great a sin it is to offend God, and reflect that those who are damned are His children, and then were to meditate upon the miserable life my brothers and sisters live, would all that suffice us? No, daughters, no! This is not the pain which is felt here, for by the assistance of our Lord we may deepen our sorrow by dwelling upon these things. But that pain does not penetrate, nor can it reach the inmost part of the soul, in the way in which this pain occurs that I am speaking about here. For it seems to grind a soul to powder without procuring such a state, or even sometimes without her wishing it.

What then is this grief? Where does it come from? Let me tell you.

A little way back I referred to the bride and how God has put her in the wine cellar and given her charity (Song of Solomon 2:4). Well, this is the situation here. The soul, having entirely resigned itself into His hands and being so captivated by His love, neither knows nor desires anything else except that God would do with it as He pleases. As far as I can understand, God will never confer this favor on any soul, except upon such as He chooses for His own. He is pleased, without it knowing how, that the soul should depart hence, signed with His seal. For here the soul does no more than wax does when a seal is imprinted upon it. The wax cannot seal itself, but it is only disposed; that is to say, it is soft. Nor does it soften itself for this object, but as it lies still it allows the impression to be made.

*God's gift of being disposed only toward Him*

Oh, goodness of God! All is at Your cost. You require only our will, and that there should be no resistance in the wax. You see, sisters, what our God does here for us so that this soul may already know that it is His. He gives it the same image that His Son had in this life, which is an exceedingly great favor.

*God takes all from us.*

Whoever desired more to leave this life than He did? So he spoke at the supper: "With desire have I desired" (Luke 22:15). Did the painful death that You were about to die present itself to You, O Lord, as something so grievous and terrible? "No, because My great love and My desire that souls should be saved transcended those pains beyond all comparison. Indeed, the many terrible things that I have suffered since the time I lived in the world—and still go on suffering—are so great that, by comparison with them, these are nothing."

**How great must be the love of Christ.**

I have often thought about this, knowing what great torments a certain soul known to me has endured and still endures by seeing how God is offended. Indeed, that soul would rather die than go on enduring it. If this soul, when it is compared with Christ, has such little love, and yet it feels such intolerable pain about sin, what then must Christ our Lord have suffered? And what a life must He have led, having all His sufferings present before Him, and always beholding the dreadful crimes which would be committed against His Father? I firmly believe that these were far greater than those which He endured in His most sacred passion, for then He saw the end of those sufferings.

Christ's joy in seeing our redemption purchased by His death and in testifying to the love that He had for His Father in suffering so much for Him no doubt had to lessen His pain. This is similar to what happens to men in this world who, through the force of love, can perform great penances so that they hardly feel them. Indeed, they would like to do more and more, for it all seems so little to them. What, then, would His Majesty feel when He found Himself able to prove to His Father His perfect obedience in fulfilling love for His neighbor? Oh, the great delight of suffering in doing the will of God!

But the constant sight of so many offenses committed against His Majesty and so many souls going to hell must, I think, have been very painful to Him. So painful was it that, had He not been more than man, one day of such torment would have been enough to put an end to any number of lives that He might have had, let alone to one.

## Part Three: Evidences of Our Betrothal to Christ

Let us now see something of what God bestows upon the soul in this state. We should always remember that we must endeavor to advance in the service of our Lord and in the knowledge of self. For if the soul receives no more than this grace, and becomes careless in its life as if it is already established, and turns out of the way which leads to heaven, there will happen to it what happened to that creature that came out of the silkworm: it leaves seed for the production of more silkworms and then dies forever. I say that it leaves seed because, for my own part, I believe that it is God's will that so great a blessing should not be given in vain, and that if the soul that receives it does not profit by it, others will do so. For as the soul possesses these virtues and desires the above virtues, as long as it perseveres in them, it will always do good to other souls by warming them with the heat of His desire. However, even after losing this, it may still desire others to profit and take pleasure in making known the graces and favors which God bestows on those who love and serve Him.

I know to whom this happened (*Life*, Ch. VII), and who although having herself gone astray (that is, by abandoning prayer for a time), yet she continued to teach others in the way of prayer who did not understand it. She also brought them very great benefits. Our Lord, in His mercy, later gave her light. For in truth, she had not as yet experienced the effects mentioned above. But how many are there whom God calls to the apostleship, as He called Judas, to whom He communicates Himself? How many does He call to a crown, as He called Saul, and who nevertheless afterwards perish through their own sin?

Thus, sisters, let us draw the conclusion that in order to gain more virtue, and not to be lost like they were, we can have no other security than "obedience" and a firm determination not to transgress the law of God. For I speak to those on whom He bestows such favors, and likewise to *all* persons.

**Obedience alone counts.**

**A true union of wills**

It seems to me that in spite of all that I have said, these Mansions still appear somewhat obscure. But since so much is to be gained by entering into them, it is good for those on whom God does not bestow supernatural favors not to consider themselves without hope. By our Lord's assistance, a true union may be obtained readily if we endeavor to procure it by having our will united only with God's will.

Oh! How many of us can say this: "We desire nothing else, and would die for this truth"? Now I tell you again, that when this is the case, we have obtained this favor from our Lord. Be not anxious about that other sweet union which I spoke about before, since whatever is most valuable in it comes from this of which I am now speaking.

What a desirable union it is! Happy is the soul which has obtained it! It will live with comfort in this life, and none of the evils of this life will trouble it unless it be from some fear of losing God, or of seeing Him offended. Neither sickness, poverty, or the death of anyone can disturb it, except the death of one which God's church might miss. Such a soul clearly sees that our Lord knows best in this matter.

Note very carefully, daughters, that the silkworms must necessarily die. This is what will cost you most of all, for death comes more easily when one can see oneself living a new life. Our duty now is to continue living this present life, and yet, as it were, to kill the worm *ourselves*. I acknowledge that this will cost us far more, but it will have its reward. So if you gain the victory, your recompense will be all the greater. But you must not doubt the possibility of this real union with the will of God. This is the union which I have desired all my life. This is what I have continually asked of my Lord, for it is most genuine and secure.

**The death even of small undetected sins**

But, alas! How few of us reach it, although the soul is careful not to offend God and has entered into the religious life thinking that it has done everything. Oh! How many worms remain undiscovered until, like the worm which gnawed through Jonah's gourd (Jonah 4:6-7), they have gnawed through our virtues. These worms are self-love, self-esteem, and censoriousness, even in little things (concerning our neighbors, lack of charity toward them, and failure to love them as we love ourselves). Even when we fulfill our obligations and apparently commit no sin, we are still far from doing what is required of us in order to be *wholly* united with the will of God.

What do you suppose is His will, daughters? Is it not that we should be entirely perfect, so that we become one with Him and with the Father, as His Majesty prayed (John 17:22)? Consider how far we are from arriving at that state. I can assure you that I am writing now with great grief, because I see that I am so much behind, and all through my own fault. To fulfill this object it is not necessary for our Lord to grant us great new favors, because it is sufficient that He has given us His Son to show us the way.

What it is to know God's will

Do not think that if, for example, my father or my brother dies, I ought to be in such conformity to God's will that I shall not grieve at their loss. Or that, if sickness and troubles come to me, that I must bear them cheerfully. It is good if we have such a disposition and sometimes it is a matter of common sense. But being unable to help ourselves, we can make a virtue of our necessity. How often philosophers used to act in this way, or in similar matters, and they were wise men indeed!

But here the Lord only requires two things of us, namely, that we should love God and love our neighbor. These are the objects that we must labor to fulfill, for by observing these laws perfectly we do His will and consequently we shall be united with Him. How far we are from doing these two things in the way that we ought to do for a God Who is so great! May His Majesty grant us grace in order that we may deserve to reach this state, as it is in our power to do so if we really wish.

The surest sign by which we discover whether we are observing these two duties is the love of our neighbor. For since we cannot know whether we love God even though

The sign of loving our neighbors

we may have strong proofs of it, these signs can be more easily discovered respecting the love of our neighbor.

Be assured, then, that the further you advance in that love, the more you will also advance in the love of God. For the affection which His Majesty has for us is so great that, as a return for the love which we show our neighbor, He will make that love for Himself increase. Of this I have no doubt.

It is very important, then, for us diligently to observe how we proceed in this matter. For if we endeavor perfectly to acquire this love of our neighbor, we shall have done everything. Because as our nature is corrupt and evil, unless it comes from the root (which is the love of God), we shall never perfectly possess the love of our neighbor. Since this is so vital, sisters, let us strive to get to know ourselves better and better, even in the very smallest things.

**Our actions and desires must be in harmony with love.**

Take no notice of all the fine plans which distract our minds when we are at prayer and which we think we will put into operation and carry out on behalf of our neighbors, in the hope of saving one's soul. For if our actions are not in harmony with these plans, we can have no hope for believing that we can ever put them into practice. I say the same thing about humility and indeed about all the virtues. For the wiles of the devil are great. He will run a thousand times around hell if by doing so he can make us believe that we have a single virtue which we really do not possess. And he is right, for such ideas are very harmful, and such counterfeit virtues are always associated with vainglory. On the other hand, those virtues which are of God are free from both price and vainglory.

It amuses me sometimes to see certain souls who think that, for God's sake, they should be glad to be humble and be put to open shame, and yet they will try to conceal even a small peccadillo. And should they be accused of anything that they have not done . . . ! God help us from having to listen to them then!

So if anyone cannot bear such a thing, be careful to pay attention to the resolutions that he has made in private.

For in fact these are not resolutions which have been made by the will as a genuine act of the will; a genuine act of the will is quite another matter. Probably they are the result of the imagination. And the devil makes good use of the imagination in the way he exercises his surprises and deceptions.

Will the devil do this with women and unlearned persons because we cannot understand the difference between the faculties and the imagination, and a thousand other things in the interior life? Oh, sisters, how clearly it can be seen what the love of your neighbor really means to some of you, and what imperfection it has reached in others! If you understood the importance of this virtue, you would not trouble about anything else.

When I see people earnestly trying to understand the kind of prayer that they are experiencing and being so self-preoccupied, not daring to divert their thoughts and so lose the slightest degree of the feelings of tenderness and devotion which they had been experiencing, I realize clearly how little they truly understand the way to attain that union with God. They think that the whole matter consists in such exercises.

*Techniques of prayer are inadequate.*

But no! Sisters, no! Our Lord desires *deeds.* So if you see a sister sick whom you can in some way relieve, do not be afraid that you will lose your time of devotion if you attend to her. If she is in pain, grieve with her and if necessary, fast so that she may have the food that you would eat. Do this not so much for her own sake as because you know that it is your Lord's will. That is true union with His will.

*Love is in deeds.*

Or again, if you hear someone being highly praised, do not be envious, but rather be more pleased than if they were praising you. This will become easy if you are humble, for in that case you will be embarrassed to be praised. But to be glad when your sister's virtues are praised is a wonderful thing. And when we see a fault in someone, we should be as grieved about it as if it were our own. We should try to conceal it then from others.

*Love is in not being envious.*

So then ask our Lord to grant you this perfect love for your neighbor. Let His Majesty do so alone, for He can bestow upon you far more than you could ever even desire. You must be submissive not to have your own will, so that your sister's will is done in everything, even though this may cause you to lose some of your own rights. You may have to forget your own good in your concern for their interest and forfeit your own pleasure in order to please them. Do this however much your own natural self may be opposed to it.

When the opportunity presents itself, try also to shoulder that same trial in order to relieve your neighbor of it. Do not suppose that this will not cost you anything or that you will find it all done for you. Instead, think about the love which we cost Him. For in order to free us from death, He Himself suffered the most painful death on the cross.

### Part Four: The Prayer Life of Our Betrothal

It seems to me that we have not yet reached the point of spiritual betrothal in this union. But it is rather like what happens in our earthly life when two people are about to be married. The first consideration they discuss together is whether they are suitable for each other, and whether they like each other, and if they are in love. Then they meet again so that they may learn to appreciate each other and know each other better.

So it is with this spiritual union. Where there is mutual consent and the soul has been clearly given to understand the blessedness of her lot, and if she is firmly resolved to do the will of her Spouse in everything, then His Majesty will be willing to take her, knowing full well if the soul has been so resolved. Then He will grant her this mercy, desiring that she should get to know Him better, and that, as it may be said, they shall meet in an interview with each other, so that He will unite her with Himself.

The whole matter is over in a very short time. For all the giving and taking has now come to an end, and it is only necessary that the soul see in a secret way Who is this Spouse that she is to take. But if she were to use her senses and faculties, the soul could not understand in a thousand years what it now understands in this briefest period of time. But the Spouse, being Who He is in His love, leaves her after that one visit worthier to be united with Him.

*The betrothal is not rationalized but experienced in love.*

The soul then becomes so enamored with Him that she does everything on her part not to break off this divine betrothal. For if the soul should grow careless and set her affection on something else apart from Him, then she will lose everything. Indeed, her loss will be as great as are the favors that He has been granting her, and these are far greater than it is possible to convey in words. So, then, Christian souls, I beseech you for His sake not to become careless; but avoid all occasions of sin. For even in this state the soul is still vulnerable to expose herself to them. It is only after the marriage has been concluded—and this occurs in the next Mansions—when there may be no further danger.

Since this communication has been no more than a single brief meeting, the devil will then make every effort to prevent these nuptials. For it is only afterward when he sees that the soul has already given herself wholly up to her Spouse that he will not dare to become so bold. He has learned by experience to fear that if he should attack her at any time, he will suffer frequently great loss and she will gain a great deal.

*The devil will try to break off the betrothal.*

I tell you all this, daughters, because I have known people with a very high degree of spirituality who have reached this state, and yet whom the devil has won back to himself with great subtlety and skill. For this purpose he will marshal all the powers of hell, for as I have often said, if he can win a single soul then he will also win a whole multitude. He has acquired great experience in this matter.

**Pray for safekeeping.**

We learn from this what it is that we should be most diligent about. First, we must constantly ask God in our prayers to keep us safe in His hand, and frequently consider that if He leaves us, we shall at once be cast into the abyss. We must never put any confidence in ourselves. This is folly.

Above all, we must walk with diligence and attention, watching what progress we make in the virtues and carefully observing that we are either going forward or else we are going back. This is to be noted especially in our love for each other and in our desire to be thought least of, and in other ordinary matters. If then we look at these things, and beg the Lord to give us His light, we shall then immediately discover whether we have gained or lost. For you must not imagine that a soul which God has brought so far will be quickly led out of His hand or that the devil can recapture it without much effort. No! His Majesty so deeply feels that it must not be lost that, in many ways, He will give the soul a thousand interior warnings of many kinds in order that the danger may be hidden from it.

**Move forward and fear when you do not.**

The conclusion of all this discourse is that we must always endeavor to move forward and to fear exceedingly when we do not. For there is no doubt that if the soul ceases to go forward, the devil will try to entrap it. The reason for this is that love can never be idle. Therefore not to progress is a very bad sign, because a soul which has resolved to become the spouse of God Himself and has already conversed intimately with His Majesty, and has now arrived at the point mentioned beforehand, this soul must not lie down and go to sleep again.

In order that you may see, daughters, what our Lord does for those souls whom He has already chosen for His spouses, let us now begin to think about the Sixth Mansions. Then you will see how really slight is all the service that we can render to Him. or all the suffering that we undergo for Him, and all the preparation which we can make for such great favors. It may be that it was our Lord's will that I should be commanded to write this work in order that we may forget our trivial earthly pleasures as we fix our eyes on the reward. Just consider how infinite is the mercy which makes Him desirous to communicate Himself to such worms as we are. Thus, fired by such love of Him, we shall run our race with our eyes fixed upon His greatness.

May He help me to explain something of these difficult things, for unless His Majesty guides my pen, I know full well that it would be impossible to write. If what I say does not help you, I beseech our Lord not to allow me to say anything. For His Majesty knows that as far as I know myself, I have no other object than that His name should be praised.

**May God help me to go on writing more about God's ways.**

Let us then strive to serve a Lord who rewards us so abundantly even in this life. May He help us to form some idea of what He will give us in heaven, where all the tedious labors and dangers which now beset us and trouble us shall no longer disturb us. What pleasure it would be for us to go on working for so great a God and Lord and Spouse were it not that we were afraid of the danger of losing or offending Him. May His Majesty grant that we may deserve to do Him such service without so many imperfections into which we are always falling, even in our good works. Amen.

# VII

# The Interior Castle
# Part 3

## The Sixth Mansions: the Prayer of Intimate Union and The Betrothal to Christ

### Part One: Greater Spiritual Favors Involve More Suffering

et us now speak with the help of the Holy Spirit about the "Sixth Mansions," the Mansions in which the soul has been wounded for the Spouse. Seeking more than ever for solitude, the soul tries to renounce everything which would disturb it in its solitude. That vision of Him (mentioned in the preceding Mansions) has so deeply impressed the soul that all its desire is to enjoy it once again. I insist that nothing which is seen in this prayer can properly be called "visionary," for it is not something that is imagined. I call it a vision simply on account of the comparison I made use of.

The soul is now determined to choose no other Spouse. But it appears that the Spouse is disregarding its yearnings for the accomplishment of the nuptials. This is because the Bridegroom wishes the soul to long after the betrothal even more earnestly and deeply, for He desires that this blessing will exceed everything in its costliness. Everything is of but slight significance in comparison with the greatness of this blessing, daughters. The proof and security that she has of possessing this gain is really no more

than is necessary to enable her to bear with its postpone-
ment.

**Living close to God all the time**

· O my God, what travail both in the interior and the
externals of life must be endured before we can enter into
the Seventh Mansions! When I really think about them, I
am sometimes afraid that if we had anticipated their intensity beforehand, it would have been extremely difficult
for us, as weak as we are, to have enough determination to
enble us to endure them or to be resolute enough to suffer
them. And this is true even when we have the advantage
of knowing that when we reach the Seventh Mansions,
there will be nothing more to fear. But I think it is right
and proper to mention to you some of these troubles
which I know for certain will have to be endured. Perhaps
not all souls may be led this way, although I doubt very
much whether those which sometimes so truly enjoy
heavenly things can ever live free from earthly trials of
one kind or another.

**The wounds of the lover**

I realize that in speaking about these trials I might give
consolation to some soul in a similar state if he can understand what is taking place in those on whom God bestows
such favors. Otherwise one might think that everything
was lost. I shall not proceed to narrate them in the order in
which these troubles occur, but only as they come to my
own memory.

I will begin with the least of these trials. This arises
from the outcry which some people make when a soul has
to face what these people think of her and their judgment
of her, even though she has not known them or communicated to them. They say, "She thinks that she is becoming
a saint!" Or, "She is only going to these extremes in order
to make everyone look less spiritual than her, while in fact
they are better Christians without these extravagances."
What they do not realize is that this is required of one who
would so search God earnestly.

Then the people whom she thought were her friends
withdraw themselves from her, and so the very people
who afflict her the most are those who think and are

grieved that this soul is, in their opinion, ruined and obviously deluded. Indeed, they are confident that all this comes from the devil. So they gossip and say that she will meet with the same end which such and such a one has already experienced who was ruined in this way. They think that, through her faults, she will drag others with her and deceive her own spiritual directors. So they scorn the poor soul and talk about her behind her back in this way times without number.

I know someone [no doubt Teresa herself] to whom all this was happening and who was so afraid that there would be nobody willing for her to confide in. There is so much I could tell you about all this, but I will not stop to do it now. But the worst of it all is that these trials do not end quickly; they endure throughout the whole of one's life. So one is sent into "social" exile by the warnings that such people give to each other.

Oh, but you say, "Surely there must be some who will speak well of her." The fact is, my daughters, that there are very few who really believe her actions to be truly good, in comparison with the many who dislike them intensely!

This leads us to a second trial and that is about when we are well spoken of; and this is worse than that already mentioned. For the soul sees very clearly that if there is no good in us, it can only be God's gift and not that of ourselves in any way. Indeed, the soul clearly sees that it was not very long ago that she was plunged into the direst bankruptcy and plunged deep into sin. So this phrase becomes an intolerable pain to bear, at least at first. It may begin to abate later for various reasons.

The first of these reasons for the pain to abate is that experience shows that people can as readily speak well of us as ill, so one should take no more notice of the one than of the other. The second reason that our Lord has shown with great delight is that although "in me, in my flesh, dwelleth no good thing," the good that can be found is truly the gift of His Majesty. So the soul bursts out in praise as if beholding the good in a *third* person that is not

**Pains suffered**

herself. The third reason is that, having seen how others have been helped by recognizing the favors which God has granted to them, the soul can turn it around and assume that it is her own virtues that are to be esteemed. In reality, of course, this is not so. The fourth reason is that as the soul goes on to prize the honor and glory of God more than its own glory, it is no longer tempted to think that these phrases which have damaged others will harm it. So the soul is freed about concern for its own reputation, provided that it can be to the praise of God's glory, come what may.

**Freedom is found in our disinterest of the false opinions of others.**

These and other reasons lessen the embarrassment that is induced by such false praises, although always some distress is still felt. It is only when the soul takes no notice whatever about them that it is free. In fact, to find the soul publicly esteemed good without reason is a far greater trial than any of those already mentioned. For once the soul has learned to care little about its reputation, it cares very much less about the other trial. Indeed, it rejoices and views this trial as the most delightful music. This is really true. For the soul is fortified rather than dejected, since experience has now taught it the great benefit which it gains in this process.

It appears to the soul that such people are not offending God in their persecution, but that really His Majesty is permitting these trials for the soul's greater gain. The soul sees this clearly, and therefore can have a special and deeply tender love for them so that she can consider them as her very best friends. They are, in fact, greater benefactors than those who speak well of the soul.

**Trials sent by God**

Our Lord is also accustomed to sending the soul grievous sicknesses. This is a much more severe trial, especially when the pains are acute. For when they are acute, then they appear to be the most severe afflictions that can be endured on this earth.

These trials affect the soul both inwardly as well as outwardly in such a way that the soul does not know what to do with itself in suffering such acute physical pains. In this state, the soul would willingly endure any martyrdom provided it was short rather than go on suffering so intensely. Mercifully God does not allow us to endure more than we can bear, so they do not last long with such intensity. Moreover, His Majesty first of all will bestow patience upon us to endure them.

But there are other great pains and infirmities of different sorts. I know someone [Teresa herself] to whom the Lord forty years ago granted this favor. There has scarcely been a day since when she has been without pain or other kinds of suffering. This is because of her poor physical health, to say nothing of the other trials that she has had to endure. It is true that she considered herself to have been so very wicked that she did not consider the pains to be anything but small in comparison with the fear of hell which she deserved.

Perhaps others who have not so greatly grieved our Lord may be led by Him along another pathway, but I myself would always choose the way of suffering, if only because I wish to imitate our Lord Jesus Christ. This I would do if there were no other advantage except doing so; but of course there are many other benefits. But oh, if I could only properly describe the *interior* afflictions so that I could make them understood! Then how trifling would these others appear in comparison. But it is impossible.

Such an experience of pain the soul does not need to reflect about in order to understand this truth about interior affliction (especially affliction which brings on depression), because the experience that it has already had of seeing itself completely helpless now makes it know its own utter helplessness. Although the soul remains in a state of grace despite all this torment, yet the experience of grace is so hidden that the soul thinks it neither has, nor ever had, the least spark of any love for God. If it had done anything good or His Majesty had granted any favor upon it, the soul seems to feel it was but a dream or vain fancy.

O Jesus! How tragic it is to see a soul so forsaken in this way and having little in the way of earthly comfort to sustain it! So do not think, sisters, that if sometimes you find

**Only God can control in such circumstances.**

yourself in this condition of depression that the rich and those who enjoy their freedom more, have a surer remedy against these times. Oh, no! It seems to me like placing all the delights of the world before people who are condemned to die, and which therefore cannot afford them any pleasure, will only increase their torment. So it is the same here. Consolation must come from above, for in this situation earthly comforts are of no avail. This great God desires that we should know our own misery and acknowledge Him to be our King.

**Examine yourself in external things.**     So what is this poor creature to do if she continues in this way for a long time? If she prays vocally, it seems as if she was not praying at all. I mean she receives no consolation from her prayers, for her inward being does not experience it. She does not even understand what she is praying for, nor does she understand herself, although she may pray vocally. As for contemplative prayer, this is not the time for it because she has no powers for it. Even solitude does her a great deal of harm and proves to be just another torment to her. She cannot endure to be in company with anyone or have anyone speak to her. However hard she strives to overcome this depression, she still has its moodiness which she cannot hide from others. It is impossible for the soul who endures this to be able to communicate it, for they are spiritual conflicts and troubles for which no name can be found. The best remedy—I do not say for getting rid of the trouble, for I know of none for that, but for enabling the soul to endure it—is to occupy oneself with external things and with works of charity, hoping in God's mercy. His mercy is never lacking to those who trust in Him. May He be blessed forever. Amen.

The devil may cause other trials which are of an exterior kind, but these will not occur so commonly nor is there any reason to speak of them, for they are not anything like the severe ones mentioned above. For, whatever these devils do, they can never in my opinion so inhibit the faculties or disturb the soul in such a distressful way. For reason remains free to consider that they can do no more than what our Lord permits them. So when one's reasoning powers are not lost, all is small in comparison with what I have mentioned above.

I shall now deal with other interior afflictions which are endured in these Mansions. I shall also speak of different kinds of prayer and favors of our Lord. Some of these, as is evident by the effects that they leave in the body, are harder to be endured than others. But they do not deserve the name of troubles, nor have we any reason to call them so, as they are such great favors of our Lord. The soul when in the midst of them knows that they are such, and yet they are not worth consideration by it. This great affliction comes, together with many others, when the soul is ready to enter the Seventh Mansions. Some of them I will mention. But to mention all is impossible.

## Part Two: A Growing Disregard for Self

It seems we have left our little dove a long way behind, but we have not in reality. For these are troubles which make her soar all the higher. Let us now begin to treat the way in which the spouse deals with herself before Him.

Clearly, the spouse belongs wholly to Him, and so He makes Himself greatly desired in many ways, some so subtle that the soul does not even recognize them. Nor is it conscious of them. Therefore they are indescribable except to persons who have had some experience of them. For some of these influences are so subtle and delicate, as they proceed from the very heart of the soul, that I know no way of comparing them for an explanation. They are very different from all that we can procure within ourselves, and likewise from the pleasures already mentioned.

Very often, without imagining them or remembering God, His Majesty awakens one by lightning without thunder, as it were. Although no noise is heard, yet the soul clearly perceives that it is being called by God. This is so obvious that sometimes the soul trembles all over, especially at first. And the soul utters groans even though it

*The call of God*

may feel no pain. For the soul feels itself to be most delightfully wounded, but it neither knows how nor by whom. It knows very well that it is a favor which is to be so prized, and it wishes never to be healed of it. The soul complains in words of love. These are external, addressed to the Spouse, for she cannot do otherwise since she knows Him to be present though not willing to reveal Himself.

This is a great but pleasant affliction. If the soul desired not to have it, it could not, nor can it ever wish to be left without it. For this afflicton gives the soul more delight than the Prayer of Quiet, which has no such distress associated with it.

I am doing my utmost, sisters, to make you understand this operation of love, but I do not know how to do so. For it seems a contradiction that the Beloved, although not seen, should let the soul clearly perceive that He is in it. He seems to call it by a sign that is so certain that it cannot be doubted, and with a whistle that shrieks so penetratingly that it cannot help being heard. For it seems that when the Spouse thus speaks to the soul, it is in the Seventh Mansions. All the other inhabitants of the other Mansions—namely the senses, the imagination, and the faculties—dare not stir.

O my powerful God! How great are Your secrets, and how different are spiritual things from all that is seen or known here upon earth! In no way is one able to express this favor, small though it is, in comparison with the very great one which You work in souls.

**It is a "call" that wounds the soul.**  So powerful is this call from You within the soul that it becomes consumed with desire and longing. Yet it does not know what to ask, because it is so strongly persuaded that God is within the soul.

If then God is so consciously within one, you may ask, what more does she desire? What is it that troubles the soul? What greater good can it possibly ask for? I cannot say: but this I know only too well that it suffers, and that this pain pierces even to the very inner parts. When He who wounds the soul draws back the dart, it seems almost as if He had torn it apart, so deeply does it desire this love.

I have been thinking just now that if I conceive of my God as a brazier of burning coals, and if a small spark should be taken from it and fall upon the soul in such a way as to make it feel inflamed yet not consumed, it will continue in that pain which is so delightful. The mere touch of such sparks gives this experience. This is the best comparison that I have been able to find.

*Yet it is a pleasant pain.*

For this pleasant pain is not really a pain, nor does it continue with the same intensity, although sometimes it may last for a long time. And at other times it will cease quickly, as our Lord is pleased to communicate it. For I insist that it is not to be attained by human efforts. Although it sometimes lasts for a long while, yet it fluctuates; in a word, it never stands still, and therefore it does not cease to inflame the soul, except when it is ready to die out. Then the spark dies and leaves the soul with a desire of suffering. Again it is an amorous pain which the spark causes.

There is no reason to believe that this experience is natural, or that it is caused by depression, or much less that it is a delusion of the devil, or the effect of a hallucination. It is perfectly clear that this experience can only come from our Lord Who is unchangeable. Its effects are unlike those of other devotions whose genuineness we may doubt because of their ecstatic character. In this experience, all the senses and faculties are never suspended, and it induces no introspection. Rather they are on the alert to discover what is going on. Their exercise as far as I can discover causes no disturbance, and they neither increase this delectable pain nor do they eliminate it. Anyone to whom our Lord has given this experience will recognize it in reading this description. Let him thank God and not be afraid that it might be a deception.

Also, so that this person is not ungrateful for so great a privilege, let him also strive to serve Him and in everything to amend his life. Then he will see what will be the salutory effect of such an experience, and how he will anticipate receiving yet more and more. One person who was granted this blessing spent several years in the enjoy-ment of it. She felt that if she had served the Lord for very many years by enduring great trials, she would still have felt it was worthwhile. May He be blessed forever and ever. Amen.

**How can one be confident about such experiences?**

You may ask perhaps how can one be so confident about such experiences? You can be most sure of this for the following reasons. First, the devil can never bestow upon the soul such delectable pain. He can indeed give certain pleasure which may seem spiritual, but it is beyond his power to unite a pain which is so intense with the quietude and joy that it effects in the soul. For all his strength is merely outward, and his trials when he sends them are never sweet or peaceful, but always restless and turbulent. Second, this delectable tempest arises from another quarter which is far different from that over which he can have any power. Third, great benefits ac-crue in the soul, which are generally resolutions to suffer for God. This cannot be from the devil. The soul is given determination to forfeit all worldly pleasures, worldly dis-course, and other such things in order to endure many afflictions.

**Such experiences are genuine.**

It is very obvious that this is no fancy, because although the devil may sometimes endeavor to do so, he cannot counterfeit this. It is so clearly experienced that in no way can it be feigned. I mean to say that it cannot seem to be what it clearly is not, nor can it be doubted what it really is. The impulses are genuine, for we clearly perceive them just as we might hear a loud noise in our ears. Nor can one confuse it with mental depression, for the fancies created by melancholy are only a figment of the imagination; this proceeds from the interior of the soul. It is possible that I may be mistaken. But until I hear stronger reasons from one who understands the subject, I shall adhere to my opinion. I happen to know someone [probably herself] who was terribly afraid of being deceived in this way, and yet who had never any fear about this kind of prayer.

Our Lord also employs other ways of awakening the soul. For example, when one is praying vocally and not thinking at all on any interior things, the soul may seem to catch fire in an abrupt and delightful manner. It is like being suddenly encountered by a most fragrant perfume so that it is diffused through all the senses. Yet I do not say literally that it is a perfume. I merely use this as a comparison in order to convey the excitement with which the soul is aroused in the presence of the Spouse and the intoxicating desire to enjoy Him. This moves the soul to be ready for any heroic act and give praise to our Lord.

*God has other ways of awakening the soul.*

The source of this favor has already been discussed. But here there is no pain, nor are such desires to enjoy God painful. This is what is most commonly felt by the soul. So I do not think there is much reason here, then, for fear. Rather we must only endeavor to receive this favor with gratitude.

## Part Three: The Soul Awakened by Locutions

Our Lord has another way of awakening the soul. Although it may seem to be a greater favor than that already discussed, yet it may prove to be more dangerous. So I will enter into some detail about it. The soul is awakened vocally in many different ways. Some of these seem to come from outside. Others come from the innermost depths of the soul. Others seem to come from above, while others again are so completely outside the soul that they can be heard orally as if uttered by a human voice.

*Discerning the types of locution*

Sometimes these may all be fanciful, especially in those who are prone to depression. I mean by this those who are affected by real melancholy or persons who have a weak imagination. No notice should be paid to these two types of persons, although they will tell us that they see, hear, and understand. Nor should we take seriously their impression that they have been told this by the devil. Rather we should look upon them as sick people. The Prioress and confessor or whoever they confide in should advise

*False locutions*

them not to pay attention to these delusions. For this is not a matter by which they can serve God, and the devil has deceived many in this fashion. Rather humor such people in a way that will not cause them more pain. It is useless to tell them that it is mental depression, for they will not believe you. They will insist that they are actually seeing and hearing it because it appears so vividly to them.

For the real solution may be to make sure that they have less time for prayer, and that, as far as possible, they should be dissuaded from attaching importance to these delusions. The devil is accustomed to make use of such weak souls as these for their own destruction or at least for the hurt of others. For both with sick as well as healthy souls there is cause for misgiving about these things until it is cleared up as to what kind of spirit is responsible. I also believe that it is better for them to get rid of such things first of all, for if they are of God, seeking to dispense with them will help us all the more to advance in His ways. When they are tested in this way, they will tend to increase. But the soul should not be allowed to be troubled too much, for then it cannot really help itself.

**Types of locution**   Let us now return to what I was saying about these "discourses" that the soul may experience. The different kinds which I have mentioned may come either from God, or from the devil, or from one's own imagination. I shall mention the traits that belong to these different kinds, and also note when these "discourses" can be dangerous. For there are many souls among people of prayer who perceive them. And I do not wish you, sisters, to imagine that you do ill either in believing them or in not believing them. When they are only for your own pleasure, or to reveal to you your defects, then it does not really matter whether they be true or false. For I warn you against such an attitude in thinking better of yourself for the experience, even though the things appear to come from God. For our Lord Himself spoke frequently with the Pharisees.

All our good consists in the way that we take advantage of His words. So pay no attention to any "discourse" which is not strictly conformable to the Scriptures, for then it is as if it came from the devil himself. For such words may, in fact, come only from your own weak imagination. Then you must consider them as temptations that test the faith. Therefore always resist them that they may gradually cease. And this they will of themselves, for they have little power of their own.

Let us now return to our first point. Unless the locutions come from God, it matters little whether we believe that they come from inside, from above, or even from the outside world. The most significant evidence that they can have in my opinion is the following: The first and truest is the sense of authority and power which such "discourses" bring with them. They are consistent in working out what they say. I will explain myself a little clearer. A soul, for example, may be quite overwhelmed by affliction and inward unrest, together with experiencing aridity and the darkness of understanding. If the whole world and all its scholars were united together in giving the soul reasons for not being grieved, they could not by all their efforts remove that affliction [here Teresa is speaking of her own experience].

*Evidences of locutions from God*

The soul may be troubled because her spiritual director and others may tell her that "she is possessed by an evil spirit." If, however, by the one word that says, "It is I, be not afraid," the soul is then freed from all fears and becomes very cheerful, and imagines that no one is able to make it believe to the contrary, then this must be a genuine experience. However anxious this soul may be about the consequences of its depression and the gloom it sees as its future, if it hears this one assurance: "Be quiet, for everything will turn out well," then the soul can be sure and without a care in the world. This assurance can have the same effect in many other ways.

*First, they comfort the soul.*

The second sign is that a deep peace will remain in the soul so that it is able to enjoy a devout and peaceful recollection and have a disposition to praise God. O my Lord! If one word conveyed by one of Your servants has such

*Second, they bring fear to the soul.*

force (at least in these Mansions), what will it be like when You are Yourself united in the soul and by such love the soul is united to You?

**Third, they are long remembered.** The third sign is that these words are not forgotten for a long time. Indeed, they will never be forgotten. This is quite unlike the words which are spoken in the world by men, however wise and learned they may be. For their words could never be so deeply impressed upon our memories, nor can we give such credit to them in comparison to these words that He gives. They can never have such a great certainty as they relate to the future, even though they are spoken about things which seem to be utterly impossible to envisage.

Sometimes doubts may arise as to their feasibility or as to whether they will prove true or false, and so the soul may waver a little accordingly. Yet there is in the soul itself such a deep security that it cannot be persuaded otherwise, although everything seems to appear contrary to what it has heard. Although some years may pass away, yet the soul remains with this confidence that God will employ other means quite unbeknown to us which, in the end, will bring these things to pass.

Nonetheless, the soul cannot help suffering when it sees so many obstacles against it. For the circumstances which she experienced at the time when she heard the words and the certainty which they left within her from God are now passed away and fresh doubts begin to arise. Do these words come from the devil, or are they just from the imagination? Yet when the soul experiences the words, it has no doubts or any fears whatever; it would even die for the truth.

**Locutions of the devil and imagination** There is much to be feared with regard to the devil and the exercise of our imagination. But if there occur the above mentioned traits, then the person may rest assured that such work comes from God. However, this may not be in the kind of way we experience spoken words relating to some important matter which involve some action on the part of the hearer, or matters which affect a third person. In such a situation, one should of course do nothing about it nor consider doing anything without taking the advice of a wise director. One should ask of God with clear insight and understanding as to whether it did come from God or not.

It is not merely a question of investigating whether it is rational or not but simply whether it is His Master's wish. For obedience to what He commands is the essential. If we experience this, then we cannot allow our spiritual director to take the place of God when there is no doubt that these words are His command. If the matter is complex, these words will help us to have courage, and our Lord will also speak to the director. If such is His pleasure, He will enable him to recognize that this is the work of His Spirit. If God does not do so, we have no further obligations. To act differently from what we have been told and to be guided therein by our own opinion is a very dangerous practice. So I warn you, sisters, in the name of our Lord, to beware lest this should ever happen to you.

There is another way in which our Lord speaks to the soul. I consider with some certainty that it really comes from Him, and that is by a certain intellectual vision about which I will speak later. This takes place in the interior of the soul. So clearly are the words heard within the soul that they are as words spoken by our Lord Himself. So intimate is the manner of their communication that the very way in which the soul understands them, together with the effects which are produced by the vision itself, convinces the soul and makes it absolutely sure that in no way can this be the work of the devil. The experience leaves such wonderful effects that these are enough to make us believe the reality of what has happened.

*Other forms of locution from God: by vision*

It becomes quite clear that this does not proceed from the imagination, and whoever reflects upon it will always be certain of this for the following reasons.

*Signs that they are not mere imagination*

First, there is a difference in the clarity of the discourse. It is so plain that the soul remembers every syllable of what

*1. Their clarity*

is heard. Likewise it knows in what particular style the words are spoken, although all may not have one meaning. In contrast, what arises in the fancy or imagination is never spoken so clearly nor so distinctly but is like something uttered by a person who is half asleep.

**2. Their sudden revelation**

Second, what is heard was often not thought of before. What I mean is that it comes unexpectedly. Sometimes when the person is engaged in conversation, an answer is given which appears only to come suddenly through our thoughts, or which has passed through them before. Often it is in things of which we had no remembrance that they had been or could be so. Hence the imagination could not have framed them. The soul is not deceived, therefore, in fancying what it had not previously desired, nor wished for, nor paid attention to.

**3. Their importance**

Third, when God speaks we are like someone who only hears. When it arises from the imagination it is as if one is composing gradually what he wishes to hear.

**4. Their amplification**

Fourth, there is a great difference in the words themselves from anything one normally hears. For example, in a genuine discourse, one word may convey a whole world of meaning which the understanding itself could never have constructed so rapidly and put into human language.

**5. Their conviction**

Fifth, it is commonly experienced that not only words can be heard but a way of hearing them is given to us which I cannot explain. There is a depth to understanding which is unutterable. It is a very subtle thing, for which our Lord should be praised.

With respect to these different ways and indeed the distinction between them there are now some persons who are very skeptical. I particularly know someone who has tried them by experience [that is, Teresa herself]. Still there may be others who could not fully understand them. But this person that I speak of has, I know, considered them with much scrutiny. For our Lord has very often bestowed this favor upon her [Teresa].

The greatest doubt which she had was whether she was imagining the whole thing when she first experienced it. For when discourses come from the devil, their source can be much more quickly recognizable, although his wiles are so numerous that he can readily deceive and reproduce the Spirit of light. I believe he does this by pronouncing his words very clearly so that there will be no more doubt about their being understood than if they were being spoken by the Spirit of truth. He is not able to counterfeit the effects which have been described so that, instead of leaving the soul in peace and light, there only ensues restlessness and conflict. So he can do little or no damage if the soul be humble and does what I have mentioned.

If the favors and gifts come from our Lord, let the soul carefully observe whether it considers itself to be better for them. If when it hears more loving expressions, it is not humbled and awed by them, then let the soul be assured that it is *not* the Spirit of God. For the greater the favor that is given, the less will the soul esteem itself. It will remember its sins all the more, and, forgetting self-interest, it will employ itself more frequently in seeking by will and remembrance only what is for the honor and glory of God. The soul will then proceed more cautiously in case it neglects to do the will of God. Likewise, it will understand more certainly that it does not deserve favors but rather deserves hell.

Since all these things and the favors it receives produce such effects, let not the soul be troubled. Trust rather in the mercy of our Lord, Who is faithful and will not suffer the devil to delude it. However, it is always best for the soul to live in fear.

May His Divine Majesty grant that we ever strive to please Him and ever forget ourselves. Amen. May our Lord grant that I have correctly explained what I intended, and may it serve as some direction for those who receive such favors.

**Part Four: Great Courage Required to Experience Such Things from God**

In the midst of all these efforts and trials, what rest can the poor butterfly take? For they all serve to enflame her desires to enjoy her Spouse. His Majesty, knowing our weakness, continues to prepare the soul so that it may have the courage to choose Him for its Spouse in these and other ways.

You may think it is absurd, and will perhaps laugh at my saying this, for courage is what you may not think is needed by a woman who would desire to be espoused to a king. Yet I believe it is so, as regards an earthly king.

But I tell you, to be espoused to the King of Heaven requires much more courage than you can imagine. For our nature is too mean and timorous for so sublime a reality. Indeed, I think it is certain that this would be impossible if God did not grant the strength for such an undertaking. Let us therefore praise Him exceedingly that He is pleased to let us know Him. Amen. Amen.

**Part Five: "The Flight of the Spirit" Called Rapture**

There is a second kind of rapture which I call "the flight of the spirit." Although it is substantially the same as an ordinary rapture, yet it is experienced in a very different way inwardly. For sometimes the soul becomes aware of such a rapid movement that the spirit seems to be swept away at great speed. At first this may cause much fear and that is why I told you that real courage was required in such an experience. Trust, confidence, and absolute resignation into the hands of our Lord are required as well to yield the soul to whatever He desires.

There is no way such an experience can be resisted. It seems to suggest that God wants the soul to be as often and truly resigned into His hands so that it has no more right to itself, and hence it is manifestly carried in this kind of motion.

This reminds us of that cistern of water that was filled at one stage quietly and gently—I mean without any noise.

Likewise this great God, Who controls all the springs of water, and does not allow the sea to overflow its bounds, here lets loose the streams and currents from which the water comes. With great force there rises up so tremendous a wave that this little ship is lifted up on high. If in such a circumstance a ship can do nothing, nor any pilot or crew has any power to control it when the waves assault it furiously, and the billows toss it about at their will, how much less can the interior of the soul remain where it would wish to be. Likewise, neither the senses nor the faculties can be in control when they are so controlled.

Merely in writing about this, sisters, makes me astounded when I reflect how vast is the power of this great King and Emperor Who is manifested by such experiences.

## Part Six: Practical Effects of Such Experiences

From the experience of such sublime favors, the soul ardently desires to wholly enjoy Him who bestows them upon it. These longings become so keen that life becomes a delicious torture and the soul even longs to die. Thus with continual tears, the soul begs of God that He would take it out of this exile. Everything that it sees in this life wearies it. In solitude it finds some ease, but then sorrow once more comes upon it.

In a word, this poor butterfly can find no lasting repose. Indeed, as the soul is so full of tender love, any opportunity which presents itself to her for rekindling this fire more and more makes her take wings. Hence in these Mansions, raptures are very common, without her having any means to avoid them, even when they take place in public. Persecutions and slanders immediately follow. For although she desires to be without fear, yet she is not left on her own, because there are many who cause them, especially confessors.

Although on the one hand she seems to have great security within the interior of her soul, especially when she is all alone with God, yet on the other hand she is in great

*Prayer is essential in such experiences.*

affliction. She fears lest the devil might deceive her, so as to make her offend Him Whom she loves so tenderly. She is scarcely affected about what other people think and say against her, especially when her own confessor afflicts her and tells her she could do more to prevent these raptures. So she does nothing but ask everyone to pray for her, and to beseech His Majesty to guide her by some other way.

But You do not need to pity her for, aided by Your power, she will be able to bear many crosses. She is determined to do so—she desires to bear them all. Stretch out Your mighty arm, O Lord! Let not her life be wasted on base things. Rather let Your Greatness appear in so low and womanish a creature that all men, seeing that she can do nothing of herself, may praise You, cost what it may. For this is what she desires, and she would give a thousand lives (if she had so many) that so by her means, one soul might praise You a little more. She would consider them all as being well-lived, knowing perfectly well that she does not deserve to suffer the least cross for You, and how much less death!

God gives souls like these the utmost desire not to offend Him in the slightest things, and if possible, of not committing even the smallest imperfection. For this reason alone, if there were no other, she would fly from all people. So she envies those who live, and who formerly lived, in deserts. On the one hand, the soul would like to plunge directly into the midst of the world in order to try to be instrumental in making only one soul praise God the more earnestly. As a woman, she grieves that her sex puts a disadvantage upon her which prevents her from doing so. So she envies those very much who have the power of crying out with a loud voice, and of proclaiming Who this great God of Hosts is.

The frailty of the soul in such experiences   Oh, poor little butterfly! You are so handicapped by many fetters which will not allow you to fly away as you would desire. Have pity on her, my God! So dispose everything that she will be able to in some degree fulfill her desires for Your honor and glory. Look not upon the slightness of her merits, nor upon her natural depravity.

For You are able, O Lord, to cause the mighty sea to retire, and the great Jordan to divide, and to do the impossible!

Such desires occur in mature people. The devil may well make them imagine they are all the more expert in their proficiency because of the number of experiences they have had. Hence it is always good to walk with a sense of fear. At the same time, I do not believe that the devil can ever fill the soul with the quiet and peace. Rather the feelings that he arouses are passionate ones, like those which we experience when we are troubled by the affairs of the world.

## Part Seven: Increased Sensitivity to Sin

Perhaps you may think, sisters, that those souls to whom our Lord communicates Himself in a special way will be so secure in their enjoyment of Him forever as never to fear or to bewail their former sins. Those who may particularly think this are those who have not been blessed by such favors. For if they ever had experienced them, and they came from God, they would understand what I am saying. But this is a great mistake, since the sorrow for sin in fact really increases all the more when more favors are received from God. For my part I believe this is because, until we arrive where nothing can disturb us, this sorrow will never leave us.

It is true that this affliction can affect us more at one time than another, and also in different ways. For such a soul does not reflect on the punishment that it deserves for its sins so much as on how ungrateful it has been to the One to Whom it owes so much, and Who so greatly deserves to be served. For by these sublime favors which He communicates to it, the soul discovers so much better the greatness of God. It is astonished at its boldness. It laments its disrespect. Its conduct seems so foolish that it can never cease to lament for it. For it remembers such base things have caused it to desert so great a Majesty.

The soul thinks more on these things than on the blessings that it has received, which although they are so great,

**A favored soul is, above all, contrite.**

these blessings seem like the central volume of water in a fast moving stream that remove it all the time. Yet its sins also appear like the muddy bottom that remains in its memory, and which is a heavy cross to it.

I do not consider it safe for a soul, however much it may be favored by God, to forget how it was sometimes in a miserable condition. Although this be a painful thought, yet in many respects it is of great advantage. Because I have been so sinful, this perhaps is the reason why it appears so to me, and why I have the remembrance always in my mind. Those who have been good will have nothing to lament over, although there are always imperfections as long as we live in this mortal body.

This pain is increased by God's forgiveness.

The pain is not relieved at all by considering that our Lord has already pardoned our sins, and forgotten them. Rather it is increased, for it beholds great goodness and mercy bestowed upon one who deserves nothing but hell. I think this must have been the great suffering which Peter and Mary Magdalene endured. For as they possessed so intense a love, and had received so many favors, and knew the greatness and majesty of God, so the remembrance of their sins must have been a very great affliction to them. They must have felt it all the more tenderly.

You may likewise imagine that one who enjoys such high favors needs not to meditate upon the mysteries of the most sacred humanity of Christ our Lord. For is the soul not already wholly employed and occupied in love? But it is impossible that a soul which has received so much from God should forget the remembrance of such precious proofs of His love.

The soul understands these mysteries in a more perfect way. For the understanding represents them to it, and they become so fixed in its memory that merely beholding our Lord prostrate on the ground in that dreadful sweat (in the Garden of Gethsemane) is sufficient to occupy it, not for one hour only, but for many days.

There are certain principles, and likewise methods, which some souls make use of who are beginning to arrive at the Prayer of Quiet. They relish the sweets and delights which our Lord gives them there. They esteem it a great thing to be continually pleasing themselves with such experiences. Now let them believe me, and not be too absorbed, for life is long and in it are many troubles. Therefore, in order to bear such troubles with perfection, we must consider how our pattern Jesus Christ and how His apostles and saints bore them.

The presence of our good Jesus is very good company. We must not leave Him. He is exceedingly pleased when we know His sufferings, although we sometimes lose our own pleasure and delight. Much more is He pleased because the delight found in prayer is not so frequent; then we may have time for everything. [Here Teresa warns those who want to indulge in raptures and ecstasies rather than to consistently meditate upon the passion of our Lord in their times of contemplation.]

## Part Eight: Do Not Desire to Seek Visions*

I will say no more about this subject except first to earnestly advise you that, although you know God bestows these favors on some souls, you must never ask Him for them, nor desire Him to lead you in this way. For although it may seem to you very desirable to be greatly esteemed, yet it is not fitting to ask.

In the first place, it shows a lack of humility to desire what you have never deserved. So I believe that whoever desires such experiences shows little humility. A working man is far from desiring to be made a king, and considers indeed that such a thing is impossible, because he does not deserve it. In the same way is a humble person far removed from wishing for such divine favors. I am certain that they will never be bestowed except on those who are humble in heart. For before our Lord bestows these favors, He gives us a true knowledge of ourselves. We ought to truly understand that the soul has a very great favor shown her in not being cast into hell. Such gratitude we should exercise.

*To seek such visions is to lack humility.*

*Part Eight in the original work of Teresa is excluded.

**It is to be suscep-
tible to deception.**

Second, such a person is very likely to be deceived, or is in great danger of it, since the devil requires no more than, to find one small door open in order to lead us into a thousand deceits.

**It stimulates the
imagination.**

Third, when the desire is strong, and the imagination is vivid, it makes one think that he sees and hears what he wants to. Such stimulation happens to those who in the daytime think upon it very earnestly and will dream of it during the night.

**It is
presumptuous.**

Fourth, it is very presumptuous for you to desire to choose a way for yourselves when you do not know what is best for you. Rather, you should refer the whole matter to our Lord Who knows you best, in order that He may lead you in the way that He thinks fit.

**It complicates the
emotional stress
of life.**

Fifth, the resultant troubles are not as few as you can imagine. Rather, they are innumerable and of various kinds which such souls endure. How do you know whether you will be able then to endure them?

**It may lead to
a loss of faith.**

Sixth, it may happen that you might lose what you thought you had gained by this very experience. This is what happened to Saul when he was made king.

So in summary, sisters, there are other reasons for not desiring visions which we must remember. Believe me that the surest thing to do is to desire only the will of God. Let us place ourselves entirely in His hands, for He loves us so much and we cannot do wrong if, with a determined will, we persevere in His love. You must also know that more glory is not merited by receiving many of these favors. Rather, we are obliged to serve Him all the more because of them.

May He be praised forever Who is pleased to reveal His glory in humbling Himself to converse with such miserable creatures. Amen.

## THE SEVENTH MANSIONS: THE PRAYER OF MARRIAGE TO JESUS AS A TOTAL TRANSFERENCE OF LIFE

### Part One: What More Can Be Said?

You may think, sisters, that if so much has already been said regarding the spiritual way, that nothing more can possibly be added. But it is a great mistake to think so, for as God's greatness has no limits, so neither have His works. Who is able to mention all His mercies and marvels? It is impossible. So never wonder at what has been said, or what shall be said, because it is all a mere fraction in comparison with what could be said concerning God. He has been very merciful to us in having communicated these things to one person [that is, Teresa herself], by whom we might be able to know them. But the more we are made aware that He communicates Himself to creatures, the more shall we praise His greatness and endeavor to have more esteem of that soul in which our Lord takes such pleasure and delight. Each one of us has such a soul. But since we do not prize it as a creature that is made after the image of God should value it, therefore we do not understand the great secrets which the soul contains.

If, however, it is the will of His Majesty to guide my pen, may He bestow upon me the favor of enabling me to explain something of the many things which are yet to be mentioned, and which He reveals to those whom He conducts into these Mansions. Earnestly I have requested this favor from His Majesty, since He knows that my only desire is to let His mercies be revealed. I hope, sisters, that He will grant me this favor; not for my sake, but for yours, in order that you may understand how important it is for your Spouse to celebrate this spiritual marriage with your souls. For it brings with it many blessings. It is also necessary that you should put no obstacle in the way.

*O Great God! Being such a miserable creature, and having to speak on a subject which I am so undeserving to understand, I tremble. The truth is, I have been thrown into great confusion, for I have been uncertain whether it is better to finish these*

**The Mansions are yet to be explored.**

*Mansions in a few words. I am so much afraid that others may think that my knowledge of it comes from experience, and this makes me feel very ashamed. The fact is, knowing myself as I do, such a thought is terrible. On the other hand, whatever Your judgment may be, it has appeared to me that this shame is due to weakness and temptation.*

Let the whole world cry out against me, so long as God is praised and He is understood a little more. I may be dead before this book is seen by others. May He be blessed Who lives and shall live forever. Amen.

When our Lord is pleased to be moved by what the soul suffers, and the soul has suffered through her desires for Him, He allows her to enter His Seventh Mansions. For He has now spiritually chosen her as His spouse for the consummation of the spiritual nuptials. For just as He has an abiding place in heaven where His Majesty dwells alone, so He must needs have an abiding place in the soul. Let us call this a sacred heaven.

It is very important for us, sisters, not to imagine that the soul is somehow darkened. Although we may not see it, we generally think that there is no other interior light except what we see, and that there is in the soul a certain obscurity. Indeed, I grant this to you regarding a soul which is not in a state of grace, because this soul is not capable of receiving the light, as I mentioned in the First Mansions.

**See the soul as a vast mystery before God.** We must not think of the soul as a limited and insignificant creature, but as an internal world that contains many beautiful Mansions. When His Majesty is pleased to bestow upon the soul the above mentioned favor of this divine espousals, He brings her into His own Mansions. His Majesty does not wish this to be as at other times, when He sends it raptures. At that moment it is united with Him as in the above mentioned Prayer of Union. Then the soul does not feel called upon to enter into its own center, as it is here in these Mansions: but it is affected only in its higher part.

However, it really matters little what is going on. Whatever it does, the Lord unites the soul with Himself.

But it becomes both blind and dumb as happened to the Apostle Paul at his conversion (Acts 9:8). This was done to prevent the soul from having any sense of how, or in what way, that favor is bestowed which it enjoys. What the soul is conscious of is the great delight of realizing it is so near to God. But when He unites it with Him, it neither understands nor knows anything; for all the faculties are lost and absorbed.

Here, however, everything is different in these Mansions. For our good God is pleased to take away the scales from our eyes, that the soul may see and understand something of the favor which He bestows upon it. He does this in a strange way. The soul is brought into these Mansions by the conviction of faith in which, by the representation of the truth, the most Holy Trinity reveal Themselves to the soul, in all Three Persons. The soul becomes enkindled as if it were enveloped in a cloud of extraordinary brightness. These Three Persons are distinct, and by a wonderful knowledge given to the soul, it understands with great truth that all these Three Persons are one substance, one power, one knowledge, and one God alone.

*Faith in the Triune God is the entry into these Mansions.*

Hence, what we behold with faith, the soul here understands, as one may say, by sight. Although this sight is not with the eyes of the body, because it is not an imaginary vision. All the Three Persons here communicate Themselves to it and speak to the soul, making it understand those words mentioned in the Gospel where our Lord said: "That He and the Father, and the Holy Ghost, would come and dwell with the soul that loves Him and keeps His commands" (John 14:23).

O my God! What a different thing from hearing these words to actually understanding how true they really are! Such a soul is every day more and more astonished, because these words never seem to depart from it. But it clearly sees (in the manner described above) that they are in the deepest recess of the soul. Since it never learned to express this, it cannot do so, but it only perceives that this divine company is within itself.

In spite of such mystical experiences, ordinary living must go on.

You might think that with such an experience the soul is so out of itself and so absorbed by it that it can attend to nothing else. On the contrary, it is more occupied than before in whatever relates to the service of God. When it is not so engaged, it is still resting in this delightful companionship. Unless the soul fails God, He will never fail it; for I believe He gives it the most certain assurance of His Presence. The soul has great confidence that God will never leave it and that, having granted her this blessing, He will not allow it to lose this confidence. Well may the soul think this, although all the time the soul walks more carefully than ever, so that He may not be displeased in anything.

Such light is more like companionship than illumination.

Experiencing this Presence within the soul is not necessarily a more dear experience than when the soul first encountered it. For it is impossible for the soul to think of anything else, or even live among men, when it has this vividness. Although the light which accompanies it may not always be so clear, the soul is aware that it is constantly experiencing this companionship.

We might compare this to the analogy of a person who is with others in a very bright room. Suppose, then, that the shutters are closed so that all the people are then in darkness. The light by which they originally could be seen has been removed, and until it is restored, we are unable to see them. Nonetheless, we are aware that they are still there. So it may be asked whether this person will look upon them again if the light returns. To do this is not in the soul's power. For it depends only on when our Lord is pleased to open the shutters of the understanding. His mercy is sufficient for the soul, for He will never leave it, and He desires that the soul should understand this clearly so.

Such companionship prepares the soul for yet a greater favor.

Yet it does seem that His Divine Majesty, by means of this wonderful companionship, is preparing the soul for some great favor. For it is clear that this soul is being greatly strengthened to advance in maturity and to cast away the fear that it sometimes had before when other favors were bestowed upon it. This proves to be so, for the person found herself [that is, Teresa] improved in everything, and she thought that in spite of all the cares and troubles she had met with, the soul seemed never to move from that dwelling place. In a sense, there was a division between her and her soul. For meeting with great troubles which occurred to her a short time after God had bestowed this favor upon her, she complained of her soul, as Martha did of Mary. For she was not always enjoying this quiet. Instead, she felt plunged into so many troubles and occupations that she would not keep her soul's company.

You may think this ridiculous, but it is what really happens. Of course, the soul is never really divided; but this impression is a very common experience. For it is possible to observe a clear difference between the soul and the spirit. Although they are, in general, one and the same thing, yet between them they may perceive a subtle distinction, that sometimes seems to work in one way different from the other. So also is the knowledge which our Lord gives them. It also seems to me that the soul is distinct from the faculties. In a word, there are so many subtle differences in our inward being that it would be presumptuous for me to attempt to explain them. In heaven we shall see them, if our Lord in His goodness shall grant us the favor of bringing us there where we shall understand these secrets.

*Teresa senses a distinction between soul and spirit yet knows it is still one person.*

## Part Two: Distinction between Spiritual Union and Spiritual Marriage

Although such a sublime favor cannot be entirely possessed within this life, let us now speak of the divine and spiritual marriage. We do so tentatively, for if we were to withdraw ourselves from God, this great blessing would be lost. The first time God bestows this favor, His Majesty is pleased to reveal Himself to the soul by an imaginary vision of His Most Sacred Humanity. He does this in order that the soul may clearly understand it, and that the soul

*The spiritual union of the soul with God is made real by Christ's Incarnation.*

not be ignorant that it receives such an immense gift. To others, He may appear in another form. But to her of whom we speak [Teresa], our Lord showed Himself—immediately after she had communicated—in a figure of great splendor, beauty, and majesty, just as He was after His resurrection. He said to her, "Now is the time that you should consider My affairs as yours, and I will take care of yours." Other words were uttered which are more fit to be felt than spoken about.

A special visitation experienced by Teresa

You may think this was nothing new, because at other times our Lord has presented Himself to this soul in the same way. But this was so very different that it left her quite overwhelmed and astonished. For this vision came with great force and with words which He spoke. In the interior of her soul, where He revealed Himself to her, she had never experienced such visions like these before. For you must understand that there is a vast difference between this and the preceding Mansions. The difference is as great as between those who are only engaged and those who are really married.

I have already mentioned that, although these analogies are used because none more suitable can be found, yet it must be understood that here the body is no more remembered than if the soul were out of it. Between the spiritual marriage and the body there is even less connection. For this secret union is effected in the interior center of the soul which must surely be where God Himself resides. He requires no door to enter.

In all that I have said until now, the effects seem to be brought about by means of the senses and the faculties, and the representations of our Lord's humanity must certainly be of this nature. But what takes place here in the union of the spiritual marriage is very different. For here our Lord appears in the center of the soul, not by images, but in the conviction of faith. This appearance is subtler than those that I have previously mentioned. He appears, just as He did to the apostles, without entering in through the door, when He said to them: "Peace be unto you" (John 20:19-22).

What God here communicates to the soul in an instant is so intimate a secret, and so sublime a grace, that the soul feels excessive joy that is incomparable to anything that I know of. All I can say is that our Lord is pleased at that moment to reveal to the soul the glory which is in heaven. This He does in a more sublime way than by any vision or other spiritual delight.

*Such experience of God is the glory of heaven.*

More cannot be said or indeed understood than that this soul becomes one with God. Being Himself a Spirit, His Majesty is pleased to reveal the love that He has for us by showing to some persons the extent of that love so that we may praise His greatness. For He has vouchsafed to unite Himself to a creature in such a way that, as husband and wife cannot be separated, so He will never be separated from the soul.

The King is in His palace, yet there may be many wars within His Kingdom. Many offensive things may be committed. Yet He does not on this account cease to be on His throne. So it is here. Although there can be many tumults and many poisonous creatures in the other Mansions, and the noise of them is heard, yet no such things can enter into these Mansions. Nor can the soul be forcibly removed from here. Although they may give the soul pain, yet it is not such as will disturb it and deprive it of its peace. For the passions are now subdued in such a way that they are afraid to enter here, because they will go away still more mortified. The whole body is in pain. But if the head be sound, no harm can be done to it.

*Nothing can disturb such union.*

I smile at these analogies, for they do not really satisfy me. But I can find no better ones. Whatever you may think of them, I have spoken the truth.

## CONCLUSION

When I began to write this discourse, I felt the confusion mentioned earlier. Yet after it was finished, I was deeply satisfied with it, and I considered my effort to be well rewarded.

Therefore, considering your very strict enclosure, and the few recreations that you have, my sisters, and the lack of conveniences which are required in some of our monasteries, I think it will be some pleasure to you to recreate yourselves within this "Interior Castle," a castle which you may enter without any permission from me or anyone else. Amen. And Amen.

# VIII
# Practical Consequences
# of a Life of Prayer

 e have said before that this butterfly dies with great joy, because she has found rest. This one knows that Christ lives within her. Let us now consider what kind of a life she leads, what is the difference between her present state and her former existence when she was alive. For we shall see by the effects whether what has been described is true. As far as I can understand, these are some of the following effects.

The first consequence is a forgetfulness of self. She truly seems, as I have said, to no longer exist. She is affected in such a way that she neither knows herself, nor does she remember that there is either heaven, life, or any honor that is destined for her. She is entirely engaged in seeking only the glory of God.

**1. Self-forgetfulness**

The words spoken by His Majesty have convinced her to mind His affairs and that He will take care of hers. So she is not troubled by whatever happens to her. She is so unconscious in her self-forgetfulness that she seems no longer to exist; nor has she any desire to go on living except when she perceives that she can in some way advance the honor and glory of God. It is for this that she would joyously lay down her life.

But do not imagine, daughters, that because of this she neglects to take any care about eating and sleeping or in doing everything which she is obliged to do by her state of

213

life. We are speaking rather here of interior matters. As regards exterior works, little can be said. Rather, it is an affliction to her to consider how all that she is able to do by her own strength is worthless. Whatever she understands will be conducive to the glory of our Lord will not be omitted by her for anything in the world.

**2. Desire to accept suffering**     The second effect is a great desire to suffer. Yet it is not like what she formerly had, for that used to worry her. The desire which such souls have that God's will may be done in them is so excessive that they receive with joy whatever His Majesty sends them. So if He wishes them to suffer, they are content. If not, they do not torment themselves about it, as they used to do on other occasions.

These souls, likewise, feel a great interior joy when they are persecuted, for then they enjoy more peace than I have ever spoken about. They do not feel the least hatred against their persecutors. Indeed, they experience for them a particular kind of affection. They love them so much that if they see them in any affliction, they feel it keenly and pity them. And they most sincerely pray to God for them that He would, in exchange, bestow these afflictions on themselves, all in order that they might not offend His Majesty.

**3. Desire to help others**     If they are so willing to endure such sufferings and afflictions and be prepared to die in order to enjoy our Lord, what about their desires to serve Him? May He be praised through their lives in this way, too?

Yes. They long to help others, and so not only do they not desire to die, but they long to be able to live many years. They will endure very many crosses in order that our Lord, by their means, may be honored, however little it may be. Although they are quite sure that, when the soul leaves the body they will immediately enjoy God, they make no account of this. And they make little about the glory which the saints possess. For they do not desire it at present, since all their glory consists in their being able to assist their crucified Lord in some way. When they see the Lord so much offended, and especially when there are so few who desire above all else to have His honor truly in their hearts, these servants only wish to live for Him all the more.

Sometimes when His servants forget their purpose, the desires of enjoying God and of leaving this land of exile come before them with tenderness. God is tender indeed considering how little they really serve Him. But immediately they return to themselves and reflect how they have Him continually before them, and with this they are satisfied. So they offer to His Majesty their willingness once more to live for Him, the most precious offering that they could make to Him. They have no fear of death, but look upon it as a sweet trance. The fact is that He Who before gave them those desires with such excessive pain, now gives this sweet desire. So may He be blessed and praised forever!

*4. A willingness to serve here rather than to be "with Christ"*

The desires of these hearts do not now long after consolation and delight, simply because they know they have Christ our Lord always with them. His Majesty now lives within them. It is clear that as His life was nothing else but a continual sorrow, so He makes theirs likewise, at least by a longing for Him. He leads them in weakness, giving them, when He sees necessary, His strength. They feel detached from everything, and they have the desire of being in solitude or engaged in those things which relate to the well-being of some soul. They have no aridities, nor internal distresses, but always a remembrance and tenderness for our Lord. They would gladly do nothing but praise Him.

*5. No need to seek comfort because of His abiding presence*

When such servants become negligent of their duties, our Lord Himself stimulates them. It is clearly seen that this impulse (I do not know what else to call it) proceeds from the interior of the soul. Here it is done with great sweetness, coming neither from the imagination nor from the memory, nor from any other thing which might suggest that the soul took initiative. This is so normal, and happens so frequently, that one can readily observe this. For like a fire which, however large it may be, does not issue its flames downwards, but upwards, so this internal motion of the soul proceeds from its very center and thus stimulates the faculties (*Interior Castle*, VII).

## SOME MAXIMS ON THE CONDUCT OF LIFE

1. However fertile untilled soil may be, it will only produce thistles and thorns; and so it is with a man's mind.
2. Always speak well of spiritual things.
3. When you are in a crowd, always speak little.
4. Be modest in all that you do or say.
5. Never contend vigorously, especially in matters which are of little importance.
6. Speak to everyone with a restrained cheerfulness.
7. Never have contempt for anyone.
8. Never reprove anyone except discreetly, humbly, and with a sense of your own inadequacy.
9. Accommodate yourself to the mood of the person to whom you are speaking. Be happy with those who are happy, and sad with those who are sad. In brief, be all things to all men so that you may gain all (1 Corinthians 9:22).
10. Never speak without carefully weighing your words, and commend them earnestly to our Lord in case you say anything that may displease Him.
11. Never make excuses for yourself, except when it is most probable that you are right.
12. Never mention anything about yourself concerning what deserves praise—such as your scholarship, your virtues, or your family background—unless you have hope that some common profit will come from it. So if you do speak about it, let it be done with humility, and always remember that these gifts come from the hand of God.
13. Never exaggerate, but express your opinion with moderation.
14. In all your conversations and talks, try always to introduce spiritual topics. In this way you will avoid

idle words and backbiting.

15. Never be dogmatic unless you are sure that it is true.

16. Never offer to give your opinion on anything unless you are asked for it, or love requires you to do so.

17. When anyone speaks to you on spiritual matters, listen humbly and as a disciple, and apply to yourself all the good things that you hear.

18. To your spiritual director disclose all your temptations and imperfections as well as your difficulties, so that he may give you advice and help you to provide a remedy to overcome them.

19. Do not stay outside yourself. Leave only for some good reason. When you do go out, ask God for grace not to offend Him.

20. Do not eat or drink, except at proper times, and then always give thanks to God heartily.

21. Do everything as if you were really in the presence of His Majesty, for by this means the soul will profit much.

22. Do not listen to bad things about or speak ill of anyone, except to properly evaluate yourself. When you begin to like doing this, you are making spiritual progress.

23. Every action you do, offer it up to God. Pray also that it may lead to His honor and glory.

24. When you are happy, do not express your joy by laughing in excess. Let it be humble, modest, affable, and edifying.

25. Imagine yourself to be the servant of everyone. Consider Christ our Lord in all that you do. Thus you will show others respect and reverence.

26. Always be ready to fulfill your vow of obedience, as if Christ our Lord, in the person of your Superior, had commanded you.

27. Examine your conscience in all you do and at all times. Having seen your own faults, seek with God's help to amend them. By following in this way you will attain spiritual maturity.

28. Do not take any notice of the defects of others, but concentrate on their vitures. Mind your own defects.

Always cherish intense desires to suffer for Christ's sake in everytl..ng, and on every occasion.

29. Every day make frequent oblations of yourself to God, and do this with great fervor.

30. Whatever you meditate upon first thing in the morning, have before you all the day long; and put into practice the desires which He has given you in your time of prayer. This will be of great benefit to you.

31. Carefully observe the thoughts with which our Lord may inspire you, and put into practice the desires which He gives you in prayer.

32. Always avoid being singular, as far as you can, for in community life to be "odd-man-out" is a great evil.

33. Read the rules and regulations of your Order frequently, and observe them faithfully.

34. Reflect upon the providence and wisdom of God in all created things. Give thanks to God in praise for them all.

35. Detach your heart from every object. Rather seek God and you will find Him.

36. Never express outwardly any devotion which you do not inwardly experience, though you may rightly conceal any lack of devotion.

37. Do not reveal any inward devotion except in special circumstances. Both St. Francis and St. Bernard say: "I keep my secret to myself."

38. Do not complain about your food, whether it is good or bad. Remember the gall and vinegar of Jesus Christ.

39. Do not speak to anyone at table and do not raise your eyes to look at another person [for Teresa's Order had silence at the table].

40. Meditate upon the heavenly table, and upon its food, which is God Himself. His guests are the angels. Raise up your eyes to the table and desire to sit down at it.

41. In the presence of your Superior, seek to see Jesus Christ. Only speak when it is necessary and with real reverence.

42. Never do anything which you would not do before everyone.
43. Never compare one person with another, for comparisons are odious.
44. When you are blamed for anything, receive the reproof with both inner and outward humility. Pray to God for the person who has given you the reproof.
45. If one Superior orders you to do something, do not tell that someone else has ordered you to do the opposite. Realize that both of them acted with good intentions and obey the order as it is given to you.
46. Do not be curious to ask questions about things that are not your business.
47. Remember to bewail your past life and your present tepidity, and how unprepared you are for going to heaven. In this way you may live in fear, which is a cause of great blessing.
48. Always do what those in your community want you to do, provided it is not contrary to obedience. Answer them with humility and gentleness.
49. Except in great cases of need, do not ask for any special food or clothing.
50. Never fail to constantly humble and mortify yourself in every way, until the end of your life.
51. Always accustom yourself to exercise frequent acts of love, for they enkindle and soften the soul.
52. Actualize all the other virtues.
53. Offer all things to the Eternal Father, in union with the merits of His Son, Jesus Christ.
54. Be gentle with everyone, but be severe with yourself.
55. On the festivals of the saints, meditate upon their virtues and ask the Lord to bestow them upon you.
56. Every night diligently examine your own conscience.
57. On the occasions when you receive communion, let your prayer consist in realizing that, miserable as you are, you will be allowed to receive God. At night, consider that you have received Him.
58. If you are a Superior, never blame anyone in anger. When your anger has passed over, then your reproof will be beneficial.

59. Seek to conduct all your affairs with devotion and with the intent to improve yourself.

60. Exercise yourself frequently in the fear of the Lord, for it keeps the soul in contrition and humility.

61. Note how quickly people change, and so how little one can really trust them. So cling closely to God, Who never changes.

62. Try to discuss matters which concern your soul with a spiritual and wise friend. Confide in him and follow him in what he suggests.

63. Every time you communicate, ask some gift of God, through the great mercy which He has shown in coming to your poor soul.

64. In times when you are sad and troubled, do not give up the good works of prayer and penance which you have been in the habit of doing. For the devil will try to persuade you to abandon them, and unsettle you. Rather, practice them more than before, and you will see how quickly the Lord will come to your aid.

65. Do not talk about your temptations and imperfections to the members of your community who have made the least spiritual progress. For if you do, this will harm both them as well as you. Speak only then to those who are more spiritually advanced.

66. Remember that you have only one soul; that you have only one death to die; that you have only one life which is short; that there is but one glory, which is eternal. If you do these things, there will be many things about which you will care nothing.

67. Let your desire be to see God; your fear, that you may lose Him; your grief, that you do not have enough fruition in Him; your joy, that He can bring you to Himself. Then you will live in great peace of mind.

> Let nothing disturb you.
> Let nothing terrify you.
> All things pass away.
> God is unchangeable.
> Patience gains everything.
> He who clings to God wants nothing.

God alone is sufficient.
(*Maxims* of Teresa of Jesus, written for her nuns.)

## ON THE LOVE OF OUR NEIGHBOR

There are only two duties that our Lord requires of us: the love of God, and the love of our neighbor. And, in my opinion, the surest sign for our discovering our love to God is discovering our love to our neighbor. Be assured that the further you advance in the love of your neighbor, the more you are advancing in the love of God.

But alas, how many worms lie gnawing at the roots of our love to our neighbor! Self-love, self-esteem, fault-finding, envy, anger, impatience, and scorn. I assure you I write this with great grief, seeing myself to be so miserable a sinner against all my neighbors.

My sisters, our Lord expects works. Therefore when you see anyone sick, have compassion upon her as if she were yourself. Pity her. Fast that she may eat. Wake that she may sleep.

Again, when you hear anyone commended in praise, rejoice in it as much as if you were commended and praised yourself. This indeed should be easier, because where true humility is, praise is prompted. Cover also your sister's defects as you would cover and not expose your own defects and faults.

As often as an occasion offers, lift up your neighbor's burden. Take it from her heart and put it upon yourself. Satan himself would not be Satan any longer if he could once love his neighbor as himself.

Endeavor, my daughters, as much as you can to be affable to all. Demean yourselves so that all who have to do with you may love your conversation, as they desire to have your way of life. Let no one be short or turned away from the life of virtue and religion by your gloom and morosity. This should concern religious women very much. For the holier they are, the more affable and sociable they should be. Never hold aloof from others because their conversation is not altogether to your taste. Love them, and they will love you, and then they will converse with you, and will become like you, and better than you.

Let not your soul coop itself up in a corner. Or, instead of attaining to greater sanctity in proud, disdainful, and impatient seclusion, the devil will keep you company there. And so he will do your sequestered soul much mischief. Bury evil affections in good works. Therefore, be accessible and affable to all, and love all. Love is an endless enchantment; it is a spell and a fascination.

Love such people as much as you like, as long as they continue in this way. They are few in number, but our Lord will not fail to make it known when there is one who has arrived at such maturity. People may say to you, "there is no need of this; it is enough for us to possess God." But I reply it is a good means of enjoying God, to be able to converse with His friends. Great benefit is always obtained from this. This I know by experience, and next to God, I owe it to such persons as these that I am not myself in hell. For I was very desirous for them to recommend me to God, and I likewise endeavor to do so myself (*The Way of Perfection*, p. 36).

## LETTERS OF TERESA

### To Philip II, King of Spain, 1577.

In defense of her friend and colleague

Jesus, the grace of the Holy Spirit, be always with your Majesty. Amen.

I have heard that a memoir has been presented to your Majesty against Father Gracian. This stratagem of the devil and his servants has indeed terrified me, because it contains a defamation of the character of this servant of God (and such he truly is, for he gives great edification to all of us; whenever he visits our monasteries, I am informed that he always fills the members with renewed fervor). His enemies are now trying to injure those houses in which our Lord is so devoutly served.

For this purpose, they have made use of two Carmelite Friars. One of them was a servant in our own community before he took the vow. But he committed himself in such a way more than once as to plainly show us that he possessed little discernment. The others who are opposed to Father Gracian (because he has power of discipline over them) have induced these Carmelites to sign such foolish charges against the nuns that I would laugh at them, were I not deeply concerned that the devil might be able to create havoc from them. Such accusations, if they were true, would be monstrous, considering the habit we wear.

I beseech your Majesty, for the love of God, not to allow such scandalous charges to be made before a court of justice. Should we give in to this occasion, the world might be inclined to believe that we have done something evil, even though our innocence would be established.

The reformation of the Order that has until now been so blessed by divine goodness might be seriously injured by the least suspicion. Your Majesty will be able to form a judgment on the matter should you be pleased to read that attestation which Father Gracian has thought proper to draw up concerning these monasteries. It includes a testimony of those who have communication with the nuns, and they are persons of much weight and holiness.

Moreover, since the motive of those who have written this memoir can easily be discovered, I beseech your Majesty to examine the matter, because the honor and glory of God are concerned. For if our enemies should see that some attention is paid to their charges, they will not hesitate, in order to prevent a visitation, to accuse as a heretic whoever will undertake to make it. This would not be difficult to do, where there is no fear of God.

I quite sympathize with the sufferings of this servant of God, which he endures with such patience and fortitude. This forces me to beseech your Majesty either to take him under your protection, or to remove the cause of these dangers, for he belongs to a family that is very loyal to your Majesty. Apart from this consideration, he has great merits of his own. I consider him to be a man sent by God.

I remain, your Majesty's unworthy Servant and Subject,

Teresa de Jesus

## Letter to Father Luis de Granada, of the Order of St. Dominic, 1577.

Encouragement
to a great writer
of devotional
literature

The grace of the Holy Spirit be ever with your Reverence. Amen.

I consider myself as one among many who love your Reverence in the Lord for having written such holy and useful works, and who gives thanks to His Majesty for having made you instrumental for the well-being of so many souls. I can think that no obstacle would prevent me from going to hear one whose words console me so much by his writings. But my sex and state of life impede me from doing so.

Independent of this matter, I am obliged to seek people like yourself to calm the fears in which I have now lived for some years. Although I have not deserved this favor, I have been consoled by the command that I have received from His Grace Don Teutonio [Archbishop of Evora] to address this letter to you. This I would not have presumed to do of my own accord. But the confidence which I place in obedience induces me to hope in our Lord that your Reverence will sometimes remember me in your prayers. For I stand in great need of them, both because I have little merit of myself, and because I am exposed to the eyes of the world. I am without a way of being able to justify the good opinion which people have of me.

If your Reverence knew how I was situated, you would be induced to grant me this favor, which I ask as an alms. You know so well the Majesty of God and can easily imagine how great must be the sufferings of one who has led such a wicked life as I have. But although I am so wicked, I have often presumed to ask of our Lord to give your Reverence a long life. May His Majesty grant me this favor, and may your Reverence increase more and more in holiness and divine love.

Your Reverence's unworthy Servant,

Teresa de Jesus, Carmelite

P.S. Don Teutonio is one of those who is deceived in their regard for me. He tells me that he esteems your Reverence highly. In return, your Reverence should visit his Grace, and tell him not to be so credulous without cause.

## Letter to Father John de Jesu Roca, Carmelite at Pastrana, 1579.

Jesus, Mary, and Joseph be in the soul of my Father John de Jesu.

*Teresa's spirit in suffering*

I received your Reverence's letter in this prison [Teresa having been imprisoned by a decree of a general chapter] where I am now filled with the greatest delight. For I endure all my troubles for my God and for my Order. But what grieves me, my Father, is the affliction that your Reverence feels for me. It is this which really troubles me. Do not, however, be troubled, nor anyone else, since I may say, like another Paul, that prisons, labors, persecutions, torments, ignominies, and insults for my Savior and for my Order are to me delights and favors.

I never knew myself to be more free from troubles than I am now. For it belongs to God to help the afflicted and imprisoned with His favor and help. I give my God a thousand thanks. It is right that we should all thank Him for the favor that He has done me by this imprisonment.

My son and father, can there be a greater delight or sweetness, than suffering for the cause of our good God? When were the saints more at the height of their joy than when they were suffering for their God and Savior? This is the most secure and certain path that leads to God, since the cross should be our joy and delight. Let us, then, my father, seek the cross. Let us desire the cross. Let us embrace afflictions, and whenever we have none, woe to the Carmelite Order, woe to us.

You tell me in your letter how the Papal Nuncio has given orders; "that no more convents of our Order should be founded, and that those already erected must be taken down, by the request of the Father General." You also mentioned that the Nuncio is exceedingly angry against me, and considers me to be a troublesome woman, and of a roving disposition. But the world is in arms against me and my sons, who hide themselves in the rocks and the mountains, and in the most retired places, in order not to be found and taken. This is what I lament—what I feel—what grieves me. That for such a sinner and wicked nun as I am, my sons should endure so many persecutions and afflictions, and should be abandoned by all. Yet not by God. For of this I am certain, that He will never forsake us, nor abandon those who love Him so dearly.

But in order that you, my son, and the rest of your brothers may rejoice, I will tell you something very comforting. But this must be in confidence between myself, your Reverence, and Father Mariano. For I would be grieved if others knew about it.

You must know then, my Father, how a certain nun [no doubt Teresa herself] of this house, being in prayer on the vigil of the feast of my Father St. Joseph, saw this saint in company with the blessed virgin and her Son. She noticed how they stood, asking for the reformation (of the Order). Our Lord told her, "that many both in hell and on earth, rejoice greatly to see, as they suppose, the Order dissolved. But that when the Nuncio commanded its dissolution, God confirmed it." He told her to have recourse to the King, who in everything would be to her and her sons as a father. Our Lady and St. Joseph said the same, and several other things I cannot mention in a letter. She was also told that within twenty days, I should be delivered from prison, God so willing. Let us then rejoice, for from this day forward the reform will continue to advance more and more.

What your Reverence should do is to continue in the house of Doña Maria de Mendoza until you hear again from me. Father Mariano must go and present this letter to the King and send another to the Duchess of Pastrana. I hope your Reverence will not leave the house and be arrested, for we shall soon be at liberty ourselves.

I am well and strong, thanks be to God. My companion is displeased. Recommend us to God, and pray in thanksgiving. Do not write to me until I tell you. May God make you a holy and perfect Carmelite.

Father Mariano advises your Reverence and Father

Jerome de la Madre de Dios to consult in secret the Duke de Infantado.

Teresa de Jesus

## To the Most Illustrious Lord Don Teutonio de Braganza, Archbishop of Evora, 1578.

Jesus, the grace of the Holy Spirit be always with your illustrious Lordship. Amen.

*Teresa's courage in the midst of intense persecution inspires others.*

It is now more than two months since I received a letter from your Lordship. I should have answered it immediately, but the reason which obliged me to postpone an answer was that I waited to see if some calm would follow the great troubles which have agitated both our nuns and brothers ever since the month of August. I was also anxious to give your Lordship an account of all that has passed, according to the command that you gave me in your letter. But matters are getting worse and worse every day, as I shall inform your Lordship in the course of this letter.

Be assured, my Lord, that a matter which is so urgently besought from God by souls desiring only that He be served in whatever they request will not fail to be heard. As regards myself, although I am so wicked, I do not forget to be very assiduous in praying for your Lordship and your servants [that is, the nuns]. Here I daily find such souls, the piety of whom embarrasses me greatly. It seems that our Lord is so pleased to bring them to these houses. He chooses them from parts which would not, humanly speaking, have any knowledge of our convents or mode of living.

Hence, my Lord, you may take courage, and doubt not for a moment that it is God's will. I have not the least doubt myself. Indeed, I am even certain that this has been ordered by God, and that His Majesty wants you now to put into execution the good desires that you have of serving Him. You have remained unoccupied too long, and our Lord stands in need of a virtuous prelate.

As for us, we can do but little, being so poor and so lowly. If God does not raise up someone to defend us, then so be His will, although we insist from Him nothing else than His holy service. For malice is raised to such a height and ambition and vanity are so much encouraged—even by those who want to tread them underfoot—that it seems our Lord, as powerful as He is, wants to make use of His creatures in order to maintain righteousness. Without them we shall not be strong enough to gain the victory. For those who in reality should be our defenders have forsaken us. Thus our Lord has chosen others who He knew would be able to help Him.

I am very glad to hear how well the affair of the Duchess of Elche has succeeded. I was deeply troubled about it until I heard of its happy conclusion. God be praised for it.

When our Lord sends us such a multitude of troubles all at once, He usually makes them serve for our greater good. As He knows, we are extremely weak, and as He does all things for our benefit, He proportions our sufferings to our strength. I think the same thing will happen with regard to the storms which have raised up against us now for some time. If I did not know that both our fathers and sisters lived in the strict observance of their rule, I should sometimes fear that their enemies would accomplish the object that they had been aiming at, namely the ruining of the beginning of the reform. The devil has such artifices, and it seems our Lord has given him leave to exert all his power in this affair.

Indeed, the stratagems and diligence which have been made use of to defame us—especially Father Gracian and myself (I am the person against whom most of their blows are really directed)—are so numerous, and the accusations against this good man have been so false, and the memorials which were presented to the King were so scandalous, that your Lordship upon seeing them would have wondered how anyone could have invented such malice. But God was at length pleased that these people should be forced to *unsay* what they had charged us with.

I was much grieved to see so many troubles raised on my account. Such great scandal has been given to the city [of Avila] and so many souls are filled with affliction, for the number of those who have been excommunicated is not less than fifty-four!

The only comfort which is left to me is the thought that I have used every effort to prevent the nuns from electing me. And surely not without reason, for it would have been one of the greatest troubles to me, I assure your Lordship, to have seen myself there as Prioress. It would have been in a house, too, where I never had one hour's good health all the time I lived in it.

I do not know how this affair will end. My great trouble is that our brothers have been taken away without our knowing where they are. But we are afraid they are closely confined [John of the Cross and Father Tostado, who were kidnapped and imprisoned by their own brothers of the order]. This makes me fearful, lest some misfortune has happened to them. May our Lord send a remedy. I hope your Lordship will pardon me if this letter is too long.

Your Lordship's unworthy Servant and Subject,

Teresa de Jesus.

### To Señor Lorenzo de Cepeda [Teresa's brother], 1577.

Jesus be with you.

Serna [the messenger] gives me so little time that I cannot write as long a letter as I would like to. Yet when I am writing you, I do not know how to finish. But as Serna is not always at hand, he must give me a little more time. When I write to Francis, I beg you will not read his letters, for I am afraid he is somewhat inclined to be melancholy, and he finds it difficult to tell me about it. Perhaps God gives him these depressions in order to deliver him from other dangers. I hope, however, to give him a remedy. I find that he is well disposed to receive it, for he believes all that I tell him.

*Practical advice to her own brother*

The book I spoke to you about [her book] is "Meditations on the Lord's Prayer." There you will find many things that may help to direct you in the prayer that you make use of, although not at such length as in my other work. I think what I say you will find in the petition, "Thy kingdom come." Read it over again, at least the Lord's Prayer. Perhaps you will find something there that will help you.

Do not be troubled about your having purchased the farm. [This was an estate about a league from Avila.] It is a temptation from the devil who tries to prevent you from being grateful to God for this great favor which He has bestowed upon you. Be assured that what you have done is for the best in many ways, for you have provided for your children something better than an estate, namely, honor.

Praise God for having given you the farm. Do not think that when you have a great deal of time you must apply more to prayer. This is a mistake. For time well spent in providing a maintenance for our children does not exclude prayer. In one instant, God often gives more than He does in a long period, for His works are not confined to times and seasons.

After the holidays are over, get someone immediately to examine your deeds, and put them in order as they ought to be. What you have spent on the farm is well-spent, and when summer comes you will have great joy in sometimes going there. Jacob did not cease to be a saint for minding his flocks, nor did Abraham, nor did Joachim. When we try to fly from trouble, everything will weary us. So it does for me, and therefore God is pleased that I should have business enough to occupy me. On these matters speak with Franciso Salcedo, who in these business matters can do more for you.

It is a great blessing from God that what gives rest to others tires you. But you must not on this account give up your business. For we must serve God not as we wish, but as He wishes.

It will not be amiss when you wake up with these holy desires for God to sit up a little in your bed, provided however that you always take the necessary sleep. Otherwise, although you may not notice it, you will finally not be able to make much use of prayer. Also take care not to expose yourself too much to the cold, for this does not suit your health.

I do not know why you desire to have these terrors and fears since God conducts you always by the way of love. Perhaps once they were necessary. But do not think it is always the devil who trys to prevent us from praying, for it is a mercy of God that sometimes we are prevented from using prayer. Indeed, I may even say that this is almost as great a blessing as when He gives us the opportunity of much prayer. There are many reasons to prove this, but now I have no time to mention them. The prayer that God gives you is without comparison much greater than thinking upon hell. For it does not depend upon you to give the preference to the one or the other. You cannot help following that which God gives you because such is His will.

Your letters do not tire me. They comfort me very much. So I should feel great pleasure in writing to you more often. But I cannot do so, because my afflictions are so troublesome. Even this very night, I have been prevented from attending to prayer. This gives me no scruples. Still it is a misery to have no leisure. May God give us some, that we may always spend it in His service. Amen.

Your unworthy Servant and Sister,

Teresa de Jesus.

P.S. I thought you would have sent us some of your verses. As for my own, they have neither head nor feet, and yet the nuns sing them. And I remember some which I once composed when I was absorbed in prayer. They seemed to give a sweet restfulness to me after I had composed them. I do not know whether these are exactly as I composed them, hence you see I am desirous of giving you some recreation:

> O Loveliness, that dost exceed
> All other loveliness we know,
> Thou woundest not, yet pain'st indeed,
> And painlessly the soul is freed
> From love of creatures here below.

> Oh, wondrous Juncture, That dost bind
> Two things that nature parts in twain,
> I know not why thou com'st untwin'd,

Since Thou canst strengthen mortal mind
And make it count its ills as gain.

Things being—lest Thou dost unite
With Being that can know no end.
Thou endest not, yet endest quite;
Unforc'd to love, Thou lov'st at sight:
Thy nothingness Thou dost transcend. *

I cannot remember any more. I tell you I must have
been very clever when I made up these lines! God forgive
you, for it is you who made me spend my time in this way;
and yet these stanzas may soften your heart and excite
some devotion in it. Do not speak of them to anyone.
Doña Guiomar and myself were together at the time. Give
my kind regards to her.

---

# A GUIDE TO DEVOTIONAL READING

Our lives are both private and public. Yet the pressures of our culture are to believe that the public activities, duties, and responsibilities are more important. Function then becomes more valued than being. Meanwhile, our souls become starved, and the inner person within us cries out for fulfillment of deeper needs. We long for deeper, more real spiritual life. For we sense we are inauthentic when we are only professors and promoters in the shallows of life. We know that we must nourish this drive to know God.

This reading guide is not a comprehensive list of principles that you must read, master, and know in order to have a "how-to kit" for spirituality. It is, however, suggestive of what might introduce you to the classics of faith and devotion and other helpful material. There is an art in devotional reading that is not exegetical, informational, or literary in its emphasis. For spiritual reading is essentially formative of the soul before God. We need, then, to read this devotional literature in such a way that it helps us be inspired and in tune with God in "the inner man." It is writing which turns us heavenward and forms our character in Christ.

Curiously, however, in spite of the spate of new books and reprints of this spiritual literature, there is little guidance offered about how the art of spiritual reading can and should be cultivated.[1] The following guidelines are suggested to help you focus on this art.

**1. Spiritual reading requires a primary emphasis on the devotional use of Scripture.**

Do not allow the excitement of entering into devotional literature detract you from the priority you give to Bible study and meditation on the Scriptures. Remember, the Scriptures are the canon of the devotion of God's people. They saw the Scriptures as God's revelation and the Holy Spirit as the Guide for its writing.

Devotional reading by theological students is made difficult by the mixture of methods used. This mixture is inevitable and not bad, provided we begin to allow the text to speak to us personally instead of being detached from it to pursue more information or mere hypothetical knowledge.

**2. Growing in the art of devotional reading is less a matter of techniques than it is a matter of attitudes of the heart.**

It is like developing a "sixth sense" of reading which is distinct from reading for information or rational understanding. So the attitude is changed from seeking information to that of being inspired and transformed.

Informational reading is more a search for questions and answers. Devotional reading is more dwelling on meanings about life's deepest issues. The former looks for transparency, the latter is content to contemplate mysteries. Again, informational reading is more dialectical and comparative, and logic is important. But devotional reading is more docile and receptive rather than critical and comparative.

Informational reading tends toward being dissective. Data is taken to pieces by analysis in order to increase one's ability to learn. But devotional reading is living and dynamic and seeks to relate the material to life. For this reason, devotional reading is more personal, allowing the reader to interpret its insights in such personal forms of assimilation as a spiritual journal and the practice of prayer. In these ways, the effects of reading for the inner man are personalized and deepened to affect and shape character, nourish the soul, and permeate the whole of one's life.

**3. Devotional reading is an art learned by facilitating conditions and circumstances rather than by improving cognitive techniques.**

It is God's grace alone which prompts us to have any desires for God and, therefore, any thirst for spiritual literature. Since we cannot invent, create, or refashion "facilitating conditions" for our own sanctity, or cognitively become better listeners to God's guiding Word, "facilitating conditions and circumstances" means to help remove obstacles to the action of grace.

In the history of the Church, as well as in the history of the soul, we experience "the desert" as such a facilitating condition. We feel "the desert within" of loneliness, "the desert outside" of relationships. Desert silence and solitude may be an experience. We relearn the priorities and essentials of life in the spiritual experiences of the desert. We discover new dimensions there of self-knowledge. We need patience, fortitude, and acceptance of desert suffering. We discover dependence and need of God in new ways. There, we reverse the worldly values of self-reliance toward dependence upon God, the dynamic of spiritual life.

A reawakening of the consciousness of indwelling sin in the believer and a sensitivity to the reality of Satan also drive us to our knees. We rediscover the great Puritan classics on the pathology of the heart, its deceptions, its hiddenness, its inaccessibility to our control. Temptation is a constant reality which requires a moral watchfulness that can be alerted by the writings of those experienced in its subtleties. Repentance becomes a lived reality that needs support and comfort. For more material on these subjects, please consult Richard Baxter's book *The Reformed Pastor* and John Owen's book *Sin & Temptation,* two volumes in the Classics of Faith and Devotion series by Multnomah Press.

A desire to reset our course of life, after failure and dishonesty with our soul, intensifies our search to learn how others have done so. Spiritual restoration is not seen as a return to the *status quo,* but as a radical change in direction into unknown territory, where we can walk "more by faith and less by sight." Seeing life with deeper meaning calls for greater spiritual resources than we previously imagined we would ever need. See *Real Christianity* by William Wilberforce and published by Multnomah Press.

Such deeper surrender to the will and purpose of God, after the defeat of self-will, creates longing in the soul for inner peace, spiritual gentleness, serenity, and spiritual refreshment. A deeper understanding and experience of the love of God creates a desire to build up covenant relations in friendships that embody the reality of God in social relationships. Moved by God's grace and compassion, we look below the marred and shattered forms of human relations to the potentials of redemption.

**4. Devotional reading has its own pace of assimilation.**

Think about the speedy insights of the mind, the transformation of thought into action, or the assimilation of deed into character—each have their own relative paces. Devotional reading does, too. The motion toward godliness is the slowest pace of human actions. Inauthenticity occurs when we move too fast, inappropriate to the nature of the transformation. Devotional reading needs its own time which is not determined by the academic calendar nor the impatience we have for "instant results." Spiritual classics cannot be read in one evening like detective novels. Such slow motion requires a regular habit of fixed times for devotional reading and an unhurried leisure to learn the disciplines of meditation and contemplation.

Devotional reading also requires space in our lives. Literally this may lead to the habit of a particular environment being developed—one spot in our room that locates an "altar" of devotion. Physically, it may require comfort, a particular chair, an accustomed posture, where we learn most readily to relax, and where the atmosphere is made for such exercise of devotion. Devotional reading requires a quiet spot, habitually frequented in solitude.

**5. Choose carefully the devotional work you want to read for the benefit of your own soul. Choose it, then, possibly with the advice of others.**

Keep in mind that the book should be chosen to open the doors of perception for you in terms of new as well as existing needs and desires. An imitation of others may not be the best reason for your choice. Because its purpose is to nurture the unique conditions of your own life, individual choice is important. At the same time, bear in mind that books we reject today may be rediscovered later because we are then ready for their insight.

Personal adoption of a book is also helped by marking the text. This may record our first reactions of approval, of help, or of questioning and rejection. It may also help to keep a spiritual journal which we feed with quotations reflected upon and assimilated from the text. Such a reflective notebook may record the immediate reactions to the text, the state of mind we were in when we read a passage, and the duties faithfully performed as a response to what we read. Recordings of ordinary feelings and happenings set within the framework of the devotional readings keep the realities of ordinary life before us. We retain and remember our thoughts if we write them down on the text. This also makes the meaning of the message clearer and more readily available to us.

### 6. Choose spiritual classics from a broad spectrum of thinkers.

Range widely and without prejudice over the classics of devotion, be they Orthodox, Catholic, or Protestant. From our perspective of history and cultural change, we can read more appreciatively of other traditions. Their encapsulation within their own culture also helps us see how likely we are entrapped by our culture as well.

Do not let the great merits of the Reformation block your view of the past so that you think there is nothing between New Testament times and the beginning of the Reformation (early 1500s) that is worth reading! See the Multnomah Press classics *The Love of God* by Bernard of Clairvaux and *A Life of Prayer* by St. Teresa of Avila. Enjoy richly the devotions of the patristic, medieval, modern, and contemporary periods alike. Discover the communion of saints as a living reality in all periods of history. Do not let modernity make you temporarily parochial.

Discern the spirits wisely by penetrating to the presuppositions and assumptions of theological stance of your writers. Learn to distinguish false from valid mysticism.

### 7. Enjoy fellowship with soul-friends so that you mutually benefit in a group, in a shared reading program.

Such a group may meet every three or four weeks to hear and discuss books reviewed in turn by members of the group. Discernment and shared enrichment are thereby exercised together. Insights may be shared of a more personal nature as confidentiality is developed. Differing perspectives may correct or add to individual impressions. The common goal of growing in Christ is emphasized as a corporate maturity that excludes no one in the group.

**8. Recognize that spiritual reading meets with obstacles to distract, discourage, or dissuade us from persistence in our reading.**

Often we do not see clearly enough what the obstacles are, and we seem to lose interest or get distracted easily by other things.

A first obstacle to remove is the time-bound and cultural or theological perspective of what we are reading. The imagery of a book like Teresa's *Interior Castle* or Bunyan's *Holy War* is bound to a particular time and culture. Nevertheless, the truths and insights contained in such works are timeless. The message of surrender and desire in the one book, or of watchfulness in temptation in the other, are timeless. Try not to be prejudiced with such labels as "old fashioned," "relevant for today," "traditional," or even "classic."

A second obstacle is the more subtle obstacle of aesthetic resistance to a text. We may not feel poetically inspired, or we may dislike allegory, or be impatient with the turgid, heavy style of a sermon. Or we may be entranced so much by the romantic imagery that we lose sight of the truth being conveyed. For being enraptured, just as much as being turned off, we may remain spectators, not really involved spiritually and personally in the text and its meaning to us. We remain connoisseurs with no real personal involvement. Many scholars are just doing literary criticism with little or no care for the spiritual food needed by the soul.

A third obstacle is moving further into the scholastic games that can be played with the text of Scripture: such are one-upmanship, where we create novelty of interpretation; name-dropping, when we review all that everyone else has said about the text; or negative listening, where we ignore all that is said positively and only draw attention to what is not said and what we think *should* be said. Such reading is shallow, in spite of its apparent scholarship, and rejects the docility and abiding in the text which we have already described as necessary for devotional reading.

A fourth obstacle is the ensuing despondency that sets in when we compare our state negatively and unfavorably with the spiritual condition of the writer. We can feel so miserable about our sinful condition that we are tempted to ignore spiritual books that show us our desperate need for God. Yet we learn precisely in this way that God can do nothing with our self-sufficiency, self-reliance, and self-respect. Acceptance of our limitations, repentance, and pleas for redemption from God—these are the bases for spiritual growth.

Finally, discouragement will rear its ugly head, even when there are signs all around us of encouragement and blessing. Patience with God's ways, trust in God's control of our circumstances, persistence when spiritual exercises seem fruitless, are all needed. The seed has to die to bear much fruit. Whether God leads us into the desert or into the garden in our devotional reading, let us follow Him. Accept mortification, as much as blessing, in your spiritual reading.

**9. Seek a balance in your reading, both between modern and ancient writings. Be sure that you nourish and strengthen a wide range of your affections by good reading.**

Remember, contemporary literature is untried, lacks vintage, and often reflects the fads of the marketplace. As C. S. Lewis has said:

> "A new book is still on trial, and the amateur is not in a position to judge it. . . . The only safety is to have a standard of plain, central Christianity ("mere Christianity" as Baxter called it), which puts the controversies of the moment in their proper perspective. Such a standard can only be acquired from old books. It is a good rule, after reading a new book, never to allow yourself another new one till you have read an old one in between. If that is too much for you, you should *read an old one to every three new ones.*"[2]

Examine also the need of balanced reading. In this same essay, Lewis gives us his preferences. Match, he argues, the somewhat "astringent" *Imitation of Christ* by Thomas à Kempis, with the "joyous" *Centuries of Meditation* by Thomas Traherne. Perhaps sandwich in between them the anonymously written *Theologia Germanica* which Luther loved. For Lewis, frequent companions were Richard Hooker's *Law of Ecclesiastical Polity*, George Herbert's poems, *The Temple*, William Law's *A Serious Call to a Devout and Holy Life*, and Francis de Sales' *Introduction to the Devout Life*. Some books, once read, may build important foundations. One such book includes Boethius' *On the Consolations of Philosophy*, which gave Lewis a firm awareness of the solidity of eternity that was more than measureless time. For every young inquirer or convert, Augustine's *Confessions* was Lewis' choice for inspiring the reality of the soul's relationship before God. However, Lewis' boon companions were G. K. Chesterton as his intellectual mentor on the sanity of the Christian faith, and George MacDonald, who fed his imagination with true devotion.

Lewis, however, would not have us slavishly imitate his fancies; he would encourage us to find devotion in heavy theological "stuff" as well as theology in the experiences of the simple things. He made friends with books in the whole range of affections we need to develop and exercise before God. Today, we tend to suffer from illiteracy of too much rapid, superficial reading—or rather mere glancing at books. Digestion, assimilation, and then a lifetime companionship with a book is a good test to see whether or not it is really a classic of faith and devotion.

James M. Houston

---

[1]Two useful Catholic aids to such material are: Susan Annette Muto, *A Practical Guide to Spiritual Reading* (Denville, N.J. Dimension Books, 1976). John Weborg, *An Introductory, Annotated Bibliography in Spirituality*, Synthesis Series (Chicago: Franciscan Herald Press, 1979).

[2]C. S. Lewis, *God in the Dock*, ed. by Walter Hooper (Grand Rapids: Eerdmans, 1970).

# Scripture Index

# Subject Index

# STUDY GUIDE FOR
# GROUP DISCUSSION

The popular notion of Christian mystics is that they are hope-lessly out of touch with ordinary mortals. Actually, they can be very contemporary for markedly independent persons; prophetic, in fact, so that they critique their culture ahead of itself. So when we are dissillusioned with "churchianity," or being merely con-ventional and nominal in faith, they are too. For they are "real people," who have a mind and a spirit of their own that does not fit them into their own culture conventionally. But they have a deep faith and a deep love for God. Teresa is one of these exemplars for us. When Pope Paul VI proclaimed Teresa a Doctor of the Church, he called her a teacher of "marvelous profundity." She is a strong woman, a towering personality, even headstrong and will-ful in youth, shrewd in business, and passionate in her devotion to her Lord. However, she knows the ways and temptations of the flesh, so she helps to lift us above our superficial tendencies of Christian living. If we lack intimacy in prayer, she excels in leading us into new realms of love.

## CHAPTER ONE

### Personality and Life Situations Help to Concretise Faith (pp. 1–3)

*Teresa insists that we take the human aspects of our lives seriously, to live concretely.*

1. How and why do we often choose the wrong mentors to help us, as she did?
2. Discuss how our personalities very often give shape to our temptations. Where was Teresa prone to be in temptable situations?
3. Because she struggled with prayerlessness for over eighteen years, Teresa illustrates the apostle Paul's central conviction of his faith, that where he was weak, there he was made strong (2 Cor. 12:10). What is the nature of your difficulties with prayer?
4. How are we also distrusting of God, as Teresa saw herself to be?

## Family Influence Upon Spiritual Life (pp. 3–6)

*Teresa's father was the son of a Jewish merchant from Toledo. His first wife died, leaving him a son and a daughter. He married Teresa's mother when she was a girl of fourteen years, but she died at thirty-three, leaving fourteen-year-old Teresa confused and bereaved. Maria was twenty-four, as serious as her father, and Juana was eleven. Seven of Teresa's brothers became conquistadores in the New World. Four of them were killed, so only Lorenzo, her favorite brother, and Pedro returned in her lifetime. Her family tried to hide their Jewish origins, so perhaps this explains why Teresa was determined to be transparent and plain-spoken.*

1. Why do you think Teresa wanted to be a Christian martyr as a child?
2. Why did her parents seem oblivious to her girlhood temptations?
3. Did Teresa's beauty make her self-conscious? In what way(s)?

## Companions and Mentors (pp. 7–25)

1. Why did Teresa look more to her cousin than her elder sister for companionship?
2. Honor held greater meaning in Teresa's world than it does today. How did she respond to its value?
3. How did family connections help her in her spiritual journey?
4. Like her studious father, Teresa liked the companionship of learned men. When can this be a help and yet also a hindrance to spiritual growth?
5. Godly spiritual directors were vital to a woman like Teresa, while the practice of private prayer was viewed with suspicion by the Inquisition authorities. What were some of Teresa's experiences with their officials?

## CHAPTER TWO

### Essentials for a Life of Prayer (pp. 27–49)

1. How can anyone teach us to pray, other than the Lord? Why is this so?
2. Why did Teresa see the importance of beneficient love—love for all—as being so necessary for growth in prayer?
3. How can we learn to practice self-detachment in our own narcissistic culture? How does Teresa's example help us?
4. Why does Teresa—indeed, all of God's saints—lay such emphasis upon the practice of humility?
5. How do temptations arise to cause us to stumble while on our spiritual journey?

## CHAPTER THREE

### Prayer, as Faith and Fervor for God Alone (pp. 51–73)

1. Can you cite personal incidents from your life that have helped you get started into a more prayerful life?
2. Many others—like Brother Lawrence, for example—also teach the essential importance of self-abandonment in the deepening of one's prayer life. Why?
3. Have you learned to link prayer with friendship as Teresa found to be so important?
4. Desire and suffering seem to go together; they certainly dominated the early prayer life of Teresa. Can you identify with this?
5. How did Teresa enter into the meaning of the Lord's Prayer?

## CHAPTER FOUR

### The Prayer Life as a Garden (pp. 75–113)

1. What biblical symbols of "the garden" help to illuminate the soul's love for God? (Perhaps it is significant that the one biblical book Teresa had access to in the vernacular was the Song of Songs, translated by Luis de Leon for his niece. He was imprisoned by the Inquisition for five years for this "crime," and was Teresa's editor of her posthumous works.)
2. How does Teresa take four ways of irrigating a garden in the dry Meseta of Spain, where she lived, to illustrate four levels of prayer?

3. How can "spiritual dryness" become beneficial in our spiritual growth?

4. Meditative prayer is what Teresa meant by "recollection" or "prayer of quiet." She is following the Augustinian reference to the role of "memory," as referring to our identity being made in the image of God. How significant is your identity as being made in God's image?

5. When God "does everything," which Teresa expressed as behing her experience, what did she mean?

6. When Teresa encountered "water from the fountain," was this what Jesus promised the Samaritan woman, that out of her "would flow rivers of living water"? (John 4:14). How does Teresa describe her involvements with this?

## CHAPTER FIVE

### The Interior Castle: Teresa's Mature Theology (pp. 115–146)

*In this work, written in 1577, five years before she died, Teresa outlines progressively what she has experienced of the life of prayer. It was written in difficult circumstances, of ill-health, heavy duties, and even political pressures against her; she wanted it to be anonymous. It is an attack on interiority or introspection as an end in itself. According to Teresa, we enter within ourselves to find the presence of God, encouraging us to enlarge our heart for him.*

1. Incommunicable experiences of God can sometimes only be spoken of in symbolic form; this is what Teresa does here. Have you had experiences like this in your own life?

2. "The Castle" is the central symbol around whose axis are the related symbols of "the butterfly" and the image of "water." But altogether in her works, Teresa uses at least fifty-three symbols. In your awareness, do symbols play much significance in your Christian life?

3. A major division of *The Interior Castle* occurs between the third set of mansions and the fourth through seventh sets of mansions, for in the last four everything is a gift of God, and all are from *His* initiative. In Christian maturity we, too, may experience this type of change, such as from being an individual with much self-will and independence of spirit to a person who relies far more profoundly upon God for everything. Discuss

your struggles with and experiences of this kind of radical change.

## The Interior Castle—Part 1 (pp. 115–146)

1. Whom do we acknowledge within our life—a unitarian or a trinitarian God?
2. Why does our soul have such dignity and beauty? Has the doctrine of the image of God ever meant much to you?
3. Discern the elements of the world still found in the first mansions.
4. Why is sin so serious a matter, when we were created in God's image? (cf. Genesis 5:1–2; 9:6; James 3:9). Do you believe that Teresa treats this seriously enough?
5. Spiritual disciplines are needed to enter the second mansions. What else is needed?
6. Many pious Christians live in the third series of mansions. What are the traits of this stage? Why is it still a spiritually precarious stage of Christian experience?

## CHAPTER SIX

### The Interior Castle—Part 2 (pp. 147–179)

1. The transition into the fourth set of mansions is when God becomes far more present in our lives. What has prevented us from being at this place much sooner? Is it possible as a Christian never to get to it? Is it our false identification, our activism, and our self-possessiveness that has kept us back?
2. Teresa experiences many struggles and much suffering in the fourth mansions. Is this what we also find in this stage of our lives?
3. We might think we have reached a deep knowledge and exercise of humility by this stage, but in the fifth series of mansions, Teresa finds she needs even more. Why is it so important that there is an ongoing, unceasing growth in humility?
4. However, there are many spiritual consolations in the prayer life of the fifth set of mansions. Which of them can you identify with?

## CHAPTER SEVEN

### The Interior Castle—Part 3 (pp. 181–212)

1. Moral realism is self-knowledge before God has deepened our awareness that "without Him we can do nothing." Now that

the desire for God is intensified, so the suffering in His name grows also. How have you experienced this?

2. What further sense of self-transcendence do we learn in the stage of the sixth mansions?

3. As God's grandeur grows, the heinousness of sin also grows. Therefore, at this stage we become far more sensitive to any presence of evil. How does prayer help us?

4. We may not experience the "locutions" that Teresa had, but how does the Word of God become more appreciated as vital for our growth?

5. How important does spiritual discernment become as we grow more intimately with our Lord?

6. Has the symbol of Christ as the Lover been as central in your devotion to Him as it appears to have been for Teresa? Bridal mysticism was very significant between the twelfth and fifteenth centuries in western Europe. Why is this no longer so, generally speaking?

7. How does Teresa interpret the seventh series of mansions as climactic? What have we learned of this stage, or does it lie still far ahead of your present state as a Christian? Do you want to go further than where you are now?

## CHAPTER EIGHT

### Practical Consequences of a Life of Prayer (pp. 213–232)

1. Like many saints concerned with mentoring others, Teresa was a faithful letter-writer. How will this ministry strengthen our prayer lives?

2. How does self-forgetfulness inhibit our tendency to engage in narcissistic ministries?

3. Discuss the collation of Teresa's maxims that she found important. What maxims would you choose to give guidance to your own spiritual life?

4. Reflect on the priorities you wish to set and carry out as taken from your study of these writings of Teresa of Avila.

Printed in the United States
1114300001B/109-123